Pedagogies of Punishment

Also Available from Bloomsbury

On Critical Pedagogy, Henry A. Giroux
On Class, Race and Educational Reform, edited by Antonia Darder,
Cleveland Hayes II and Howard Ryan
Pedagogies of Taking Care, Dennis Atkinson
Critical Pedagogy for Healing, edited by Tricia M. Kress, Christopher Emdin,
and Robert Lake
Wonder, Vlad P. Glaveanu
Against Sex Education, Caitlin Howlett
Children, Religion and the Ethics of Influence, John Tillson

Pedagogies of Punishment

The Ethics of Discipline in Education

Edited by
Winston C. Thompson and John Tillson

BLOOMSBURY ACADEMIC
LONDON • NEW YORK • OXFORD • NEW DELHI • SYDNEY

BLOOMSBURY ACADEMIC
Bloomsbury Publishing Plc
50 Bedford Square, London, WC1B 3DP, UK
1385 Broadway, New York, NY 10018, USA
29 Earlsfort Terrace, Dublin 2, Ireland

BLOOMSBURY, BLOOMSBURY ACADEMIC and the Diana logo are trademarks of
Bloomsbury Publishing Plc

First published in Great Britain 2023

Copyright © Winston C. Thompson and John Tillson and contributors, 2023

Winston C. Thompson and John Tillson and contributors have asserted their right under the
Copyright, Designs and Patents Act, 1988, to be identified as Author of this work.

Cover design: Grace Ridge
Cover image © William Holbrook Beard, *School Rules*, 1887, oil on canvas, 18 × 24 in.
Courtesy Crystal Bridges Museum of American Art, Bentonville, Arkansas. Photography by
Steven Watson.

All rights reserved. No part of this publication may be reproduced or transmitted
in any form or by any means, electronic or mechanical, including photocopying,
recording, or any information storage or retrieval system, without prior
permission in writing from the publishers.

Bloomsbury Publishing Plc does not have any control over, or responsibility for, any
third-party websites referred to or in this book. All internet addresses given in this
book were correct at the time of going to press. The author and publisher regret any
inconvenience caused if addresses have changed or sites have ceased to exist,
but can accept no responsibility for any such changes.

A catalogue record for this book is available from the British Library.

A catalog record for this book is available from the Library of Congress.

ISBN: HB: 978-1-3502-7570-6
PB: 978-1-3502-7569-0
ePDF: 978-1-3502-7571-3
eBook: 978-1-3502-7572-0

Typeset by Deanta Global Publishing Services, Chennai, India
Printed and bound in Great Britain

To find out more about our authors and books visit www.bloomsbury.com and
sign up for our newsletters.

Contents

List of Illustrations   vii

Introduction   *Winston C. Thompson and John Tillson*   1

Part I   Punishing Children: Foundational Analyses

1. Should School Children Be Punished? *Joan F. Goodman*   13
2. Punishment, Pupils, and School Rules *John Tillson and Winston C. Thompson*   37
3. Responsibility and the Prospect of Punishing Children *Larisa Svirsky*   62

Part II   Punishment in Practice and at the Margins

4. Justice for Trans Youth: Imagining Education Without Cisgenderism *Jenna Scaramanga*   75
5. Racialized Childhoods, Educational Goods, and "No Excuses" Schools: In Defense of Play and Agency *Abigail Beneke*   90
6. Punishment in Early Childhood: Do Exclusionary Practices Threaten Children's Moral Rights? *Joy Dangora Erickson*   106
7. A New Look at Shaming in Schools *Clio Stearns and Peter Stearns*   125

Part III   Due Process, Standing, and the Authority to Punish

8. Due Process: Fairness in Procedure and Substance in the Public Schools *Todd A. DeMitchell*   143
9. Taking Hypocrisy to School *Kartik Upadhyaya and John Tillson*   161
10. The Punitive Classroom: Punishment and Punitive Feelings between Adults and Children *Ruth Cigman*   178

Part IV   Exploring Alternatives to Punishment

11. What We Talk About When We Talk About Punishments and Consequences *Avi I. Mintz*   199
12. Praise and Positive Behavior Management *Zoë A. Johnson King*   217

13 Nudging School Discipline *Viktor Ivanković*   236
14 Making Sense of Student (Mis)behavior: A Critical Pragmatist
    Alternative to Pedagogies of Punishment *Barbara S. Stengel,
    Elizabeth A. Self, and Rebecca A. Peterson*   255

List of Contributors   269
Index   274

Illustrations

Figure

11.1   Plotting outcomes according to authority and arbitrariness   210

Table

6.1   Time-Out and Articles 28, 19, 12, and 37   118

Introduction

Winston C. Thompson and John Tillson

Schools proscribe various activities including absenteeism, tardiness, failure to complete work, leaving the school site, swearing, wearing makeup, eating in class, and noncompliance with teacher instructions (also expressed and subjectively judged as insubordination, often to the detriment of racial and gender minority students). They enforce them via means as various as reprimand, detention, community service, paddling, internal exclusion, suspension, and permanent expulsion, and they index their responses against infractions differently, even where they have the same rules and pool of responses. These facts are so deeply woven into the fabric of educational institutions that they are rather often unquestioned by the onlooking families and educators adjacent to the experience of being punished in schools. Surely punishment must happen in schools, right? They ought to be doled out in roughly the ways they have always been delivered, otherwise the school would devolve into the chaos of youth.

Of course, local, national, and perhaps international headlines are made when a particular punishment is especially egregious or seemingly cruel. And, indeed, much is made of patterned overrepresentation of this or that identity group in a school's punishment practices. But these are hardly ever accompanied by calls for a fundamental analysis of school punishment *qua* school punishment. That is, the underlying ethical questions of punishment in school are given relatively little attention in relation to questions of efficacy and empirical outcomes.

This is especially odd when compared to the probing and dynamic field of ethical work conducted on criminal and other similar forms of punishment. For example, in addition to empirically framed inquiries into the efficacy of, say, solitary confinement in prisons, one can relatively easily read ethical arguments against the implementation of the same. Despite the fact that far more school children are likely to be suspended or excluded from school than incarcerated citizens are so confined, the attention to the former is almost nonexistent in comparison to the latter.

These and similar observations have motivated our continuing work in exploring with others the ethics of school punishment. With an eye to the stakes of these matters, we have sought to reinvigorate normative attention on this all too familiar, yet strangely under-discussed aspect of education.

There is need, we think, for systematic moral theory about when and why punishment is morally acceptable in school contexts. The proliferation and enforcement of arbitrary requirements are problematic partly, as Joan Goodman (2006) argues, because it tends to undermine effective moral communication by eroding schools' and teachers' testimonial credibility, sending the wrong moral messages and missing easy opportunities for effective communication. However, apart from downstream consequences, misguided and arbitrary impositions are intrinsically wrongful. This is fundamentally because there is reason—albeit overridable—not to limit the freedoms of and impose burdens on people, children included, because they have a conditional claim to direct their own lives as they see fit and because limiting those freedoms and imposing burdens can be experienced as distressing and unwelcome. Imposing limits and burdens can be justified, but the onus rests on the actors imposing them to produce a justification. Wherever they are unjustifiably imposed, children are treated wrongly.

In our view, developing a theory of just school punishment is valuable for the following reasons.

1. *Conforming with morality.* Conforming with morality means acting in the right way for any reason whatsoever (more precisely, it means acting as close to the right way as one can without having whatever motivations help constitute the right way, proper). Of course, the behaviors required of students and the expected range of responses to perceived noncompliance vary widely across schools and political jurisdictions, holding children to different standards in different ways for different reasons. While some permit girls to wear trousers, others forbid this, and while two schools may proscribe the same target behavior (e.g., swearing), some respond to it more harshly than others. Schools differ in whether they consider the circumstances of rule infraction in deciding how to respond (e.g., "zero-tolerance" stances do not) and in the range of responses they permit themselves to use (including forms of isolation or exclusion). Even where schools respond to the same violations in the same way, they may do so for different reasons—some may visit their response as a form of "just desert," others as ways of deterring offenders or, more generally,

third parties from similar behavior, yet others as a form of development or education. These differences in school policies and practices call for normative evaluation and guidance. It is likely, given this variation, that some schools are performing punishment wrong, thereby wronging their students. They might punish the wrong things or fail to punish the right things or punish the wrong people in the wrong way for the wrong reasons. Knowing why punishment is sometimes justified helps all parties to identify permissible and impermissible instances of punishment and non-punishment, and to ensure that punishment and non-punishment conforms with moral requirements. Even if a wide variety of punitive practices are morally justified, part of what a theory of moral punishment should show is what kind of variety is morally permissible (and why) and what lies outside this permissible range.

2. *Complying with morality.* Complying with morality means acting in the right way *for the right reason.*[1] It is plausible that punishing for good reasons is partly constitutive of good punishment and that mere conformity with a true theory of punishment is morally defective. If that is correct, those good reasons need to be known by the punisher and must motivate the action. When agents hold themselves (and each other) to a publicly stated standard, this can help them to act for the right reasons rather than select whichever justification is most convenient for doing whatever they happen to want to do. While valuable, compliance is not as easily measured and enforced as conformity. It also seems less valuable—actors should not sacrifice conformity to generate more compliance. Additionally, it matters more that people are treated in (almost) the right ways than that they are treated so for the right reasons (albeit, the right reasons are sometimes constitutive of the right treatment).

3. *Knowing why.* It is plausible that knowing why one is being punished (to the extent that one can) is partly constitutive of being punished well. This is because it is good in itself to know when one is being treated justly or unjustly, especially where one could easily confuse one's treatment with an injustice. If this is so, it means persuasively explaining a true theory of just punishment to those who are punished in accordance with it. It is also good to know why one's punishment is just, because it enables the knower to comply or better conform with justice.

4. *Palimpsest.* Even if actors do not quite accurately perceive or understand the principles of just punishment, it is important to state them so that

they can become the shared object of critical scrutiny and improved on to better realize goals 1–3.

These needs for clarity and accuracy have informed much of our initial and ongoing work in this project.

Our concerted work on this subject, under the header "Pedagogies of Punishment," began in 2018. One of us (Tillson) had previously been working on questions about how children's outlooks and identities could be permissibly influenced (2019). Having previously set aside questions about punishment in that work, he turned to consider the morality of punishment as an influence. The other of our pair (Thompson) had a long-standing interest in the intersection of education and justice, especially when considered under nonideal social-political circumstances. Our conversations were generative, and we soon found ourselves submitting a grant proposal to the Center for Ethics & Education. With success in that effort, we began to plan conferences, symposia, and workshops, taking care to invite a multidisciplinary group of scholars who might advance normative thinking on our subject. That criterion yielded satisfying outcomes as the meetings led to a good number of high-quality publications (Thompson and Tillson, 2020)—and a project website featuring interviews with contributors, a series of blogposts, and teaching resources.

Our appreciation of multidisciplinary approaches to our questions has, by design, persisted into the present. Rather than featuring only valuable yet abstract theorizing, we wanted to involve varied approaches to the book's core concerns. In our view, this provides a richly nuanced set of perspectives, each drawing from slightly or decidedly different domains of expertise. Instead of resting upon a shared lattice of assumptions, we find that this approach challenges disciplines, fields, and professional communities to rethink some fundamental issues. We hope that this approach to organizing philosophers, psychologists, social scientists, educational generalists, legal scholars, and more might increase the likelihood that the volume, read as a whole, will offer meaningful progress in untangling the knotty ethical threads of school punishment.

We intend this book to be of practical value to readers with various identities and roles. Normative theorists will likely find that most chapters raise interesting questions of subtle attention and specificity, thereby improving the quality of discussion regarding the ethical details of school punishment. Policymakers and administrators will find much to inform the design and implementation of disciplinary policies under their control. Practitioners and educators, often tasked with the ethically weighty work of enacting the aforementioned policies, often by use of their individual and collective judgment, will find both nuanced distinctions and language for interpreting and discussing their options, and guiding their choices. Finally, the students and families who are most directly impacted by the receipt of punishments in schools may find that the book helps to inform and clarify a sense of justice in school discipline worth hoping and petitioning for.

Not all of the chapters in this collection are similarly addressed to each of the groups described earlier. Instead, some are intended for lay audiences, while others make advances at the cutting edge of academic work on punishment. Since chapters are mostly entirely self-contained and independent, making no reference to one another, readers can steer their own path through the book reading parts of particular interest to them. However, we have arranged the chapters into a reasonably natural order of progression. We suggest reading Part I first since it introduces and discusses some of the most general and fundamental questions about the nature and justification of school punishment, and we suggest reading those chapters in the order given. The chapters in Part I are so ordered that earlier ones illuminate later ones, introducing concepts, arguments, and choices that later chapters presuppose or come down on a particular side of. The other parts might be read in any order. But again, we have organized chapters into clusters whose members complement each other well by speaking to similar themes.

Part I ("Punishing Children: Foundational Analyses") probes core questions about the nature of punishment and its justification in the case of children. Likely of interest to those who are looking for elucidation of concepts that recur across subsequent chapters, it offers a ready entry into the constituent concerns that might be engaged in any normative analyses of punishment. That written, Part I is far more than only preparation for what lies ahead. Instead, it offers substantive arguments and significant conclusions. Novice readers might spend time with this part first, to not only understand some of the concepts invoked in other chapters but also return to it having read more of the book, to reconsider its arguments in light of later chapters.

In the first chapter, Goodman forwards a thoughtful set of distinctions between various forward-looking and backward-looking concepts in schools' responses to student behavior. In this, the chapter advances an argument regarding permissible and impermissible responses in the abstract and in practice. Retribution (as a significant aspect of punishment) is discussed in some detail.

In Chapter 2, Tillson and Thompson provide some ground clearing that offers a broad analysis of the nature and justification of punishment in order to begin the creation of a specific theory of punishing school children. The chapter explores what rules schools may establish, how schools might respond to students' breach of these rules, and the role of autonomy in those determinations.

Chapter 3 highlights a number of important foundational distinctions, as Svirsky clears confusion regarding the fuzzy boundaries between punishment and other methods of disincentivizing behavior. In this work, Svirsky insightfully distinguishes between a child being "responsible" and being "held responsible" for a behavior. Locating punishment as a subcategory of the latter, the chapter asks how, through an analysis of what is required to hold a child responsible, one might become confident that a given punishment is appropriate.

Part II ("Punishment in Practice and at the Margins") shifts reader attention to the real-world circumstances that complicate the ambitions of more general and systematic normative analyses of punishment in schools. Here, matters of group identity and social practices are foregrounded in contextualizing the ethical questions addressed in these chapters. Readers primarily interested in how particular populations are ill-served by existing punitive practices or background assumptions may do well to focus their attentions here. The chapters in this section do not only offer practical commentary and guidance on punishment in and of those communities; they also provide insight into how better understandings of the (in)justice of punishment at the margins enable improvements to understanding punishment across contexts.

In Chapter 4, Scaramanga offers urgent and sober analysis of the role of cisgenderism in punishing trans youth in schools. Through this analysis, the chapter articulates a vision of what a just degree of safety in schools might require for trans youth in particular and how punishment often sits in opposition to that goal.

In Chapter 5, Beneke addresses the important pattern of racialized injustice that, as a form of school punishment, limits play for children of color. With a focus on "No Excuses" schools, the chapter suggests that safeguarding experiences of play has a special significance for those communities most expected to behave as adults.

Chapter 6 motivates careful attention to the student by focusing analysis on the early childhood educational context. Given the special vulnerabilities of that group, this context allows the chapter to pose questions that reverberate across the age spectrum as it asks whether exclusionary practices can be well defended from a moral perspective.

Throughout Chapter 7, Stearns and Stearns provide the reader with a probing take on shame. Rather than an essentializing account of shame as a desirable or undesirable aspect of school punishment, the chapter asks far more subtle questions of the role of shame in classroom punishment practices.

Part III ("Due Process, Standing, and the Authority to Punish") scrutinizes procedures by which punishment may permissibly be implemented in schools. In addition to a focus on laws regulating school punishment, this part explores how persons come to have the right types of relationships to one another such that just punishment is even a possibility. Readers interested in legal and relational analyses will find much to engage here.

With impressive legal acuity, in Chapter 8, DeMitchell shares a framing of due process as a template for fairness in deliberations and decisions regarding punishment. This chapter observes the ways in which schools must adhere to jurisdictional statutes even while it offers an analysis that implies an analogy regarding the relationships between a legitimate state and its citizens on the one hand and the student and the school on the other. Importantly (in both contexts) due process serves as a check against excessively unjust outcomes of wrongful punishment.

Chapter 9 gives serious consideration to the familiar feeling of being a child held to standards transgressed by a seemingly hypocritical teacher. Upadhyaya and Tillson use this scenario as an entry into a deeper exploration of just what engages that sense of ethical wrong in the case of punishment by the hypocritical authority figure and what its broader implications are for how teachers should hold their students to account.

In Chapter 10, Cigman skillfully directs attention to the relationship between children and adults and asks whether children can punish adults, as a matter of conceptual intelligibility, and under what conditions they may rightly do so. The chapter traces these analyses to compelling conclusions regarding the ability to justly punish another.

Part IV ("Exploring Alternatives to Punishment") asks whether punishment might be better understood by comparative analysis with its alternatives and whether it ought to be wholly or partly replaced or supplemented by alternative approaches to managing bad behavior and cultivating good behavior. The stakes of punishment are on display in this section as the chapters demonstrate that alternatives to punishment might engage significantly fewer ethical problems. Still, these alternatives are not without their burdens. Readers interested in thinking about what ethics might require in the response to student behavior may find this section of particular interest.

In Chapter 11, Mintz wonders whether punishment can be avoided in pursuit of a more neutral response to behavior, namely, consequences. By exploring the literature on the concept of disciplinary consequences, the chapter connects with the possibility of adults setting aside punishment in favor of this alternative.

Chapter 12 finds Johnson King providing an impressive analysis of the moral importance of praise. Set alongside blame and blameworthiness, this chapter's focus on praise offers a theoretical and normative analysis to more equally complement the empirical evidence of praise's efficacy.

In Chapter 13, Ivanković provides a promising account of nudging as an alternative to traditional punitive practices. By examining how crafting an environment that encourages some student behaviors over others may simultaneously differentially impact students at dissimilar developmental milestones, the chapter provides a view of how nudging decisions might be made well.

In Chapter 14, Stengel, Self, and Peterson demonstrate a critical pragmatist approach to student behavior. The chapter suggests an "improvisational" account of response to student misbehavior. This educative context challenges teachers to construct the breach of a norm or a rule as an opportunity for skillful pedagogy over punishment.

We are excited about the new ground broken in this volume and about the ways some of its chapters build on previous outputs of the Pedagogies of Punishment project. While we have learned much from the work of our contributors across all of these sites and platforms, there remains much work to be done. Most obviously, since our contributors' papers, chapters, and blogs do not always directly and self-consciously respond to one another, a more integrated vision is still necessary for exploring how the different topics cohere with another. Such a vision would show the extent to which the views our contributors defend are consistent with one another, on the one hand, and where choices between them must be made, on the other. However, still further questions remain largely unconsidered altogether, beyond where they fit into the wider puzzle.

Scholars in this area of research may ask why some people have the moral authority to punish, while others do not. It is simple to think that an original right to punish originates with some or another omniscient deity who delegates small bundles of this (e.g., rights to punish children or citizens of various lands) to mortal persons (e.g., parents or monarchs of various lands) and that these individuals can further delegate powers (e.g., to teachers and judges), but this is not a view which commands much agreement in the contemporary world. It is also simple to think that each individual has a natural right to punish all other individuals for any violation, in so far as can be proportionately done, and that individuals can (and must) mutually abdicate this power to a trustworthy central authority that can more reliably punish on the collective's behalf. If something like this view is right, its connections to the authority of teachers and parents to punish surely need further exploration.

Additionally, from our perspective, more work is needed on a variety of nonideal circumstances. For instance, the question looms regarding whether wrongful punishment (and non-punishment) is itself rightly punishable. These include circumstances of conscientious objection, wherein teachers are required not to punish but think they should or in which teachers are expected to punish but think they should not. They include questions about protections to err and the limits of these protections—where teachers err too often or too far. The field may also ask whether there are any constraints of legitimacy, rather than of justice (distributive or otherwise), that invalidate rights to punish and dissolve duties to submit to or cooperate with punishment. This possibility urges consideration that there may be a wide permissible range of punishments that can be implemented in schools with some level of injustice, without full loss of legitimacy.

Also, in Chapter 2, we raise but do not resolve the following issue: if we think of young children (unlike adults) as *never* being liable for punishment due to wrongful choices, we might still also think that punishments and other burdens can be imposed (as side effects or essential mechanisms of strategies we use) to guide their choices in ways that reduce harms they do. If so, we then face the question of how these burdens and benefits are to be distributed justly and so we have to bring issues of distributive justice into matters of school punishment. A further quandary emerges about whether schools should punish in less-than-ideal ways, if parents wrongly threaten to remove their children from schools that punish justly.

Chapter 2 also makes use of Tadros (2019) in arguing that insofar as children are autonomous, they may not be treated paternalistically, and insofar as they are heteronomous, they are not liable for certain punitive purposes (general deterrence in particular). A question that needs further careful thought is whether the capacities and conditions that make paternalism wrongful are identical with the practices and conditions that render individuals liable for punishment for purposes of general deterrence.

A final question that still needs further consideration is what punishments (if any) are appropriate? Much has been said about isolation, exclusion, and corporal punishment; many accounts rule these out. We suspect that a good deal more could be said about which punishments are permissible and why. Working toward resolution on these and other matters ought to be priority.

Self-interestedly, we are excited to have worked on this collection. The questions answered by our contributing authors have been intellectually satisfying even as they kindle curiosity and prompt new areas of further attention. As engaged as we have been with the ideas within these pages, we are equally anticipating the good outcomes of making these analyses public.

Our ongoing work under the project title "Pedagogies of Punishment" has been rewarding for many reasons. Not least among these has been the pleasure of inviting new perspectives to these important and perplexing ethical issues. While this book is a self-contained contribution to the field, we also hope it will be an invitation to others to engage with the arguments and expertise on display. Schools and students deserve good justifications for the punitive practices. Refining the views on these matters as shared by stakeholders and scholars will be of importance for as long as punishment remains interwoven within educational institutions.

We hope you will join us.

Note

1 This compliance/conformity terminology is due Joseph Raz, but the distinction goes back at least as far as Plato's dialogues.

References

Goodman, Joan F. (2006) "School Discipline in Moral Disarray." *The Journal of Moral Education* 35 (2): 213–30, 218.

Tadros, Victor (2019) "Punishing Children." *Pedagogies of Punishment Website*. https://www.pedagogiesofpunishment.com/blog/2019/8/20/punishing-children.

Thompson, Winston C. and Tillson, John (2020) "Pedagogies of Punishment." *Theory and Research in Education* 18 (1): 3–9.

Tillson, John (2019) *Children, Religion and the Ethics of Influence*. London: Bloomsbury.

Part I

Punishing Children: Foundational Analyses

1

Should School Children Be Punished?

Joan F. Goodman

Disciplining children at school is a pervasive practice and inevitably so because, except under utopian circumstances, teachers and students are often at cross-purposes.[1] No one better described these tensions than Richard Waller almost a century ago (Waller, 1932). As he boldly stated: "Teacher and pupil confront each other with attitudes from which the underlying hostility can never be altogether removed." The "relationship is a form of institutionalized dominance and subordination. The teacher represents the formal curriculum, and his [sic] interest is in imposing that curriculum; . . . pupils are much more interested in life in their own world than in the desiccated bits of adult life which teachers have to offer" (195–6). To maintain stability, teachers must therefore develop management systems enforced by discipline. Though Waller's description is perhaps overly bleak and exaggerated, it remains true that the top priority for teachers is instructional success, often demonstrated by student test scores, while the priority of students tends to be peer status, often threatened by obedience to teacher authority. When the inevitable disruption occurs a teacher's perceived obligation is, naturally enough, to regain and retain control by stopping the behavior (Pace and Hemmings, 2006; Tom, 1984). Obtaining voluntary consent from students is currently made yet more difficult by standards-based curricula that restrict the development of lessons geared to student interest (Pace and Hemmings, 2007). Critics of education should therefore be cautious in objecting to discipline. Even those committed to a progressive rather than autocratic disciplinary approach, that is who emphasize individual autonomy, choice, character development, and self-control, rather than behavioral suppression and obedience, must acknowledge that when a teacher is confronted with resistant students who are "out of line" (either literally or figuratively), disturbing others, and "off-task," her first imperative is to speedily and authoritatively quell the disruption, even if discipline is "top-down," stirs student resentment, or weakens self-confidence.

Yet, with full recognition of both the teacher's plight and the obvious need for school discipline, its administration need not be haphazard. All discipline is not equivalent in its impact or justification. In this chapter I attempt to separate *educative discipline* from punishment. This is not an easy task for the differences are often subtle. While a school will advertise its disciplinary policies are intended as remedial and educative (Coverdale, 2020), the practices may (perhaps inadvertently) drift from educative to purely punitive. In part, the drift occurs because of a tendency to lump punishment with discipline (Hand, 2020) or to view the punitive on a continuum with the educative. Both blur distinctions and obscure the crucial retributive element integral to punishment. I make a cautious case in favor of discipline rather than punishment.[2] While educators generally frown on punishment, by including it as a form of discipline they lose sight of the crucial contrast in purpose that puts it at odds with educative discipline. The object of punishment is to restore a moral equilibrium by inflicting suffering on an offender for a past offense. The object of educative discipline is to redirect an offender through a remedial action that will ameliorate future learning.

I initially attempt to disambiguate theories of discipline and punishment by describing each, drawing particular attention to retribution. This turns out to be a daunting task because one person's punishment is another's discipline separated more by teacher and student construal than overt acts of misbehavior and consequent censure (see Mischel and Shoda, 1995, on behavioral consistency as a matter of psychological interpretation rather than situational sameness). Moving away from theory, the next section looks at punishment and discipline as understood in school practice. Using major texts, I point out existing confusions resulting from an inadequate conceptual and practical separation. Neither wrongs committed by a student nor actions taken in response can be categorized as punitive or disciplinary because they emerge from student and teacher interpretations. Although not made explicit in the texts, what emerge as the major differentiating features in practice may be less what the teacher objectively does than what she *intends*. Then, it returns to the salient criteria for punishment laying bare their ill-suitedness for a school setting. Finally, I suggest that despite my punishment critique there are occasions that do merit punishment. Concluding thoughts follow.

Discipline in theory

Discipline, according to the highly regarded educational theorist R. S. Peters (1967), is submission to rules. "The rules may be those of what is learned, e.g., the rules of grammar or of morals; they may be those of the method of learning, e.g., rules of practice and training; or they may be more general rules necessary for something to be learned, e.g., rules relating to silence, posture, and diet. . . . 'Discipline' is thus a very general notion which is connected with conforming to rules" (173–4), the methods used to inculcate obedience and order (also Newman, 1985). Broadening the concept still further discipline can refer to fields of study (e.g., history and math, see Gardner, 2016) or it can be a good in itself (self-discipline) unrelated to the learning enterprise. This discussion is limited to a narrow perspective, conforming to rules. It omits the omnibus notion of discipline as subject of study, methods for subject mastery, self-regulation, and felonious acts that fall beyond the purview of a teacher. As described concisely in a major educational text, discipline is "the act of responding to misbehaving students in an effort to restore order" (Burden, 2020, 11). In schools the most common cause for discipline is students' defiant and disruptive behavior in classrooms (Bear and Manning, 2014).

The essential warrant of discipline, then, is to correct misbehavior and prevent future disruption so that a learning atmosphere is sustained. For some that atmosphere can be informal and student centered. For others it will be hierarchical and rule governed. Regardless of preference, the teacher's justification for exercising authority is that acquiescence to classroom mores is necessary for instruction. Interventions can cover a broad spectrum from a reminder, redirection, admonishment, detention to shaming, suspension, and expulsion. Whether mild or severe, however, all target an improved learning context. The question arises, in furthering these purposes, how far does the teacher's prerogative extend? When nonpunitive methods fail, is she entitled to punish? The answer to be developed is that punishment is not simply a linear expansion moving from mild discipline to more severe consequences. It requires a justification that goes beyond preservation of classroom procedures. Punishment should not be a component of discipline, for in shifting from educative discipline to punishment both methods and purposes change. The distinctions are clarified when punishment, unlike educative discipline, is understood as imposing pain, making moral judgments, and attributing culpability. The behavior addressed is judged not only a school wrong, to be corrected and hopefully not repeated, but a display of bad character to be condemned. Educative discipline, by contrast, seeks to alter those behaviors that forestall learning without judging the morality of either the act or person. When punishment is subsumed into discipline the distinction between the purpose of educative discipline—to remediate—and that of punishment—to condemn—is lost. Before mounting a critique of punishment at school, however, an attempt to clarify it in theory and then practice follows.

Punishment in theory

An aspect of discipline. Punishment, as with discipline, has both omnibus and narrow definitions. The most inclusive description, often advanced by those with behaviorist leanings, is any unpleasant event following a behavior that reduces its repeated occurrence (Bear, 2010; Also, Levin and Nolan, 2014; Skiba and Rausch, 2015; Wolfgang, 2009). It includes withholding positive reinforcement through such behavior modification techniques as time-out, logical consequences and loss of privileges, along with adding aversive stimuli (Burden, 2020). Equally unspecified are the boundaries of punishment described as any acceleration of consequences when other measures have failed (Landrum and Kauffman, 2006). Presumably, the behavior deserving of punishment can be relatively innocuous, like repeatedly whispering to a neighbor, or seriously harmful, like throwing a can and hitting a student's head; the procedure can be simply withdrawal of attention or ratcheted up to detention; the objectives minimal—the student becomes rule-obedient—or maximal, it brings about rule-acceptance, a reform in student attitudes and freshly grounded commitments. The justification is completely outcome based. In this interpretation, one resorts to punishment to curb a behavior.

Punishment as retribution. At the opposite pole of an all-inclusive omnibus description, punishment is narrowly circumscribed as an inherently retributive practice, condemnation for moral misdeeds by the perpetrator (Kleinig, 1982; Mackie, 1982; Moore, 1997; Murphy, 2003; Waller, 1932). In contrast to the behaviorist's description, success is judged *not* by outcome measures—did the child conform to expectations—but by standards of fairness/justice—did the child receive just deserts? Fairness is not to be eclipsed by perceptions of efficacy, as in any unpleasant event that reduces the reoccurrence of a behavior. Its primary attributes are the infliction of *pain* for a *moral wrong* of which the student is *culpable* administered for *past offenses* by someone with proper authority to do so (Kleinig, 1982; Peters, 1967).

As distinct from discipline, "punishment is a deliberate, presumably unpleasant, imposition on or interference with a person because of (that is, as a retribution for) that person's moral failure" administered by a legitimate authority (Kleinig, 1982, 223; also, Feinberg, 1988; Moore, 1997; Morris, 1968). Accordingly, there is no justification for punishing a student who fails to follow a host of school regulations around decorum, procedures, and work products. They are nonmoral and therefore nonpunitive offenses. For a retributivist, if the wrong committed is not worthy of moral censure, that is, harm to others, it would not precipitate a punishment, strictly a tool for the expression "of attitudes of resentment and indignation, and of judgments of disapproval and reprobation" (Feinberg, 1965, 400). Pain inflicted may consist of moral condemnation alone or it can be an addition, but pain without moral condemnation (as in having to attend school after hours to make up an assignment) is not punishment (Feinberg, 1988).

Limiting the term still further, to merit punishment the offender must not merely have committed the wrong but also be culpable (Moore, 1997). If a student commits even a seemingly moral misdeed but does so because she is under extreme pressure (if she didn't fight with x she would fall victim to a vindictive gang), doesn't appreciate the gravity of the offense (everyone does it), or the harm it does to others (copying answers or stealing from a classmate), she would not deserve condemnation for her moral culpability is minimal to nonexistent.

Beyond the core elements of retribution—pain infliction, moral wrong, and culpability—punishment is further constrained by two related considerations. First, retribution is not a means to prevent future misdeeds but always a response to past wrongdoing, justified as a simple matter of fairness, of upholding justice (Feinberg, 1988). It is deserved for someone who intentionally deviated from the prevailing accepted order, not for someone who has difficulties abiding by that order and needs help in conforming to it. The value of punishment as retribution is that "someone who deserves it gets it" (Moore, 1997, 87). In a school setting, retributive punishment should not be considered a pragmatic tool for ensuring future obedience to a teacher's authority. "Punishment's real function is not that of crime control, in terms of which it is rather ineffective, but rather that of moral affirmation" (Garland, 1999, 24). It underscores foundational principles and policies, the boundaries between what is morally permissible and impermissible. One does not ask of retribution, does it work? Second, punishment is not intended to reform the offender nor serve as a deterrent on others. If it does have such payoff these are merely "surplus good effects" (Moore, 1997, 153)—welcome but not critical. In sum, retribution subscribes to administration of pain for a moral wrong of which the student is culpable, oriented to the person for a past misdeed to uphold justice.

Educative discipline, by contrast, "is not retributive but teleological" (Kleinig, 1982, 223). Correctives are administered for a school wrong of which the student may not be culpable, oriented to ameliorating future acts to improve educational performance. Given their different functions it is a mistake to collapse into a single entity discipline-inclusive-of-punishment and to implicitly permit whatever efficiently curbs a behavior. For present purposes, I take retribution to be the critical feature separating punishment from discipline, for there can be no punishment without it and no discipline with it.[3]

Mixed theory. A broader, intermediate definition (sometimes referred to as modest retributivism or mixed theory) moderates the pain criterion while adding ameliorating consequences (deterrence and personal reform) as critical ingredients of punishment. Jean Hampton (1984) has called this the "moral education theory of punishment." Whereas consequences are immaterial to the pure retributivist, in the mixed theory they are essential and embedded in it. Indeed, punishment is only justified if in addition to retribution it is productive of good consequences (Berman, 2016; Mackie, 1982).

Diluting the pain requirement may make educators more comfortable but further obscures the demarcation of punishment from other school impositions. A hardship may or may not be painful. Here, too, it depends on interpretation. Students undoubtedly find many school activities, even required attendance alone, as unwanted hardships yet not painful because they buy into the purposes. Mandatory attendance is therefore not to be interpreted as a punishment unless it is severed from its educative purpose, for example if extended through weekends for no discernable rational reason. If hardship is substituted for pain infliction, punishment will likely be used promiscuously for a range of misbehaviors. As a result, the seriousness and tall bar it should meet will be lessened.

According to the intermediate theory, infliction of any pain is acceptable *only* when it is oriented toward deterrence, rehabilitation, and reform. Deterrence is directed to both the individual who committed the offense (specific deterrence) and others who witnessed it (general deterrence). As a result of being punished an individual will *theoretically* forswear the same behavior in the future (rehabilitation) and acceptance of the moral wrong she perpetrated will produce a reconstitution of character (reform). It is future oriented (Meyer, 1968). These effects are not contrived, an add-on to retribution, but inherent and impossible to eliminate from punishment, for the mere threat of serious censure, reproach, and possible pain infliction serves as a natural deterrent (Hampton, 1984). The discomfort aroused from moral disapproval will naturally burnish the offender's moral convictions, inspire remorse and guilt over misdeeds and, in the school context, prompt a resolve to further community and classroom values (Scribner and Warnick, 2021). Further, the resulting reorientation will be premised on conviction, not obedience and fear of authority (reform). The "ultimate goal of the punishment is not merely to deter the child from performing the bad action in the future, but to deter her *by convincing her* (as well as other children) to renounce the action because it is wrong" (Hampton, 1984, 218, italics in original).

The emphasis on deterrence through censure for breaking a moral norm is a departure from the retributive view of punishment. It is included in the mixed theory because alone, the theory goes, rational explanations about wrongness are unlikely to harness sufficient desire and willpower. Only serious disapproval will spur the offender's desire not to repeat misbehaviors and, vicariously, motivate those witnessing the punishment (specific and general deterrence). However, the added affliction need not be severe. A minimal amount may be sufficient as, for instance, depriving a student of participating in other activities by placing her in after-school detention or requiring her to talk with a principal. But why is affliction necessary when the goal is remedial and the student understands it as such? If the desired outcomes—deterrence, reform, and rehabilitation—were achievable without it, say through a thoughtful but unthreatening talk with a student, that would surely be the preferred option. To assume a student requires serious disapproval and censure from a teacher, rather than a rational and sympathetic encounter, is to believe the child cannot grasp the rule or that she is willfully disobeying it. In either case harshness is more likely to induce a merely temporary inhibition rather than a changed conviction. Instead, for example, consider the case of a student who steals. Why not explain without harshness, "because you repeatedly have taken x's lunch and added it to your own, for the time being you need to store your food in plain view on your desk without access to cubies at lunch time." Such an intervention need not attribute malign moral motives to the student—maybe she truly does not understand the nature of stealing—while correcting a behavior. By merging components of punishment—a touch of retribution, disapproval, and censure—with educative discipline—a focus on amelioration—the mixed theory obliterates the distinctive message each is potentially delivering. Better, as discussed later, preserve the retributive and painful elements of punishment, and then consider its limited justified use in school. First, however, a look at school practice where discipline and punishment are also poorly separated.

Punishment and school practice

Confusion. *Hanna, a middle school student, constantly gets up from her desk when asked to do seat work. She walks around the room, claims she needs to sharpen* *a pencil, whispers to another student, or asks repeatedly to go to the bathroom. At first her teacher ignores the walking, stands silently by her desk for a moment making eye contact, reminds her that the classroom rules prohibit leaving her seat during this work-completion time, and finally says a private word to her after class. All ineffective. Next, the teacher deprives her of any opportunity to use the pencil sharpener. That too fails to curb the wandering. Upping the ante, the teacher has Hanna sit at a desk on the front row and, when that makes no impression, begins deducting recess time until she isn't allowed out for recess at all. Hanna's resistance to the sitting-still rule continues; the teacher finds her roaming increasingly disruptive. Harsher consequences follow: no talking at lunch, a call home, after-school detention, the possibility of suspension.*

Are any or all these interventions punishment? Whereas forced silence, detention, and suspension seem so, the teacher's private and gentle talk about how to correct a misdeed seems clearly not. Reminding a student of the rules hardly ranks as a disciplinary moment, probably no more than an instruction akin to "take out your notebooks." What about the other interventions? Once the teacher starts "costing out" the unacceptable behavior, making Hanna "pay" for her wrongdoing (cannot use the pencil sharpener, banned from recess), have we entered the realm of punishment? According to (1984), punishment is any loss of freedom and autonomy. This is what makes jailing a punishment, no matter the treatment. But this definition does not work in the educational context, for many students find just being at school a serious deprivation of freedom and autonomy compounded by the deprivations of discipline—like missing recess.

Schools, as mentioned, frequently present punishment as the farther end of a discipline continuum, to be avoided whenever possible and used only when all else has failed (Bear and Manning, 2014; Good and Brophy, 2008; Levin and Nolan, 2014). The slide from nonpunitive to punitive is largely a pragmatic decision seemingly dependent on the extent and severity of the misbehavior as well as the success of nonpunitive measures. Further contrasts that might cabin the two types of discipline, so that the choice is more deliberate and principled, are not drawn.

As a result, prominent texts on discipline are confusing in their descriptions of punishment. For example, Levin (2014), who accept the omnibus definition of punishment as "any adverse consequence of a targeted behavior that suppresses the behavior" (162), describe two forms: "removal of privileges and painful—physical or psychological—experiences." Although contradicting their just-given definition, the authors add: "Either form may or may not suppress misbehavior" (162). Burden (2020), who appears to adopt the continuum theory popular with many educators, distinguishes mild (nonpunitive) from moderate (punitive) responses to an offense. A mild response to a low-level offense might be to "*provide* non-punitive time-out" (176, italics added, such as to calm down, reorganize); a moderate response for a more serious offense "intended to be punitive" (182) is to "*place* student in a time-out" (176, italics added). The difference between the two time-outs? Presumably *providing* gives the student a chance to reorganize while *placing* is exacting a punitive payment. A teacher might be hard put to distinguish the two.

Desired outcomes also are undifferentiated. The purposes of mild responses, according to Burden (2020), are to "get the student back on task" (180), "*correct* the student's behavior" (178, italics added), provide guidance for appropriate behavior" (170), stop off-task behavior, and restore order. The purposes of moderate responses are to "*decrease* unwanted behavior" (176, italics added). Again, what is the difference between *correcting* a behavior and *decreasing* a behavior? Finally, many examples of moderate interventions—such as picking up a dropped paper from the floor or cleaning the desk one has messed up—do not strike one as particularly punitive. These practices are grouped together as logical consequences. And in what category do logical consequences fall? Burden sees them as punitive; Levin and Nolan are more equivocal. This contrasts with Rudolf Dreikurs, originator of the logical consequence theory, who advocated them in opposition to punishment (Dreikurs and Grey, 1968).

Without being explicit why *guiding* and *correcting* are placed under mild (educative in our terms) and *decreasing* behavior is placed under moderate, Burden hints at a distinction between punitive and nonpunitive. Guidance perhaps is not deemed useful once a student's offense becomes quite troubling. Deterrence (deceasing behavior) is now to be accomplished by punishment. Is this not a distinction without a difference? Both mild and moderate are meant to stop the misbehavior. Levin and Nolan (2014) recognize that the same intervention might or might not be punitive: if a student is daydreaming in class and the teacher denies her recess to complete the work, this is not punitive. It becomes a punishment only if the logical consequence is delivered in an "aggressive, hostile, or demeaning tone of voice" (162) or if she imposes a consequence unrelated to the poor behavior, like cancelling a trip for the student. So, contrary to the definition, punishment is not "any adverse consequence of a targeted behavior that suppresses the behavior," only those harshly delivered or nonlogical. Are the authors singling out the harsh interventions because they are "often designed only to cause discomfort and get even" (162)? In other words, because they are retributive? Here we have the essence of a plausible separation for schools to consider. Punishment is distinguished from the nonpunitive less by what the teacher does than by what she intends (determined by language and tone) and the student's interpretation. Devoid of these subjective aspects the sanction cannot easily be classified.

Intent. Let us go back to Hanna. Several efforts by the teacher—standing silently by her desk, depriving her of recess, and changing her seat—could be either discipline or punishment depending on the presentation by the teacher and understanding by Hanna. Assume at first that the teacher interprets the wandering as due to forgetfulness and distraction. She wants to help Hanna refocus, hence a gentle reminder to instigate behavioral self-awareness and disrupt possible preoccupations. When that is ineffective the teacher has Hanna sit by her desk to curb wandering impulses with a gentle touch. She tries other interventions: asking Hanna's friend to remind her of the rule when she starts to leave her seat and permitting her a brief walk in the hall or taking frequent stretches. Restricting use of the pencil sharpener is also meant to help Hanna stay on task. When cancelling recess, she explains this as an opportunity for Hanna to make up neglected work. All this I interpret as educative discipline.

However, as the wandering continues, the interpretation and intent change. The teacher gets understandably frustrated and is short on time. Sympathy for the child turns into exasperation and exasperation into anger. Presumably, she sees her effort to preserve order as sabotaged by deliberate insubordination. The misbehavior is now an affront against her and the demands of civility. Her goal shifts from educative to punitive, from assisting Hanna to punishing her. While enacting the same behavioral restrictions—on seating, recess, pencil sharpening—she does so now in a scolding harsh tone.

Of course, it takes two to tango. Without knowing why Hanna wanders and fails to complete assignments, even constructive interventions may misfire. Perhaps Hanna is in over her head and wants to hide her ignorance, has an undiagnosed attention deficit, or is angry at the teacher and unwilling to exert herself. If so, any move by the teacher will be received as censure for wrongs committed, as punitive not educative. And the reverse is true as well. A teacher, infuriated by a student's behavior, may intend to administer a retributive punishment but the student does not receive it as such. Hanna might not *feel* punished although the teacher grows harsh and means to be punitive; perhaps she even perceives more severe interventions as useful. She is grateful to have a strict teacher who curbs her impulses and forcefully jolts her willpower. After all, how often does an ex-student exclaim: "she was the strictest teacher I ever had and the best." If

Hanna experiences "tough love" as cared for, then she is not being punished. Or she may be indifferent, indeed proud of receiving a punishment. Obedience holds no attraction and disobedience may win her peer approval. The teacher is hard-pressed to sculpt an educative intervention without knowing the motives behind a behavior, motives that are often inaccessible, and the likely reception to that intervention. Ideally, unveiling the psychology of a child would be a large assist in determining interventions and understanding should certainly get priority over condemnation. But that knowledge is rarely available. The fact that schools must sanction students with limited contextual knowledge surrounding a behavior lessens the justification for punishment.[4] A still stronger argument is that retribution, while perhaps right in a court of law, with all its protective procedures and investigation of context, is not appropriate for children at school given punishment's criteria.

Meeting the criteria for punishment at school

Although there is disagreement as to whether punishment, in addition to being retributive, can have a deterrent, reform, and rehabilitative impact, I claim the three criteria—imposition of pain for moral wrongs of which the student is culpable—are primary. A look at each in the school context suggests that mostly they cannot, and in any case should not, be applied to the school context.

Pain. One assumes that visiting suffering upon an erring student would not be an educator's priority. To deliberately hurt a student even if she has hurt another (just deserts) is a response that replicates and thereby increases the totality of harm. Let us assume Child A deliberately lashes out (verbally or physically) at Child B, the weaker of the two. Is making A suffer the right response? Will that "teach her a lesson"? The goals of a school, I imagine, would chiefly be to prevent a reoccurrence by activating regret in Child A, compensate Child B for the harms committed by Child A, uncover and try to resolve the issues between the children through mutual understanding but not to take revenge. Administering pain is still less appropriate for the breach of rules that are victimless. Hanna's problem appears to be with rule following, not with adversarial relationships. It is hard to see any equivalence between her wrongful acts—upsetting a routine— and deliberately causing her pain.

Were it nonetheless determined that an offender merits some deprivation and/or suffering, the threshold for its administration is obviously high. Pain inflicted, particularly on a minor, must be in accordance with her desert and calibrated to that desert. Yet, determining desert and pain are deeply subjective. What criteria are useful? Contenders might be odiousness of the act and/or incorrigibility of the child. When a student makes teaching impossible by repetitively and intentionally disrupting the classroom, for example, perhaps she merits a painful sanction, assuming other discipline has failed. But how does an authority determine just how awful the disruptions are and then measure the degree of pain deserved? School codes of conduct tend to rank disruptiveness/subordination as more serious than, for example, cheating on a test (Goodman, 2006). It seems likely this is due to the disruption rather than its intrinsic evil. Academic cheating is a more obvious moral wrong—and punished severely in higher education—than at least some forms of disruption. The codes also rank frequency as a determinant. The more often a bad act is repeated, the greater the pain warrant. Clearly insulting a teacher a half dozen times is worse than insulting her once, but some disruptions are less blameworthy than others. Is talking out of turn ten times worse, more deserving of punishment, than throwing wadded paper into the trash or insulting a fellow student? Doesn't it depend as well on the student's understanding of the misbehavior?

Assuming one could count frequency and awfulness of an act, there is no parallel metric for degrees of suffering (just deserts). Presumably the more a punishment is extended, the greater the pain—a week of imposed silence is worse than a lunch period. But again that does not factor the student's experience. What is barely noticed by some, say a long look from a teacher, can deeply humiliate another. One child might find a day of suspension severe, especially if her parents pile on more pain for her misdeed, where another might rejoice in having a day without school. We can be pretty sure that whipping a child, especially in front of others, will be physically and psychologically painful. Yet, it is also possible that substantial numbers of students have developed avoidance strategies to punishment. Rather than experiencing pain, they proudly see themselves as having successfully provoked a teacher's anger and experience the punishment as a mark of status, a badge of courage.

Moral. Commonly, descriptions of punishment, excepting those that equate discipline and punishment, claim it is applicable only for moral wrongs. The function of punishment is not behavior control but affirmation of shared moral values. These overriding mores bind students, teachers, and administration together, uniting them with the larger community. They basically concern the foundational requirements of decency and respect with which we must treat one another as predicates for a viable community. By this reasoning there are hosts of acts prohibited by school rules that should not qualify for punishment because they are not moral violations. As seen in the case of Hanna, much of her misbehavior consists of nonmoral wrongs that a school wants to correct for the sake of future performance. Many commonly disobeyed school rules fall into what John Dewey (1977) and others have called the conventional domain (also Durkheim, 1925/1961). They express the customary values of a particular institution or social group and lack the universality attributed to morality. They are rules of convenience and efficiency and, though perhaps important to the smooth running of a classroom, without moral standing. Accordingly, the daily commission of such offenses as violating a dress code, poor posture, not tracking a teacher, talking out of turn, and tardiness would require other discipline methods, reserving punishment for clear moral violations that harm other students or adults through such acts as deliberate disruption, disrespect, bullying, and aggression (for more contemporary authors on these distinctions, see Nucci, 2001, 2008; Turiel, 2002). However, separating a conventional from moral wrong is often muddy.

Like pain, morality has subjective and contextual elements. Consider swearing, widely forbidden at school, sometimes precipitating suspension and expulsion. Does it fall into the conventional or moral category? According to Joel Feinberg (1985), swearing is merely a nuisance, an act of bad manners like belching, but not the breach of a moral code. Schools, trying to teach students the accepted and expected language codes used in the broader society, can legitimately prohibit swearing because most believe it degrades the language and is therefore not suitable for an educational environment. Still the wrongness would appear to be school-based and the offense conventional—or is it? There is a difference between swearing as an exclamation (it was a fucking hard test; we had a fucking good time) versus as an insult (you fucking ass hole). The former merely underscores a point; the latter is an offensive weapon indistinguishable from other bullying taunts. When swearing is used in attack mode to injure a student, it would qualify as morally wrong.

A further complication is that swearing simply to amplify a statement may nonetheless be offensive to adults. In the past swear words have been strongly prohibited and generally disallowed. A teacher might well feel students using such language are displaying inconsiderateness and disrespect, if not blasphemy; they are insulted. As the violation is repeated, the wrong is perceived not just as breaking a conventional school rule but as intentional insolence/insubordination. A harm that lies in the interpretation of an act but is not intrinsic to it becomes a derivative moral wrong. The teacher has taken a conventional rule—no swearing—perhaps important to the culture of the school—and transformed it into a moral transgression (Goodman, 2006). Because teachers cannot fulfill their role unless they are either feared or respected by students, many school prohibitions serve to protect them from derivative wrongs. When conventional rules, such as Hanna's sharpening a pencil, are broken and the teacher has lost control, she understandably finds students at moral fault even if the behavior in question is by itself not a moral failing. Yet sometimes the student does not need to sharpen her pencil and takes pleasure in upsetting the teacher. The act then is insolent and the derivatively moral becomes morally blameworthy. Once again, in the moment, untangling the contrast is often just not feasible for the educator.

Culpability. Of the three punishment components probably the most difficult to determine is culpability. Because culpability means responsibility, the initial question is what does it mean for a child to be held responsible? In the school context, culpability would be the willful flouting of established mores, yet students tend toward the impulsive and nonrational. They have restricted perspectives; they act first and think later, if at all. We should be wary therefore of assuming they possess the requisite agency to be held fully responsible (Murphy, 2003). Consider the following: the teacher witnesses student A carrying a pile of books when one smashes on student B's foot. Was it an accident? A deliberate assault? Compelled by student C who threatened dire consequences if A did not commit the battery? Payback by A for the teasing and bullying she received from B? Students can commit wrongs and not be culpable (accidents) or be culpable and not commit wrongs (failed attempts to injure). Teachers, however, deal with observable behavior; they are not connoisseurs of motivation and intention. Given imperfect information and an interest in fairness, the teacher is persuaded to treat like acts similarly. She might wish to pursue who is accountable for what (as would a parent adjudicating among her own children), but while a class is watching and ready with its own fairness judgments, equality takes precedence over individualizing relative blame. Judges may award sentences only after all the circumstances involved in a misdeed have been examined thoroughly with the participation of opposing advocates. Teachers are understandably unable and unwilling to make such subtle judgments. Their justification is more on enforcing compliance and deterrence than on just desert—*behave or you'll be punished.* One can be sympathetic to such a consequentialist position while still noting that it stretches punishment beyond its proper restrictions. Subjugating Hanna to condemnation and blame without knowing she is culpable—that is, assuming she could will herself to sit still if she tried—is hard to justify.

Focus on intention. There is an irony here: while punishment and discipline are frustratingly alike and extremely hard to disentangle because they depend on intention and reception, they are sharply discordant in meaning. However, the attitude of the teacher is more readily surfaced. And that is likely pivotal. A student who after disturbing her classroom is sent to help in a kindergarten classroom will decipher if the teacher intends to provide her a useful opportunity for reform or censor her for disruption depending on how the assignment is formulated.

Sometimes teacher intention is obvious by the consequences delivered: the teacher sends the disruptive student to the office with the injunction "The principal could use your help with her paper-work and give you a break from class" versus "The principal will keep you after school in her office because of the disturbance you caused." Sometimes intent is made verbally explicit: "You need some space and time to collect yourself" versus "I'm sending you to the office because you cannot follow the classroom rules." Or even more to the point, "To help you settle down I'm . . ." versus "because of the harm you have done I'm . . ."

Yet it must be acknowledged that motives are often mixed, and intent is not always obvious to teacher or student. A teacher may raise her voice out of frustration, and thereby mortify a student, when her intention was constructive criticism. Ideally, she will note the effect of her tone and quickly moderate it explaining to the student that she meant to be helpful not angry. Or a teacher may be uncertain as to the student's motives and the appropriate response: Did the student deliberately sabotage the classroom or fall apart because of personal stress? In such instances the teacher may try to clarify matters in a private conversation with the student before determining what to do. Understandably, these are subtle decisions requiring deliberation and careful judgment by the teacher. Whether successful or not, however, the thrust of the discipline policy can be for teachers to review the culpability of a student before disciplining her and then make clear her intentions when she administers consequences. It means going beyond the mere act—you do x and y follows—to judging whether educative discipline or a punishment is required. It means taking into consideration the circumstances of an act rather than using cookie-cutter responses for misbehavior. It means sensitizing students to the notion that fairness is not always treating like offenses alike.

Is punishment ever justified in schools?

For the most part a retributive approach fits poorly with educational goals: to teach and ameliorate behaviors that interfere with learning. Punishment is both too draconian and too limited: too draconian because of the pain and culpability requirements; too limited because schools must regulate students' nonmoral offenses. Given the reluctance to hurt a student as well as the complexities of determining a student's culpability and just deserts, punishment should be a reluctant choice. Even if the requirements of punishment are met, it is generally ineffective. Before imposing punishment the authority must be certain it is deserved. Mere repetition of nonmoral offenses, such as breaking the dress code or not completing work, does not usually merit punishment although, as mentioned, what begins as a nonmoral violation such as challenging a teacher or teasing a student can, when repeated, become hurtful (derivatively moral) and deserving of punishment.

Even justifying punishment for breaching foundational norms is often problematic because cultural diversity and generational changes can result in shaky adherence to what presumably are universally accepted norms and because the context surrounding a wrong must be factored into the calculus. We need to be more uncertain about moral certainties. Take hitting. When one student starts punching another without apparent provocation, would the teacher be justified in administering a punishment? Is she certain the no-hitting norm is broadly accepted? Is she sure there was no provocation? I suspect in most instances the perpetrator would plunge into self-justification by retorting along the lines of: "She has been calling me names"; "My parents told me to get even when insulted"; "She deserves it for flirting with my boyfriend." The teacher, not in a position to debate the justification for retaliation, perforce falls back on the argument that hitting is not allowed *in school*. In so doing she is demoralizing the norm, turning it into a school rule subject to discipline but not punishment. What appears cruel to the observer may look reasonable to the perpetrator.

Even taken-for-granted norms such as truth-telling and prohibitions on stealing may be challenged. Lying is acceptable to protect others or oneself from unfavorable exposure ("I am not a squealer." "I lied to stay out of trouble."). Stealing from a store to feed a hungry family or because a proprietor charged too much may also be seen as permissible. Schools have the prerogative to generate rules required for smooth functioning. But they are in a poor position to insist on moral norms about which there is widespread disagreement—such as prohibitions on lying and stealing or duties of compassion and generosity. While they can turn such prohibitions and obligations into school rules, they are on weak grounds establishing them as absolute moral norms. Further, personal/cultural considerations are likely to override instruction. Students are unlikely to buy into school values discrepant from those of the home.

For an authority to mete out pain is a big deal in a relationship premised on care. Given the relatively weak position of students who live under the authority of school personnel, they should be given as much due process as feasible. As an aid in determining desert for serious wrongs—and punishment is inappropriate for nonserious wrongs—a panel of faculty and students might be consulted in assessing the adequacy of the evidence (including context and motives). Another approach to guard against arbitrariness is restorative justice (Ahmed et al., 2001; Brathwaite, 1989, 2000). It seeks both to prevent wrongdoing by establishing a school-wide culture and set of practices accepted by all members of the community and to resolve conflicts through collaboration of all parties. Methods used include restorative circles (inclusive of community members as well as school parties), conferencing, peer mediation, justice panels, public apologies, service, and reflection circles. Conflicts and misbehaviors are not automatically dealt with through punishment but resolved by the working together to restore relationships (Gardner, 2016). However, punishment is not ruled out. Censure and condemnation resulting from conferences are appropriate. Shaming a student is also sometimes called for when it is a prelude to repentance, remorse, and reintegration into the community. Because the process encompasses so many parties deliberating together, there is an opportunity to bolster foundational norms and for consequences to be perceived as just.

Employing penalties is another means of avoiding punishment. Although again there is no red line of separation, penalties fall on the discipline side of the ledger because their purpose is to correct/compensate nonmoral misbehaviors (Newman, 1985; Kleinig, 1982). They have been described as payment for pursuing a prohibited interest. Whereas punishment expresses resentment, indignation, disapproval, condemnation, and denunciation, penalties—paying a fine for failing to return a library book, sitting out when breaking a rule in sports, having to keep an extra uniform at school because of repeated dress-code violations—largely lack the symbolic significance of punishment (Feinberg 1965). Good and Brophy (2008) call such sanctions "response costs" and give as examples restricting the use of materials if they have been misused and suspending recess privileges for repeated fighting. Also included as penalties might be logical/natural consequences (destroy property you must replace it). Although again a penalty may be saddled with pain for the student, it is unlikely to produce guilt and remorse because no moral wrong has been committed. A student may make the calculation that she wants to keep a book for the weekend and incur the consequent fine without feeling guilty. However, if she knows another student is depending on the book to prepare a paper or the sport's rule she broke was a deliberate attempt to hurt an opposing player, then we are back in the moral domain and a mere penalty may be insufficient.

Objections to punishment would be mitigated were it effective in deterrence or reformation. However, unless students are already on board with the rules that punishment is enforcing, they are apt to resist and resent it, showing obedience only out of prudential fear of getting into trouble. Insofar as punishment does deters, the motivation is likely fear of the sanction. Punishment will produce remorse, expiation, and reconciliation only when a student is convinced of her wrongdoing (Feinberg, 1988; Murphy, 2012; Nucci, 2006). As John Dewey pointed out long ago, and contrary to Hampton's (1984) claim that punishment can persuade offenders to reform, "[T]he child and the man yield to force in such a way that their sense of duty is developed only in case they recognize, implicitly, the force or the authority as already *right*" (Dewey, 1969, 332, italics in original). Punishment may even boomerang when flouting a teacher yields the reward of peer group attention, power, and attention (Kleinig, 1982). The research consensus is that any short-term benefits, such as student submission, is outweighed by increased frustration, fear, anger, cynicism, shame, lower grades, and an antagonistic school climate (Bear, 2010; Bear and Manning, 2014; Brophy, 1996; Good and Brophy, 2008; Levin and Nolan, 2014; Osher et al., 2010; Perry and Morris, 2014). While shame and coercion are appropriate sanctions in some circumstances, they do not improve learning (Coverdale, 2020). To compound the problems, studies have long shown punitive techniques not only fail but disproportionately target poor and minority students (Balingit, 2018; Gregory, Skiba and Noguera, 2010; Skiba et al., 2011). By contrast, if discipline is not perceived as a scolding but as integrated into the learning process, it is unlikely to provoke indignation. While a student may not profit from the disciplinary action, a teacher's good intention will more likely be appreciated than resented.

Still, it would be a mistake to prohibit punishment in schools. Despite a general antipathy to it, teachers, like the rest of us, when faced with an unruly class may deliver one because the students have exceeded her frustration tolerance; she has run out of patience and mistakenly punishes a student who might have received more lenient treatment were there only one culprit in the room or this the first incident of the day. She should not be punished for punishing. More importantly, there are occasions and students that may call for it. When a student knowingly, willfully, and repetitively violates the basic morality of the school, foremost the prohibition on deliberate harm to others, punishment is required to uphold the moral norms. Schools are institutions that perforce must regulate student interactions; it is therefore mandatory the impermissible is clear. If the line is crossed a sanction is in order. It then serves to support the moral order of the classroom and larger society. Surely there are norms—prohibitions on bullying, gratuitously stealing prized possessions from peers, lying to take advantage of another student, abusing the weak and marginalized, vandalism, assaulting a teacher—that broadly offend most students' sense of justice. When a student, unprovoked, maliciously pushes a classmate bound to a wheelchair down a flight of stairs she deserves a punishment. If punishment is used rarely, against a backdrop of agreed-upon norms, the emotional impact may stimulate students' remorse, guilt, and arouse a sense of justice. Even if an intervention does not ameliorate the behavior, punishment demonstrates the teacher's legitimate authority to enforce the community's shared basic values.

Concluding thoughts

In an ideal school, students and teachers have similar ambitions and rules set up to further the common goals are accepted. However, since we don't live in an educational utopia not all rules are accepted or obeyed. When breached, the teacher's responses fall into two major categories—punishment or educative discipline (although there are others such as penalties and mediation). The intuitive appeal of punishment is that it serves justice: the wrongdoer has incurred a social debt by upsetting a moral equilibrium; punishment absolves the debt and restores the equilibrium. Beyond the fairness of punishment, it is merited by the wrongdoer; not to be punished denies her equal rights. (Lewis, 1987; Morris, 1976). Moreover, treating-like-cases-alike gives the appearance of fairness premised on equality. It silences objections raised by other students for whom differential treatment can look like favoritism. Finally, it is expedient. Examining extenuating factors that cause similar behavior to merit different interventions is largely beyond the school's investigative resources.

Were schools primarily justice-enforcing institutions, these arguments might have purchase. Were we dealing with adults out in the world, rather than minors in educational institutions, when one person injures another—directly by assault (verbal and physical) or indirectly (lying, cheating)—she may well deserve retribution that expresses society's condemnation for violating fundamental values, subject of course to due process protections. But for schools, strict justice is secondary to the formative educational mandate and students are still in the process of becoming. As an example, were justice the prime objective then persistent truanting might trigger punishment, for the attendance requirement is a well-established communal obligation coded in law and school rules. But where remediation is foremost, it behooves a school to investigate causes of the truanting—in the child and her circumstances—than help resolve them. Because students are enmeshed in complex circumstances with diminished responsibility, the argument that students deserve punishment is vanishingly small.

Those who believe the response to misbehavior should be framed as a remedial opportunity must still interpret the wrong, not obvious from a single act. The student who "talks back" to a teacher is possibly insolent or, alternatively, is exercising a practice common to her culture—no insult was intended. Similarly, the teacher's action also requires interpretation. She may intend to punish but her action is met with student indifference or the intention to remediate interpreted as punishment. Punishment is best understood as a *looped interaction* rather than an act: the teacher intends to inflict it; the recipient closes the loop experiencing it as intended. But the loop is short-circuited when the experience of teacher and student are discordant.

These subjective aspects of wrongful behavior (context and motives of both student and teacher) must be factored into any disciplinary determination. Cookie-cutter lists of rules and consequences, focusing solely on objective behavior, fail to account for them. When in doubt, remediation should be the default position. Retributive punishment for Hanna's misusing the pencil sharpener retribution would be a mistake for there is no indication of deliberate malfeasance. We do not know the cause of her roaming and defiance is just a guess. Rather than an undeserved punishment, such as a recess prohibition, why not have her collect and distribute pencils or sharpen those that have gone dull? While objectively the difference may seem slight, not so to the student. In one instance she perceives the teacher as vindictive, in the other as supportive.

For teachers to consider the distinctions between educative discipline and punishment, and to squelch their retributive impulses, is a big ask, especially given all the nonacademic burdens imposed on them. The isolated teacher in a busy classroom can hardly stop to unravel what precipitated an event or to clearly communicate the intention of her response. Just what additional resources would be most helpful is a determination best left to them in collaboration with other school personnel. The quick and dirty resolution is always to go to the rule book and pull out a response. To ask them to go further we, the askers, must do so as well.

Notes

1 I accept the presumption that discipline is a constant in educational settings. This is not to deny the enormous influence of community mores, school environment, curriculum, relationships, and pedagogy on discipline. They are just not relevant factors to this discussion.
2 Although I advocate that schools resist the punishment of students, this does not mean parents should forswear punishing their children at home where circumstances and relationships are so different. As Jean Hampton wisely noted: "[A] parent who is responsible for the full maturation and moral development of her child is naturally thought to be entitled to punish her children for many more offenses and in very different ways, than the children's schoolteacher" (1984).
3 This, of course, is opposed to the behaviorist definition that a stimulus is a punishment only if the target behavior is diminished, whereas retribution is not focused on behavioral changes.
4 This is another reason why caretakers, with a deeper knowledge of what prompts a child's behavior, are more justified in the use of punishment.

References

Acosta, Joie, Augustine, Catherine, Chinman, Matthew and Engberg, John (2019) *What Two New Studies Reveal About Restorative Justice*. https://www.rand.org/blog/2019/04/what-two-new-studies-reveal-about-restorative-justice.html.

Ahmed, Eliza, Harris, Nathan, Braithwaite, John and Braithwaite, Valerie (2001) *Shame Management through Reintegration*. Cambridge: Cambridge University Press.

American Psychological Association (2008) *Zero Tolerance Task Force*. http://www.apa.org/pubs/info/reports/zero-tolerance.aspx.

Augustine, Catherine, Engberg, John, Grimm, Geoffrey, Lee, Emma, Wang, Elaine, Christianson, Karen and Joseph, Andrea (2018) *Can Restorative Practices Improve School Climate and Curb Suspensions? An Evaluation of the Impact of Restorative Practices in a Mid-Sized Urban School District*. Santa Monica, CA: Rand Corporation. https://www.rand.org/pubs/research_reports/RR2840.html.

Balingit, Moriah (2018) "Racial Disparities in School Discipline Are Growing, Federal Data Show." *Washington Post*, April 24, Washington, D.C.

Bear, George (2010) *School Discipline and Self-Discipline: A Practical Guide to Promoting Prosocial Student Behavior*. New York: Guildford Press; also, Levin, James and Nolan, James, *Principles of Classroom Management*, 7th ed., 2014. New York: Pearson; Skiba and Rausch, 2015.

Bear, George and Manning, Maureen (2014) "Best Practices In Classroom Discipline." In Peter Harrison and Alex Thomas (eds.), *Best Practices in School Psychology:*

Student-Level Service, 256–67. Bethesda, MD: National Association of School Psychologists.

Berman, Mitchell (2016) "Modest Retributivism." In K. Ferzan and S Morse (eds.), *Legal, Moral, and Metaphysical Truths: The Philosophy of Michael S. Moore*, 35–47. Oxford: Oxford University Press.

Braithwaite, John (1989) *Crime, Shame, and Reintegration*. Cambridge: Cambridge University Press.

Braithwaite, John (2000) "Shame and Criminal Justice." *Canadian Journal of Criminology* 42 (3): 281–98.

Brophy, Jere (1996) *Teaching Problem Students*. New York: Guildford Press.

Burden, Paul (2020) *Classroom Management: Creating a Successful k-12 Learning Community*, 7th ed. Hoboken, NJ: Wiley.

Coverdale, Helen (2020) "What Makes a Response to Schoolroom Wrongs Permissible." *Theory and Research in Education* 18 (1): 23–39.

Dewey, John (1969) "The Idea of Obligation." In Jo Ann Boydston (ed.), *John Dewey: The Early Works, 1882–1898, vol. 3, 1889–1892*. Carbondale, IL: University of Southern Illinois.

Dewey, John (1977) "The Moral Training Given by the School Community." In Jo Ann Boydston (ed.), *John Dewey: The Middle Works, vol. 4, 1899–1924*, Carbondale, IL: Southern Illinois University Press.

Dreikurs, Rudolph and Grey, Loren (1968) *The New Approach to Discipline: Logical Consequences*. New York: Penguin.

Durkheim, Emile (1925/1961) *Moral Education: A Study in the Theory and Application of the Sociology of Education*. Glencoe, IL: The Free Press.

Feinberg, Joel (1965) "The Expressive Function of Punishment." *The Monist* 49 (3): 397–423.

Feinberg, Joel (1985) *The Moral Limits of the Criminal Law, vol. 2: Offense to Others*. New York: Oxford University Press.

Feinberg, Joel (1988) *The Moral Limits of the Criminal Law: vol. 4: Harmless Wrongdoing*. New York: Oxford University Press.

Gardner, Trevor (2016) *Discipline over Punishment: Success and Struggles with Restorative Justice in Schools*. New York: Rowman and Littlefield.

Garland, David (1999) "Durkheim's Sociology of Punishment and Punishment Today." In Mark S. Cladis (ed.), *Durkheim and Foucault: Perspectives on Education and Punishment*, 19–35. Oxford: Durkheim Press.

Good, Thomas and Brophy, Jere (2008), *Looking in Classrooms*, 10th ed. New York: Pearson.

Goodman, Joan (2006) "School Discipline in Moral Disarray." *The Journal of Moral Education* 35(2): 213–30.

Gregory, A., Skiba, R. and Noguera, P. (2010) "The Achievement Gap and the Disciplinary Gap: Two Sides of the Same Coin." *Educational Researcher* 39: 59–68.

Hampton, Jean (1984) "The Moral Education Theory of Punishment." *Philosophy and Public Affairs* 13 (3): 238–98.
Hand, Michael (2020) "On the Necessity of School Punishment." *Theory and Research in Education* 18: 10–22.
Kleinig, John (1982) *Philosophical Issues in Education*. New York: St. Martin's Press.
Landrum, Timothy and Kauffman, James (2006) "Behavioral Approaches to Classroom Management." In C. Evertson and C. Weinstein (eds.), *Handbook of Classroom Management: Research, Practice, and Contemporary Issues*, 47–71. Mahwah, NJ: Erlbaum.
Levin, James and Nolan, James (2014) *Principles of Classroom Management*, 7th ed. New York: Pearson.
Lewis, Clive S. (1987) "The Humanitarian Theory of Punishment." *Issues in Religion and Psychotherapy* 13 (1, 11): 147–53.
Mackie, John (1982) "Morality and the Retributive Emotions." *Criminal Justice Ethics* 1 (1): 3–10.
Meyer, Joel (1968) "Reflections on Some Theories of Punishment." *The Journal of Criminal Law, Criminology, and Police Science* 59 (4): 595–9.
Mischel, Walter and Shoda, Yuichi (1995) "A Cognitive-Affective System Theory of Personality: Reconceptualizing Situations, Dispositions, Dynamics, and Invariance in Personality Structure." *Psychological Review* 102 (2): 246–68.
Moore, Michael (1997), *Placing Blame: A General Theory of the Criminal Law*. New York: Oxford University Press.
Morris, Herbert (1968) "Persons and Punishment." *Monist* 52: 475–501.
Morris, Herbert (1976) *On Guilt and Innocence: Essays in Legal Philosophy and Moral Psychology*. Berkeley: University of California Press.
Murphy, Jeffrie (2003) *Getting Even: Forgiveness and Its Limits*. New York: Oxford University Press.
Murphy, Jeffrie (2012) *Punishment and the Moral Emotions: Essays in Law, Morality, and Religion*. New York: Oxford University Press.
Newman, Graeme (1985) *The Punishment Response*, 2nd ed. Albany, NY: Harrow and Heston.
Nucci, Larry (2001) *Education in the Moral Domain*. New York: Cambridge University Press.
Nucci, Larry (2006) "Classroom Management for Moral and Social Development." In C. Evertson and C. Weinstein (eds.), *Handbook of Classroom Management: Research, Practice, and Contemporary Issues*, 711–31. Mahwah, NJ: Erlbaum.
Nucci, Larry (2008) "Social Cognitive Domain Theory and Moral Educ." In L. Nucci and D. Narvaez (eds.), *Handbook of Moral and Character Education*, 291–309. New York: Routledge.
Osher, David, Bear, George, Sprague, Jeffrey and Doyle, Walter (2010) "How Can We Improve School Discipline?" *Educational Researcher* 39: 48–58.

Pace, Judith and Hemmings, Annette (2006) "Understanding Classroom Authority as a Social Construction." In J. Pace and A. Hemmings (eds.), *Classroom Authority: Theory, Research, and Practice*, 1–31. New York: Routledge.

Pace, Judith and Hemmings, Annette (2007) "Understanding Authority in Classrooms: A Review of Theory, Ideology and Research." *Review of Educational Research* 77 (1): 4–27.

Perry, Brea and Morris, Edward (2014) "Suspending Progress: Collateral Consequences of Exclusionary Punishment in Public Schools." *American Sociological Review* 79: 1067–87.

Peters, Richard (1967) *Ethics and Education*. Atlanta: Scott, Foresman.

Scribner, Campbell and Warnick, Bryan (2021) *Spare the Rod: Punishment and the Moral Community of Schools*. Chicago, IL: University of Chicago Press.

Skiba, Russell, Horner, Richard, Chung, Choong-Geun, Rausch, M. Karega, May, Seth and Tobin, Tary (2011) "Race Is Not Neutral: A National Investigation of African American and Latino Disproportionality in School Discipline." *School Psychology Review* 40 (1): 85–107.

Skiba, Russell And Rausch, M. Karega (2015) "Reconsidering Exclusionary Discipline: Efficacy and Equity of Out-of-School Suspension and Expulsion." In E. Emmer and E. Sabornie (eds.), *Handbook of Classroom Management*, 2nd ed., 116–38. New York: Routledge.

Tom, Alan (1984) *Teaching as a Moral Craft*. New York: Longman.

Turiel, Elliot (2002) *The Culture of Morality: Social Development, Context, and Conflict*. New York: Cambridge University Press.

Waller, Willard (1932) *The Sociology of Teaching*. New York: John Wiley.

Wolfgang, Charles (2009) *Solving Discipline and Classroom Management Problems: Methods and Models for Today's Teachers*, 7th ed. New York: John Wiley.

2

Punishment, Pupils, and School Rules

John Tillson and Winston C. Thompson

Introduction

In this chapter, we consider what behavioral requirements schools may establish for students and which (if any) they may enforce through punishment, during compulsory education. Punishment, as we use the word, is the intentional imposition of burdensome treatment on someone—usually on the rule breaker—for having broken a rule, partly because the treatment is burdensome. We aim to identify principles that should guide and constrain which behaviors schools punish and how and why they punish them. In brief, we develop the following principles regarding legitimate requirements that can be made of students and the ways punishment may be used to enforce those requirements. Before children are autonomous, schools may establish both paternalistic and other-regarding requirements but not requirements imposed from within comprehensive conceptions of the good.[1] They may punish children in order to ensure a fair distribution of the burdens and benefits of social arrangements. Schools may punish children for paternalistic reasons, including developmental reasons, but not for reasons of general deterrence. When children become autonomous, compulsory schooling may establish only other-regarding requirements of student conduct.[2] They may punish to ensure a fair distribution of the burdens or benefits of social arrangements; this includes punishing for reasons of general deterrence, due to children's responsible choices enhancing their liability, as well as for other-regarding developmental reasons.

We acknowledge that more or less detail may be given for operationalizing and implementing these principles. Given the generality of our task, we offer limited detail in this regard. A yet more comprehensive account would explain by what authority schools may make and enforce requirements, and to what extent (if any) students or parents should have a role in deciding the requirements. For our present purposes, we highlight that however this authority is distributed, there are better or worse decisions that can be made. In this chapter, we seek only to guide the *content* of these decisions through identifying appropriate goals for and constraints on school discipline.

The concept of punishment

Philosophers define punishment in different ways, sometimes weaving justifications into their definitions. Following H. L. A. Hart, we keep justification and definition separate. We also keep justifications of systems of punishment separate from justifications of particular instances of punishment within systems. Punishment, as we use the word, is the intentional imposition of a burden (or, equivalently, hard treatment) on someone—usually on the rule breaker—for having broken a rule, partly because the treatment is burdensome.[3] Typical school impositions (e.g., setting homework, class learning activities, wearing uniform, and requiring attendance) are often burdensome for those upon whom they are imposed. Indeed, some may wonder whether compulsory schooling is, itself, a form of punishment. As we are concerned with burdens imposed in response to rule-breaking, we do not count it or the other impositions mentioned earlier as punishments. This is so even if they are often *enforced by* punishments. Furthermore, some burden-imposing responses to rule-breaking need not count as punishments. Our qualification that a particular treatment has to be imposed *because* it is burdensome requires the burden imposed to feature in the punisher's intentions as either a means or an end, rather than as a merely foreseen side effect. For example, school exclusions intended only to avert rule-breaking impose a burden on the excluded student as a side effect. Such exclusions also respond to rule-breaking in a way which differs from punishment—namely, by regarding it as evidence of *prospective* rule-breaking, which serves as the real motivating consideration. We give some attention to these burden-imposing responses to rule-breaking but do not regard them as punitive. The qualification "on someone—usually on the rule breaker" is intended to account for group punishment in which a whole group is punished for the perceived rule-breaking of only some of its members.[4] It is interesting to wonder whether the punished party's and wider community's reactions are constitutive of punishment, whether, for instance, their experiencing treatment *as* punishment is necessary or sufficient for that treatment's being punishment.

We think that success in punishment rather than a failed attempt at punishment requires that the party punished experience their treatment as burdensome. So far, we have stated a definition of punishment. Ultimately, we want to say when and how it might be justified.

Kinds of requirements of student behavior

It is important for a theory of school punishment to consider what kinds of behavior schools may require, since it is these very requirements that schools claim a right (or duty) to enforce through punishment. We distinguish three kinds of requirements: *moral, ethical, and prudential*.

Moral requirements. Schools should generally require (and teach) students to behave in non-wrongful ways. Alongside demands not to harm, deceive, demean, or discount others, more controversially, *moral requirements* may also demand that we behave in ways which show due concern and respect for ourselves (e.g., by not self-harming, self-demeaning, or self-corrupting).[5] We may distinguish between points on a continuum of moral principles, with those principles that are least contingent at one end and those which are most contingent at the other. The least contingent principles may find themselves realized in more particular ways as more details about the circumstances are determined (e.g., a general, conditional duty to do no harm may mean obeying a particular principle of following a technician's instructions when using dangerous chemicals in a laboratory). Similarly, students may have contingent, particular (but no less moral):

- Duties to cooperate on fair terms with others (giving them a duty to skill-up within a certain range of skills that are useful in that society), and/or
- Duties of prospective citizenship (giving them a duty to practice civility in whatever form that takes in schools).

Schools often require that students attend, are punctual, obey dress codes, eat in certain venues in allotted windows of time, complete assigned work, obey teachers' reasonable directions, are neat in various ways,[6] bring prescribed equipment, and follow human traffic rules. Rules which enable schools to run in a sufficiently orderly way to achieve their legitimate, *morally required* mission are contingent moral rules. Plausibly, such morally required missions might include giving all students a fair chance of flourishing, ensuring that they and their fellow students respect one another's moral rights and become capable of socially useful work. Such a raison d'être for some school rules gives a reasonably clear justifiability test, which may prove difficult to pass (it may not warrant prohibitions on swearing or requirements to wear particular uniforms, attend religious worship, or display subordination to high-status individuals). At any rate, the various requirements of orderliness in school are highly circumstantial and do not exist across all contexts. Additionally, we may distinguish *ethical and prudential requirements*.[7]

Ethical requirements, such as requirements to eat according to Kosher or Halal standards, are requirements nested within particular comprehensive doctrines or outlooks. Such requirements may be *politically* or *epistemically* controversial. Politically controversial requirements are those which are (or can be) in dispute among citizens who comply with basic moral requirements. Epistemically controversial requirements are those not decisively supported by such evidence and argument as is available.

Prudential requirements are not nested within any particular comprehensive doctrine but are of benefit to the person who conforms with them, though that person is under no moral duty to do so. The benefit is that it enables them to more optimally flourish now and later (e.g., by developing character traits and capacities).

In what follows, we consider whether behavioral requirements of the kinds delimited earlier may be justified in schools or justifiably enforced through punishment. Before considering which of the aforementioned kinds of requirements (if any) schools should make, we consider why schools may make or enforce requirements at all.

Which requirements?

Which (if any) of the kinds of requirements delineated previously should schools make and enforce?

Students are under many moral requirements. These can include duties to abide by such institutional expectations as maintain a sufficiently educational environment. On this understanding, in many cases schools' job is only to hold students to standards that are morally required of them in any case—sometimes to standards enabled by contingent features of the institutional context, sometimes to standards that hold outside of that context. May schools equally require students to comply with the ethical and prudential reasons which apply to them?

Political theorists part ways at a major fault line about the use of coercive power. We distinguish perfectionist, anti-perfectionist, and (what we dub) perceptionist positions:[8]

> Perfectionist: coercive power *may* be exercised by [some authority] over [some subject] in ways that reflect the most credible account of flourishing.
>
> Anti-perfectionist: coercive power *must not* be exercised by [some authority] over [some subject] in ways that reflect an account of flourishing [the subject] can reasonably reject or has not voluntarily submitted to.
>
> Perceptionist: coercive power *may* be exercised by [some authority] over [some subject] in ways that reflect [that authority's] understanding of [that subject's] flourishing.

As the content of the square brackets indicate, the authorities and subjects can be specified in different ways and one may take perfectionist, anti-perfectionist, or perceptionist stances depending on how they are specified. For instance, some may think perfectionism is justified for parents with respect to children in their custody but not justified for states with respect to their citizens or for bosses with respect to their employees. Perfectionists emphasize authorities' duties of concern (to safeguard or promote subjects' flourishing).[9] Anti-perfectionists emphasize authorities' duties of respect (for subjects' rights to form and pursue their own conceptions of the good) and regard perfectionism as wrongfully paternalistic. Perceptionists emphasize the natural authority of some agents (e.g., parents) over some subjects (e.g., their custodial children). Perceptionism and perfectionism are stated as permissions, but they can be restated as requirements. While popular, once made explicit, perceptionism does not look credible as a requirement. It would require authorities to require subjects to behave in ways which are in fact contrary to their well-being, if the authorities' views about flourishing are mistaken enough. A more credible version of perceptionism restates the view as allowing for a permissible margin of error for a perfectionist requirement.

In acting paternalistically, schools must decide how thick or thin a conception of welfare and harm they may act on and on whether to treat children of different ages alike. Perfectionist schooling will hold that coercive power *may* (or must) be exercised by schools over students in ways that reflect the most credible account of well-being. It may aim to ensure behavior that *complies* (rather than merely conforms) with a detailed, particular conception of the good life. It may aim to ensure this just for younger children or for all children. While anti-perfectionist schooling objects to this, in addition to making moral requirements for self- and other-regarding reasons, it may also make *prudential requirements* of, at least, its younger students for paternalistic reasons. In doing so, it will aim to ensure behavior that complies with an inclusive conception of well-being compatible with a wide range of more particular conceptions (e.g., by developing Rawlsian primary goods). Whether schools may oblige and enforce conformity with ethical and prudential requirements depends in part on the moral status of paternalism, to which we now turn.

Paternalism

In summary, our view on the matter is as follows: we think that before children reach an age at which the majority of children become autonomous (in a given domain), schools may establish both paternalistic and other-regarding requirements (in that domain). These include moral and prudential requirements but not ethical ones. When adolescents reach an age at which the majority of students are autonomous (in a given domain), schools may establish only other-regarding requirements of student conduct (in that domain). These include moral requirements but not prudential or ethical ones. Paternalistic requirements are inappropriate. As students become older the range of domains within which they are autonomous will increase.

A central question of political philosophy concerns when and why agents may legitimately compel others to do things or have things done to them. Sometimes other-regarding reasons are cited to justify coercion (e.g., the protection of first- or third-party interests), other times paternalistic reasons are cited (i.e., the protection of the coerced party's interests). Paternalism is often regarded as hard to justify because it can be disrespectful—subordinating *respect* for autonomy to *concern* for welfare. Call that property which properly warrants *respect* and which largely overrides *concern* for welfare, "autonomy." Respect for autonomy requires us not to do things to or with others (unless for compelling, other-regarding reasons) without their consent.[10] Those who think of respect as a weighty consideration independent of concern for welfare may think of some level of ruin as sufficiently bad for considerations of concern to win out. However, they will think that above that threshold people's lives may drop considerably beneath optimal levels of well-being without trumping considerations of respect.

What, then, is the test for deciding when someone is generally autonomous or, more locally, when a single choice of theirs is sufficiently autonomous to warrant respect? A promising answer suggests that children are autonomous when they meet a "control" condition, whereby their actions are under their control.[11]

A too-stringent test is whether a person always identifies and complies with whatever the strongest reasons available to them recommend. Attractively, this enables instrumental and noninstrumental rationality to be the test of control. However, on this view, nobody's actions are under their control. A weaker test for this control condition might be whether an individual generally makes choices of sufficient quality that interference would not improve their lives. However, this test would not take respect seriously since it would leave people with little opportunity to make something of their lives that they can endorse: an opportunity limited only by a lack of effectiveness of means of interference. A more intermediate test might ask whether people sufficiently identify and comply with whatever the strongest *moral* reasons available to them require, this enables them to have a life to live, while still allowing rationality to be the test of control. However, it seems arbitrary to restrict the relevant standard of rationality to rationality within the moral domain.

A better test for whether people meet a respect-conferring standard of control in general might be the following tripartite criterion of action that agents: (a) meet a threshold of instrumental and noninstrumental rationality that is (b) reflected in choices that are (c) non-disastrous, on almost any view.[12] It will involve being able to reflect on, endorse, reject, and prioritize desires (noninstrumental rationality), and to think of things that would count as realizations of these, efficient means to their realization, and ways of combining their realization (instrumental rationality). It will preclude acting on alienated desires (i.e., not acting on desires they wish they did not have).[13] This capacity will require a level of general knowledge that makes the world intelligible and navigable. For individual choices, possessing all relevant information is too high a bar: it may be that individuals can make autonomous choices without some important knowledge (e.g., when a Jehovah's Witness refuses a blood transfusion on the understanding that this refusal is required by a deity or when a manager endorses an employee's plan without hearing it, saying, "Spare me the details—I trust you"). However, at least some level of relevant knowledge (or opportunity for it) is required in these cases. In deciding whether to permit people to exercise control over their lives in potentially harmful ways, it often makes sense to ask whether people are sufficiently informed to make a judgment about the balance of probabilities, payoffs, and harms in prospect.[14] If they are not sufficiently informed, the control condition may not be satisfied. We will return to this control condition in our discussion of liability to punishment.

As applied to the context of schools, one might ask when paternalistic reasons are (relevant and) sufficient for the imposition of compulsory education: for requiring attendance and participation in education for students' own benefit, rather than first- or third-party benefits. Our answer is as follows. First, *concern for children's autonomy-in-prospect* means not doing anything that would frustrate its development and aiming to promote it to at least the level at which it merits respect.¹⁵ Second, if a student is autonomous (tout court, or within some particular sphere), it is wrong to force anything on them in their own interests (tout court, or within that sphere). If they are heteronomous (tout court, or within some prudentially important sphere), it can be permissible to force things on them in their interests (tout court, or within that sphere), especially if doing so is intended to bring about the conditions that would allow them to make autonomous choices about the matter/s at hand. As such, paternalism is part of a moral educational project, attempting to bring heteronomous students to greater moral autonomy by coming to understand the relevant factors, stakes, and consequences of their choices. This would be so even when evaluated from within anti-perfectionist understandings of schooling. However, under anti-perfectionism the coercive power exercised must not reflect an account of flourishing that the student can reasonably reject, where reasonableness is a moral notion measured in compliance with enforceable duties.¹⁶

Institutional practices often wisely settle upon age-based recognitions of autonomy. For the test to be passable by the vast majority of people aged over eighteen or twenty-one (depending on the context), it has to be fairly low— low enough that it is often achieved by many before they reach that age. For this reason, while the capacity-based test of autonomy detailed earlier can make good sense of paternalistic attitudes toward younger children, as Andrew Franklin-Hall (2013, 224) points out, it struggles to accommodate "middle and late adolescents (roughly ages 14–18)." However, he observes that treating adolescents as adults "is in serious tension with our educational aims, which strive to foster much more than the minimal competence for independence in a liberal society" (2013, 224). Rather than age or competence, Franklin-Hall contends that "life-stage" is a permissible watershed for ending paternalistic interventions since (a) it can be compatible with "global autonomy" (immunity to interference in determining the shape of our lives), (b) "paternalism at the beginning of a life is much less intrusive," and (c) it can simply be "a normal period of preparation for assuming full authority" (224, 236).

However, disrespect early on is not the same as respect for all. While compulsory education is less intrusive earlier than later, it is intrusive. It is not on a par with forcing people to wear seat belts, for instance, by failing to conflict with still-developing conceptions of the good. It cuts away a significant chunk of people's lives which they may no longer autonomously govern. On the other hand, compulsory education for other-regarding reasons—when placed at the beginning of life—would reduce the cost to the individual by minimizing its interference in people's life plans, and this insight marks a change in the kinds of requirements we can make of children at different ages. Though Franklin-Hall thinks that discriminating against people on the basis of age is an injustice, we take more seriously the observation that in the course of a normal life, nearly everyone reaches such an age, and large societies need some kinds of efficiencies to enable the transition from one set of powers and liabilities to another. As such, these capacity-tracking age-based statuses are broadly defensible.

The distinction between heteronomy and autonomy captures the foundational importance of autonomy in our arguments regarding punishment in the context of schooling. In what follows, we demonstrate how our previous analyses of autonomy and paternalism might be used to determine what might be required of students and how this might be enforced. In this we offer two guiding principles. In summary, in this section, we have argued that different kinds of requirements can be justified for autonomous and for heteronomous students.

Why punish school students?

With this understanding of justified requirements guiding student behavior, we now turn our attention to justifications for punishing students as a response to violations of these requirements. These can be understood as a subset of reasons that might be thought to render individuals liable for harm (i.e., reasons why a person would not be wronged if they were harmed).[17] Here, it may be helpful to provide another advance summary of our views. Ahead, we will argue that schools may punish both autonomous and heteronomous children to ensure a fair distribution of the burdens and benefits of social arrangements. Schools may punish heteronomous children for paternalistic reasons but not for reasons of general deterrence. When children become autonomous, schools may no longer punish for paternalistic reasons but may punish for reasons of general deterrence, as well as for other-regarding developmental reasons. Justifications for punishment are often divided into the familiar categories of purely backward- and forward-looking justifications and admixtures, in these terms we accept one forward-looking justification and one admixture. We begin by rejecting purely backward-looking views.

Backward-looking justifications. Some deontic views say that some proportionate amount, degree, and kind of suffering for wrongdoers "fits" their wrongs. The deontic approach does not require that punishment be instrumental to any further good or that it reward the efforts by constituting a better state of affairs than would obtain had punishment never occurred. Joan F. Goodman (2006) provides a nuanced retributivist position on punishment in schools. On her account, pupils' culpable moral wrongs *deserve* punishment. This is in contrast with breaking conventional rules. While the culpability condition "would largely eliminate punishment for children up to their teen years" (224), for Goodman,[18] the word "largely" allows for exceptions. On her account, "children can be knowingly and wilfully malicious; therefore deserving of punishment" (Goodman, 2006: 224). On our reading, this notion of "desert" seems vengeful. Though Goodman does not defend moral retribution as the sole valid justification of punishment, the offered analysis seems to assume it throughout. She provides an example that may be persuasive to some:

> A teacher insists a young boy apologize for hitting a girl, and "make it up to her" in some way; a way is suggested to him when he cannot think of a way himself.

This example is not well understood as retributivist. Goodman suggests the victim does not benefit from the intervention and that the primary intention is to give him a deserved, and unpleasant, experience. A more plausible interpretation sees the intervention as imposing an additional burden of moral training in the practice of compensation.

In her chapter for this volume, Goodman invokes expressions that intimate different kinds of justifications for punishment: for example, retributive punishment "absolves the debt," "can be deserved," "restores" an "upset moral equilibrium," and ensures "equal rights." We do not find these suggestive locutions and appeals attractive or persuasive. First, we regard our own approach as protecting and reflecting equal rights, without being retributivist. Second, we do not accept suffering as a noninstrumentally valuable response to wrongdoing. Third, while wrongdoing does create obligations, such as compensation or apology, and makes urgent the need to reform any character defects, it is hard to see how someone's suffering harm is, in itself, any defensible improvement in states of affairs. Finally, punishment (and even compensation and apology) cannot undo wrong, even though they can make things better than they otherwise would be.

Following Victor Tadros, we hold that "just desert" is unattractive as a punishment justification, even in the case of adults. First, other things being equal, burdens, pains, and negative experiences should be avoided and never sought. Second, whether these burdens and pains are sometimes rightly sought noninstrumental goods is controversial; as such, it would violate political neutrality to act on such a principle. Third, the aim of "just deserts" does not appear so desirable that it could justify associated costs such as reduced rewards and opportunities for learning. Having rejected desert-based views, we now consider consequentialist views in the school context.

Forward-looking justifications. Burdens are sometimes intentionally imposed because they are means to good consequences. The primary good consequences that punitive burdens are thought to conduce to are character reform and/or offense reduction. This view can look suspicious. If punishment truly works as a general deterrent, then why are there any offenses at all? If it effectively reforms characters or works as a special deterrent (i.e., deters those punished), then why are there re-offenses? The most credible version of the view holds that such mechanisms do not work infallibly but sufficiently. On the forward-looking view, a condition for the justness of doing harm (by imposing burdens) is that the good consequences obtained through harming outweigh the harm done. More precisely stated, this view suggests that the net balance of value is higher; the state of affairs is best from an impersonal perspective, or *impersonally best*. On an unconstrained consequentialism, all harms, no matter how they are produced, are alike in disvalue and producing a net increase in value is a sufficient enabling condition for doing harm.

However, it seems that (other things being equal) it is worse to intentionally do or allow harm, rather than do harm as a foreseeable side effect. We might call this view *byproduct discount*. The *byproduct discount* clause has consequentialist and deontic readings. On a consequentialist reading, one intentional harm might be worse than two merely foreseen harms, and doing one intentional wrong better than letting two intentional wrongs (by others) occur (i.e., what is *impersonally best*). In contradistinction, the deontic reading allows an *agential* perspective that usually trumps the impersonal perspective and says that without their consent, we are not permitted to use people (especially not in harmful ways), even to produce a greater good (i.e., bring about what is impersonally best). On the deontic reading, harming one person is wrong even though *impersonally worse* than letting two people be similarly harmed by someone else (although, at some point, consequentialist reasons may dissolve deontic constraints; perhaps harming one person is not wrong to avoid similar harm to millions).[19]

Additional considerations about which states of affairs are valuable add further variety to this family of views. For instance, if one holds that suffering is generally intrinsically dis-valuable but intrinsically valuable when attached to wrongdoers, a quite different picture emerges than would if one were indifferent about who suffers. Further questions concern which distributions of benefit are most valuable. We have already rejected the idea that suffering is intrinsically valuable when attached to wrongdoers. We discuss the distributive question later in this chapter.

Notice that neither unconstrained consequentialism nor the version constrained by a consequentialist reading of *byproduct discount* gives a principled limitation on who may be burdened to produce good consequences. There is no special permission, for instance, for injuring culpable wrongdoers to a greater degree than innocents. If false accusations of wrongdoing produce a valuable, lively sense of injustice, they are justified.[20] We find this consequence unattractive in the case of autonomous adults and favor the deontic reading of byproduct discount. However, the deontic restriction on doing harm seems to make it impermissible to intentionally harm people in most cases. It licenses only acting in ways that generate proportionate negative side effects of being denied opportunities to harm others. But these are not punishments as they are not intentional impositions of harms in response to wrongdoing. First, it is only in an attenuated sense that the harms inflicted are *responses* to wrongdoing (i.e., as evidence of a danger of further wrong and not cause in their own right), and second, the harms are side effects rather than intentional impositions. However, exceptions exist. If pain is imposed for the good of the person upon whom it is imposed (*qua*, say, character development), then it can be justifiable to punish people in response to their wrongdoing if (a) they have given their consent to such treatment or (b) their consent is not required for such treatment. In the case of young children, it might be thought that such consent is not required (cf. Tadros, 2020).[21]

A hybrid justification. A modified forward-looking view integrates a backward-looking component and says that potential punishing authorities may harm wrongdoers where doing so fulfills a protective duty to the community accrued in doing wrong (via a mechanism of general deterrence), but only up to the level of harm they have a duty to sustain in the course of that protective duty (i.e., Victor Tadros's "duty view" of punishment).[22] A "lesser evil" principle says that if that duty can be executed in either a more or less harmful way, the less harmful way is preferable. This view introduces a principled reason for injuring culpable wrongdoers but not innocents (it restricts use of the kinds of hard treatment associated with punishment to use in responding to wrongdoing). In the case of liability unenhanced by responsible choice, apportioning impositions of punishment becomes a matter of distributive justice—a matter we will turn to shortly.

Paternalistic punishment

How might punishment benefit the punished individual? Here are three suggestions:

1. *Compliance*. Punishment itself might be thought to help develop compliance with just rules by developing relevant dispositions (e.g., knowledge and attitudes) in the party punished.
2. *Conformity*. Alternatively, it might be thought to help ensure conformity with just rules, which is less bad in itself than breaching these rules.
3. *Enablement*. Punishment might enforce and thereby enable valuable activities (e.g., learning, cooperating) or reduce general chances of being harmed.

The idea that punishment enables compliance by engaging students' rationality (rather than bypass or subvert it, or appeal entirely to prudential reasons) is popular in the literature. Punishing actions is thought to communicate:

1. That an action is wrong (Hampton, 1984, Morris, 1981)
2. Why an action is wrong (Hampton)
3. The seriousness of the wrong (Morris, 1981, Hobson, 1986, Hand, 2018)
4. The depth of the punisher's attachment to standards of conduct (Morris, 1981).

Hobson suggests that it may be essential for understanding the concept of wrongness at all. Others think that punishment trains us. Michael Hand takes this kind of view. In Hand's view, although differential punishment can convey an understanding of gravity, its main justification is for conditioning us. Hand illustrates this with the case of parents smacking their children.

> When a mother smacks a child for, say, tripping up his younger sister near the top of a staircase, or next to a busy road ... she is attempting to convey to her son the seriousness of his wrongdoing and to establish in him a visceral aversion to putting others in danger. Although she intends to cause her son temporary pain, she does not intend to injure him or cause him harm. Her purposes are educative,

and while it is not self-evident that smacking is an effective educational tool, nor is it self-evident that it is not. (2018, 81)[23]

Paternalistic harms and punishment (whether of a special deterrent or educational kind) may look suspicious here too. Similar to the deterrence arguments analyzed earlier, if paternalistic punishment works, one wonders why there are re-offenses? A plausible response is that while the practice is not fail-proof, it works reliably enough that persons have good reason to think that it will be in the punished individual's interests (to comply or conform with just expectations), such that it is worth enacting, at least as a general practice. A failure rate that would defeat this practice would need to be specified.

However, the crucial premises that punishment is necessary (if not sufficient) for communicating the wrongfulness of action (Hampton and Morris), the degree of wrongness, or the idea of wrongness in general (Hobson) are left undefended. It is plausible to think there are sufficiently communicative, nonpunitive strategies. For Hampton, punishment alerts the punished person to the reasons it was wrong. However, it is hard to see how punishment directs the punished to a sense of the reasons, except perhaps seeing what it's like to suffer in the way one caused or risked causing suffering. It is hard to see that as essential, or even contingently integral, to communication. In Hand's case, the claim that it is not self-evident that smacking is not an effective educational tool is not strong enough to warrant the practice. It seems that it would have to evidently be the least harmful means of achieving a necessary goal. The same holds for punishment in general. While we doubt that punishment is needed to promote compliance, we accept that it is more likely to promote conformity and enable valuable activities.[24] But why confer such benefits on others? What reasons support or motivate these interventions? We hold two candidates in mind:

1. Perhaps an authority *owes them* some good (as an entitlement).
2. Perhaps an authority is permitted to provide them with some good (preferentially, perhaps). On this understanding, the use of punishment seems optional (unless required for other reasons).[25]

However, approximating a wrongdoing sensitive burden-imposition might be the thought that while all of us are liable to assume burdens for the sake of improving social conditions, some punitive-looking sanctions are only effective at improving social conditions when imposed on those who have done wrong.

Both on the forward- looking and on the hybrid account, we will find that some duties are unenforceable:

it may sometimes be undesirable for the government to attempt to enforce certain duties or political values. This might be due to different reasons. Some of them are related to feasibility problems. At other times, attempting to enforce a duty might violate the duty (or the value) it aims to enforce. Another reason for nonenforceability may be that enforcing one duty involves the violation of a different duty (or the value that a duty is supposed to serve), which overrides the first duty. (Moles, 2015, 660–1)

Before discussing liability unenhanced by choice and concluding, we now turn to discuss liability enhanced by choice (i.e., distribution of harms and benefits).

Capacities for control and responsibility

A minimal sense of responsibility might be stated in the following way: persons are responsible for an outcome if they are the proximate cause of that outcome. A more demanding sense (to a first approximation) might be stated as follows: persons are responsible for an action to the extent that they could have chosen to avoid it.[26] Where the action is wrong, and a person lacks a valid excuse, the person is *to blame*. It is often thought that responsibility for wrongdoing means that an individual becomes liable to having more harm visited on them. But young children, at least infants, are generally agreed to lack responsibility and so not be *to blame*. While they might be at fault in having acted wrongly, they lack the fault of having been sufficiently responsible to enhance their liability. More accurately, children's capacities are thought to evolve and in doing so, children are thought to become more responsible for their actions. Eventually, they are thought to (often) be fully responsible for their actions or often sufficiently responsible for their actions to warrant more harmful responses to their actions.[27]

What kind of responsibility matters for how people may be treated, why should any kind of responsibility matter at all, and why does more of it license different treatment? This question will foreground our discussion of what responses are left in cases where individuals' responsibility is evolving. The relevant lens through which we should discern morally salient differences between kinds and degrees of agency is one provided (or inspired) by Hart: a person is responsible if they had fair opportunity to do otherwise. This can be scalar; a person can be liable for more punishing treatment in proportion with their degree of responsibility. This can manifest in external features (e.g., freedom from duress) and internal conditions (e.g., having suitable capacities).[28] As Nelkin (2016) observes, "what determines blameworthiness is whether one has had a fair opportunity to avoid wrongdoing, where whether one has such an opportunity depends on both one's capacities and one's situation."[29] Let us assemble and consider respects in which responsibility might be differentially scored, paying particular attention to suitable capacities. We judge them as relevant because they effect the degree of difficulty and effort required to comply with requirements and, in their absence, an actor lacks a fair opportunity for such compliance.[30]

1. Having or having access to relevant moral, factual, and normative knowledge (i.e., of the relative weight of reasons).[31]
2. Having self-control. Self-control is composite into four dissociable, scalar capacities. These are capacities for deferred gratification, to maintain goals despite distraction, to suppress inappropriate impulses, and to cancel a started action.[32]
3. Context control: Students in compulsory schooling may lack one means of avoiding wrongdoing: we can avoid testing our self-control by controlling the situations we are in, if we cannot do that, we are perhaps less responsible for where we give into temptation and so on.

What is the threshold of these conditions that must be met by people's choices in order to render them liable for use in general deterrence for wrongdoing? If one thinks that the majority of adults can make choices which make them liable for use in this way, then one will think that some or even many adolescents will be liable for use in this way. However, again, we note that large societies need some kinds of efficiencies to enable the transition from one set of powers and liabilities to another.

Distributive justice: Liability without responsible choice

Suppose control never made a difference to how burdens and benefits should be distributed. What then? It seems that discipline regimes should be assessed in terms of (non-desert based) distributive justice alone. Tillson and Oxley (2020a, 48) offer the following:

> Arguably, if a child, Sandra, consistently and significantly undermines the weighty interests of others (e.g., the physical or mental well-being of other children or educational opportunities), teachers might reasonably aim to

prevent this from happening, and exclusion might be a means of the last resort. This might even be to Sandra's detriment so long as

1. other strategies have been exhausted,
2. the detriment is not disproportionate to the interests others are protected in,
3. is as minimal as affordable and
4. is not for its own sake but a by-product (e.g., of the effective protection of others' weighty interests, such as educational opportunities to some level which is fair on them).

They clarify disproportion in a footnote.

> For instance, if other children were to be protected in their opportunity to learn one fact each, and it came at the expense of Sandra knowing nothing at all, this condition would not be met. (fn 17)

Elsewhere, Tillson elaborates this differently.

> If removing a child from a school community will diminish their educational opportunities, that's a reason not to do it. And if keeping them in the school diminishes other people's educational opportunities that's a reason to remove them. So which should you do? One way to think about this is to focus on the adequacy of education. If keeping that child in the school gives them access to an adequate education and doesn't diminish anyone else's education below a threshold of adequacy we may not have a reason to remove them yet. Even though removing them would improve everyone else's education. If removing them improved everyone else's education a just little bit, but it wasn't inadequate in the first place, and put this child in a situation where they get an inadequate education it looks like you shouldn't remove the child from the school because it visits upon them a disproportionate harm and that can be so even though removing them will produce more education in general. More education in general isn't what matters, what matters is how it is distributed: we should ensure, so the thought goes, that everyone has an adequate education, not that more learning happens in general. (Tillson and Oxley, 2020b 15:06–16:40)

These arguments might seem to advance a view that evaluates circumstances only in reference to educational outcomes. But, of course, more matters in a life than only education: sometimes a better education might have a remedial effect (or counterbalancing effect) on poor quality family life—so that people with worse family lives might have a claim to more education than others. People with better family lives might have less of a claim. If this is so, children from loving families might have to put up with more misbehavior from children from unloving families than children from unloving families would have to put up with from children from loving families. Tillson and Oxley float a sufficientarian approach to distributive justice. Our point is not to say that they are right about this,[33] but that they are right to draw attention to the importance of principles of distributive justice to work out the distribution of harms and benefits when it comes to protection from wrongdoing.

There may be nonideal situations in which loving families tend to be wealthy and have power and choices and leverage for less tolerance toward the behavior of children from unloving families than justice requires, and they may use this leverage to get what they want: if schools do not equally respond to equal *actus reus*, they will remove their child and this may diminish the quality of education more widely. Full engagement with these arguments may mean that national-level laws must be enacted and, perhaps, international treaties created and endorsed, such that this kind of power cannot be exercised.

Conclusion

Before children are at an age at which the majority of children are autonomous, schools may establish both paternalistic and other-regarding requirements. These include moral and prudential requirements but not ethical ones. When adolescents reach an age at which the majority of students are autonomous, schools may establish only other-regarding requirements of student conduct. These include moral requirements but not prudential or ethical ones. Since autonomy-relevant capacities come in degrees and can be sufficient to warrant respect in certain domains before they warrant respect more completely, as students become older the sphere of domains within which they are autonomous will increase.

How may these requirements be enforced? Consider moral requirements first. Consider a developmentally typical child, a middle adolescent, and an adult who each violate some moral requirement. Paternalism warrants treatment that helps make the child behave better (or otherwise avoids their doing wrong) for their own sake but not the adult. It may not (ideally) warrant such treatment for the middle adolescent, but reasons of efficiency may make it permissible. Distributive considerations of general or background liability (undisturbed by responsible choice) warrant treatment that helps make the child behave better for the sake of others. A similar but inverse pattern holds when we consider liability enhanced by responsible choice. Choice-enhanced liability warrants treatment of adults that deters similar wrongdoing by others but does not warrant such treatment of children. It may (ideally) warrant such treatment for the middle adolescent, but reasons of efficiency and the avoidance of injustice in discretion may make it impermissible.[34]

Now consider prudential requirements. Consider a developmentally typical child and a middle adolescent who each violate some prudential requirement. Paternalism warrants treatment that helps make the child behave better (or otherwise avoids imprudent behavior) for their own sake. It may not (ideally) warrant such treatment for the middle adolescent, but reasons of efficiency and injustices that may arise in making the matter discretionary may make it permissible. That said, disobedience of legitimate authorities pursuing legitimate duties of their office (which includes the promotion of prudence) in a legitimate way might warrant some burdens designed to ensure conformity or promote compliance. Such duties and permissions will gradually disappear as the child approaches majority (i.e., as their range of local competencies increase). The expressive content of this treatment is as follows: "I am entrusted with your good and this action is for your own good. Until you're mature enough to decide your own good or otherwise override it, I have duty to ensure you behave in accordance with your good, and I am permitted to place proportionate burdens on you to ensure that you do so." While that is surely a complicated message likely too difficult for most young students to understand, it nevertheless captures important elements of the view we advance.

Students can be responsible for violating prudential requirements but not blameworthy for doing so. Heteronomous students may be punished if it conduces to conformity with such requirements. Autonomous students may not. Pupils can be blameworthy for violating moral requirements. Autonomous individuals can be punished for reasons of general deterrence where they are blameworthy. As to whether reactive blame or its expression is appropriate, we remain agnostic in this chapter. We note that it is often natural and where it is hard to avoid, but bad, it might be excusable or permissible but to be avoided. On the other hand, if it is peculiarly educational in shaping our habits toward justified thoughts, feelings, and actions, in ways that spares us cognitive burdens, this educational payoff may warrant teachers' faking reactive attitudes where they don't feel them. At a minimum accurate diagnostic blame and its articulation are appropriate where pupils are blameworthy. Where students are only minimally responsible and their behavior is wrongful (or requiring improvement), they are apt to be corrected and trained to "make up for it."

Acknowledgments

Thanks to Matthew Clayton, Jeff Howard, Tom Parr, Bill Wringe, J. Adam Carter, Neil Levy, Ian MacMullen, Laura Oxley, Kartik Upadhyaya, and Viktor Ivanković, and to an audience at The Ohio State University Political Theory Workshop seminar.

Notes

1. It is, we think, never justifiable to impose on children requirements from within comprehensive conceptions of the good. It is not justifiable in private schools or in public schools, in contemporary Britain or in medieval Britain. However, despite this, doing so may be excusable in some nonideal circumstances. For instance, while not justified to punish in line with a comprehensive doctrine, a punisher who has been indoctrinated to think only in terms of that comprehensive doctrine might be forgiven or otherwise excused for having done so. Additionally, we acknowledge that autonomous adolescents and adults may sometimes voluntarily enter private educational institutions that enforce requirements from within comprehensive conceptions of the good. However, as a condition of permissibility, punishment within the boundaries of these institutions can only be excused if alternative, institutions of comparable quality are available for student attendance as determined by any separable secular educational goals that those institutions serve (such as legal education). We thank Ian MacMullen, Neil Levy, and Bill Wringe, respectively, for pressing us to clarify these related points.
2. Viktor Ivanković points out, correctly, that a single requirement can be motivated by both paternalistic and other-regarding justifications. In such cases, a single rule may be justified for both children and adolescents—justified in two ways for children and in just one way for adolescents. In cases where rules are only justifiable in one way or the other, then they are only justifiable for one group or the other.
3. We thank Bill Wringe for suggesting the qualification "partly or wholly because the treatment is burdensome" so as to more clearly express our position elaborated beneath.
4. We thank J. Adam Carter for pointing out a helpful counterexample to our previous formulation.
5. The relevant standard of well-being may be anti-perfectionist (i.e., one that is broadly agreeable across morally permissible comprehensive doctrines, perhaps so that one might yet commit to any one of these) or perfectionist (i.e., the most evidence-responsive account of well-being).
6. Apple (1982) emphasizes neatness among school expectations.

7 Of course, one might be tempted to introduce legal requirements as a fourth category: *legal requirements* are whatever the law happens to require teachers and schools to require of students as well as whatever the law requires of students. We resist this temptation as legal requirements shift focus from *what* is required to *whose* requirements they are. What the law *ought* to require schools to require is a question of the kind we said at the outset we would bracket, namely a question about how decision-making authority should be distributed rather than which decisions should be made, however it is distributed. It may be worth noting that in nonideal contexts, unjust laws can form part of the conditions which effect what teachers are justified or excused for requiring and punishing.

8 This statement is indebted to Clayton (forthcoming). For further discussion of antiperfectionism in schooling, see Clayton (2006, 2015).

9 Some versions of perfectionism, like Joseph Raz's preferred principles of state governance, can be liberal in a few ways. First, they can regard ethical requirements as impermissible to enforce (albeit providing for perfectionist government action through taxation is a form of enforcement). Second, they can regard there as being many and various ways of satisfying ethical requirements (e.g., of living a sufficiently flourishing life). Third, they can regard uncoerced, unmanipulated choice as partly constitutive of well-being.

10 Some philosophers subsume respect under concern, saying that the reason we should not interfere with people for paternalistic reasons is that it undermines their well-being. This could be for different reasons: (1) because people are most likely to know what is in their own interests, (2) because the uncoerced choice of activities is a precondition of, or enhances, the goodness of the things chosen, (3) because coercion tends to be the third best to people's choosing what is suboptimally good for them.

11 Another prominent answer is that children's identities are sufficiently integrated. Schapiro (1999) and Richards (2010, Ch. 6) take such a view.

12 The position is somewhat similar to that of the soft paternalist who endeavors only to limit harmful actions that a person has not *freely* chosen Feinberg (1983) and who aims to intervene to support freedom of choice rather than positive outcomes, but we adopt the nomenclature of control and allow non-disastrousness of outcomes as a test of adequate control.

13 Frankfurt (1971).

14 Regarding specific choices, Joel Feinberg (1986, Ch. 18) recommends a twofold test for paternalistic intervention. Both insufficient voluntariness (understood as an expression of will) and potential harmfulness are required before interference is permitted. Connecting this with schooling, it may be suggested that children in general lack sufficient voluntary control of their actions to warrant respect and that regular and constant paternalistic intervention and guidance are permitted. While that might seem right, it seems strange to suggest that children's imprudent actions cannot express their wills. We recast voluntariness in terms of a control condition, but our position is much like Feinberg's.

15 Plausibly the human good consists partly in autonomous action (even if, in the end, respect for autonomy requires prioritizing it over welfare) and so it seems likely that considerations of welfare require the development of autonomy. See Feinberg (1992).
16 This chapter's authors are a little divided on the question of whether to be perfectionists or anti-perfectionists. Tillson argues for perfectionism in various places (Tillson, 2017, forthcoming). Thompson takes a more anti-perfectionist approach (Nikolaidis and Thompson, 2021; Thompson, Beneke, and Mitchell, 2020). That said, given the current state of evidential and argumentative play, perfectionism may have scant resources to provide more detailed guidance than anti-perfectionism: there is no decisively attested conception of flourishing. Even perfectionists can regard paternalistic *coercion* as wrongful and, therefore, adopt a broadly Rawlsian approach, regarding individuals as autonomous when they are able to form and pursue a conception of the good, encouraging them to recognize requirements of justice, and permitting them to pursue their conceptions of the good only so far as they respect these constraints.
17 Harms are various. One kind of harm can be the deprivation of opportunities. For instance, having access only to plastic cutlery reduces one's opportunity to hurt someone with a dangerous implement but at the cost of being able to cut food with ease, and, depending on the context, it may be experienced as an indignity.
18 Goodman cites Piaget and Kohlberg in support of this claim.
19 Compare Nagel (1986, Chapter 4).
20 Thanks to Matthew Clayton for this suggestion.
21 Tadros sketches a defense of this view (2019).
22 This view has interesting consequences (e.g.) if you cannot deter murder by elongating sentences further than two years, say, then murderers may only receive custodial sentences of two years. In this case, further protective duties might still be owed and might be repaid in some other manner (perhaps through community service).
23 Hand regards whether smacking is permissible as a matter of reasonable disagreement.
24 Finally, it might be thought that punishing children *as if* they were responsible actors when they break a rule contributes toward forming their capacities for control.
25 Relevant considerations to determining whether these hold include whether there is a just distribution of responsibilities for doing good, whether the costs of providing the benefit (costs to the benefactor, beneficiary, or others) defeat a permission or duty to do the good, and whether the advantage conferred by punishment unfairly advantages them over others who receive less punishment.
26 This may be regarded as false due to Frankfurt-examples (although, to varying degrees, we each remain sceptical) or if hard-determinism should be true. Levy (2014) describes Fischer and Ravizza's alternative view (1998): "responsibility requires not regulative control—actual access to alternative possibilities—but

only guidance control. Roughly speaking, we exercise guidance control over our actions if we would recognize reasons, including moral reasons, as reasons to do otherwise, and we would actually do otherwise in response to some such reason in a counterfactual scenario."

27 We should note that judgments of agency do not entail (all by themselves) judgments about what responses are appropriate—so this last thought indicates how people often index responsibility against degrees of punitive response (e.g., responsible enough for this harsher form of response). At this level and stage of analysis, we are identifying principles that might guide us in determining relative degrees of response rather than specifics of the response itself.

28 True, a bad upbringing (external) might result in poor capacities, but it's the capacities that matter here rather than the history (that's just the explanation for the lack of capacity). That said, poor capacities can be our own fault—if we had sufficient capacity to improve/maintain our capacities but didn't take advantage—a bit like drinking alcohol.

29 Nelkin also cites degree of sacrifice, which seems more relevant to excusability.

30 Another strategy could be to take a person with a guilty mind, then isolate and subtract elements, asking after each distillation whether they are still guilty.

31 Rosen (2004).

32 Churchland, Patricia (2013) "On Self Control," *Philosophy Bites*, with David Edmunds and Nigel Warburton. An alternative (Aristotelian) view is that we are responsible for an action when it reflects a stable character trait. Sometimes this is called an expressive view of responsibility (as opposed to a control theory) (Levy), sometimes it is called an attributability view of responsibility (as opposed to an accountability view) (Nelkin).

33 For example, for Tillson, a Dworkinian hypothetical insurance model of distributive justice may be an improvement.

34 There are questions about on which side one should err. On the one hand, erring so as not to punish for reasons of choice-enhanced liability adolescents who are not sufficiently autonomous to have incurred preventative duties might be contrasted with, on the other hand, the potential error of imposing the good on adolescents who are sufficiently autonomous to be owed respect. Actors have a choice about who the system will err so as to wrong and in which way.

References

Apple, Michael (1982) *Education and Power*. Boston: Routledge and Kegan Paul.
Churchland, Patricia (2013) "On Self Control." *Philosophy Bites*, with David Edmunds and Nigel Warburton. https://philosophybites.com/2013/12/pat-churchland-on-self-control.html.

Clayton, Matthew (forthcoming) *Independence for Children*. Oxford: Oxford University Press.

Clayton, Matthew (2006) *Justice, Legitimacy and Upbringing*. Oxford: Oxford University Press.

Clayton, Matthew (2015) "Anti-Perfectionist Childrearing." In A. Bagattini and C. Macleod (eds.), *The Nature of Children's Well-being*, 123–40. Dordrecht: Springer.

Feinberg, Joel (1983) "Legal Paternalism." In Rolf E. Sartorius (ed.), *Paternalism*, 3–18. Minneapolis: University of Minnesota Press; Reprinted in Feinberg, *Harm to Self*.

Feinberg, Joel (1986) *Harm to Self*. Oxford: Oxford University Press.

Feinberg, Joel (1992) "The Child's Right to an Open Future." In Joel Feinberg (ed.), *Freedom and Fulfilment: Philosophical Essays*. Princeton University Press.

Fischer, John Martin and Ravizza, Mark (1998) *Responsibility and Control: A Theory of Moral Responsibility*. Cambridge: Cambridge University Press.

Frankfurt, Harry G. (1971) "Freedom of the Will and the Concept of a Person." *The Journal of Philosophy* 68 (1): 5–20.

Franklin-Hall, Andrew (2013) "On Becoming an Adult: Autonomy and the Moral Relevance of Life's Stages." *Philosophical Quarterly* 63 (251): 223–47.

Goodman, Joan F. (2006) "School Discipline in Moral Disarray." *The Journal of Moral Education* 35 (2): 213–30, 218.

Hampton, Jean (1984) "The Moral Education Theory of Punishment." *Philosophy & Public Affairs* 13 (3): 208–38.

Hand, Michael (2018) *A Theory of Moral Education*. London: Routledge.

Hobson, Peter (1986) "The Compatibility of Punishment and Moral Education." *Journal of Moral Education* 15 (3): 221–8.

Levy, Neil (2014) *Consciousness and Moral Responsibility*. Oxford: Oxford University Press.

Moles, Andrés (2015) "Nudging for Liberals." *Social Theory and Practice* 41 (4): 644–67.

Morris, Herbert (1981) "A Paternalistic Theory of Punishment." *American Philosophical Quarterly* 18 (4): 263–71.

Nagel, Thomas (1986) *The View from Nowhere*. Oxford: Oxford University Press.

Nelkin, Dana Kay (2016) "Difficulty and Degrees of Moral Praiseworthiness and Blameworthiness." *Noûs* 50 (2): 356–78.

Nikolaidis, Alexandros C. and Thompson, Winston C. "Breaking School Rules: On the Permissibility of Student Noncompliance in an Unjust Educational System." *Harvard Educational Review* 91 (2): 204–26.

Richards, Norvin (2010) *The Ethics of Parenthood*. Oxford: Oxford University Press.

Rosen, Gideon (2004) "Skepticism about Moral Responsibility." *Philosophical Perspectives* 18 (1): 295–313.

Schapiro, Tamar (1999) "What Is a Child?" *Ethics* 109 (4): 715–38.

Tadros, Victor (2019) "Punishing Children." *Pedagogies of Punishment Website*. https://www.pedagogiesofpunishment.com/blog/2019/8/20/punishing-children.

Thompson, Winston C., Beneke, Abigail J. and Mitchell, Garry S. (2020) "Legitimate Concerns: On Complications of Identity in School Punishment." *Theory and Research in Education* 18 (1): 78–97.

Tillson, John (forthcoming) "On Deciding the Aims and Content of Public Schooling." *Educational Theory*.

Tillson, John (2017) "When to Teach for Belief: A Tempered Defence of the Epistemic Criterion." *Educational Theory* 67 (2): 173–91.

Tillson, John and Oxley, Laura (2020a) "Children's Moral Rights and UK School Exclusions." *Theory and Research in Education* 18 (1): 40–58.

Tillson, John and Oxley, Laura (2020b) "The Pedagogies of Punishment Project: Morally Legitimate Punishment." *The Emotional Curriculum*. https://podcasts.apple.com/gb/podcast/s02-e16-pedagogies-punishment-project-morally-legitimate/id1484954368?i=1000476359982.

Upadhyaya, Kartik, "Why Hypocrisy Is Wrong" (PhD 2020).

Responsibility and the Prospect of Punishing Children

Larisa Svirsky

Introduction

Children do all sorts of things for which those close to them think it is appropriate to hold them responsible—for example, biting their siblings, not picking up their toys, or distracting their classmates. For parents, teachers, and other caregivers, the reasons for holding children responsible are ordinary and not mysterious: holding responsible is an essential part of moral education, and from fairly early on, there are many things we can reasonably expect children to do. As such, children can genuinely be responsible for living up to those expectations. A parent who sees their child biting his sister, for example, might say to the child that he knows better than to act that way.

Despite the ordinariness of these kinds of scenarios, philosophers working on responsibility have rarely addressed the question of whether children are responsible. For most responsibility theorists, the paradigm example of a responsible agent is a rational, self-controlled, and otherwise psychologically typical adult, and capacities like rationality and self-control are what make an agent responsible. These commitments, often held by responsibility theorists, obscure the idea that children, who are generally regarded as relatively deficient in such capacities, can be responsible and be appropriately held responsible. Those who have written on the possibility of holding children responsible either have mostly characterized it as a matter of pretense or have said that there are degrees of responsibility, and children are responsible to a lesser degree.[1] I have argued elsewhere that these approaches miss one crucial feature of our social practices of holding children responsible, namely that actors' relationships to children are essential to determining whether or not they should hold them responsible.² While a parent ought to hold their child responsible for not biting his sister (e.g., by giving the child a time-out), it seems odd and perhaps morally inappropriate for a stranger to offer a similar intervention.

Relationships as sources of norms

It is relatively uncontroversial that one is not born a responsible agent but rather becomes one. I take it as a given that robust social practices of holding children responsible exist, though these practices have been undertheorized in the philosophical literature on responsibility. Moreover, I have offered an account of why one's relationships to children play a vital role in determining whether or not it is appropriate for one to hold these children responsible. On this account, one's relationships to others are sources of normative expectations.³ The norms in question are what I refer to as "relationship-based norms." For example, when the parent in the previous example is holding their child responsible for not biting his sister, they are doing so in virtue of enforcing a norm that had previously been established with the child, namely that we do not bite others. There are two characteristics of relationship-based norms that distinguish them from other sorts of norms: first, the norms in question are created in a particular, token relationship, and second, the parties in that relationship have a special authority to hold each other to those norms that others outside the relationship lack.

One might be skeptical of the idea that each token parent-child relationship has its own set of relationship-based norms and is a source of those norms. Given that children have to complete the same general sort of developmental tasks and that parents are charged with facilitating a significant portion of children's moral education, one might assume that the majority of norms that hold between parents and children flow from the *type* of relationship they have. I agree that parents are largely responsible for aiding their children's development and moral education. As such, there may be a lot of similarity between norms that arise in all parent-child relationships. Nonetheless, there is also a lot of difference. In one family, the children might be expected to volunteer in their community, while in another they might be expected to attend religious services or to cook dinner for their younger siblings on the nights their parents have to work late. These are all examples of relationship-based norms that do not arise in every parent-child relationship. Even with respect to norms that we might expect there to be some version of in every parent-child relationship, there may be variations in the sorts of responses parents have, which makes these norms distinct from each other in my view.[4]

The special authority that children's caregivers have to hold them to relationship-based norms is evidenced by shared judgments that often strangers who attempt to hold children responsible, and especially to blame or punish them, are overstepping their bounds. Elsewhere, I have offered the example of a child screaming in a restaurant because he is bored. In this example, the child is in violation of a relationship-based norm that exists between him and his parent.[5] Though it is the restaurant staff's business to ensure that other patrons are able to enjoy their meals in relative peace, and perhaps it would be appropriate for them to say something to the parent in question, most observers would be unlikely to judge that it is likewise appropriate for the staff to hold the child responsible for his behavior. This is a matter not just of the restaurant staff knowing less about the child and what is reasonable to expect of him but rather of the special authority the parent has to enforce a norm that she has created with her child.

Though all persons might be subject to relationship-based norms (take, for example, the norms that exist between romantic partners about how frequently they communicate), their existence is more noticeable in cases involving children. This is because young children come to learn about the norms of the wider community through their close relationships with parents and other caregivers. Young children are often subject to relationship-based norms whose content overlaps with the norms that are expected to be upheld by most members of the moral community, other things being equal. For example, most people are expected to understand that it is inappropriate to scream in a restaurant simply because they are bored, where this is something they understand they owe to the wider community. Before they have this understanding, however, children can understand this expectation as something that is owed to a parent and therefore be responsible to the parent for upholding the relevant norm. In my understanding of responsibility, to be responsible is always to be responsible to someone for something—that is, to be responsible is to be subject to norms in our relations with others.[6] Therefore, children are responsible full stop (not "pretend-responsible" or "responsible to a lesser degree"), though community expectations of them look different in various ways from the expectations typically held of adults. That is, though children are truly responsible, *holding* children responsible is a matter of some nuance. The remainder of this chapter attends to many of the details of that distinction.

The distinctiveness of punishment

To establish that children are and should be held responsible, however, is not yet to show that it is appropriate to punish children. Punishment is just one sort of mechanism for holding responsible and one that seems to stand in need of its own distinctive moral justification. In part, this is because it seems more ethically problematic to punish those who are undeserving of punishment than to reward those who are undeserving of reward. Under normal circumstances, punishment is something people wish to avoid, which is why it is often regarded as a disincentive with respect to the behavior for which someone is punished. So, it seems of special importance to ensure that punishment is accorded fairly and only to those who deserve it.

In order to get clear about what a justification for punishing children might consist in, I first identify what distinguishes punishment from other modes of holding responsible, and in particular, other modes of holding responsible meant to dissuade children from engaging in similar behavior in the future (i.e., the imposition of negative consequences or disincentives). The view I will be defending here is that punishment, by nature, is a response to wrongdoing, and thus the category of punishments is narrower than the category of disincentives. Moreover, punishment has a communicative aim, meaning it involves communicating to the one punished that they have acted wrongly, which is not true of all disincentives. Though there will be many reasons to disincentivize certain behavior, for now I want to highlight two such reasons that are distinct from the judgment that someone has engaged in wrongdoing. First, one might disincentivize conduct that is not inherently wrong or even undesirable in order to protect the interests of others. For example, a teacher might suggest to a student who raises their hand immediately in response to every question that they hold back on occasion in order to encourage other students to speak. The teacher need not judge or communicate to the student that their contributing to class discussions is wrong, and asking the student to hold back in these circumstances is not a punishment. Instead, it is meant to disincentivize the student's habitual behavior for the sake of the larger classroom dynamic.

Second, one might disincentivize conduct that is undesirable for various reasons but do so in the absence of a norm that the person in question is violating. In my view, such a norm is a necessary condition on the person having engaged in wrongdoing. In other words, the judgment that someone has done something wrong entails the judgment that they have violated a normative expectation to which they are subject. Sometimes, teachers and parents offer disincentives in an aspirational way. They do not yet believe it is reasonable to expect the child in question to avoid the relevant behavior and so have not created a norm with the child regarding that behavior yet. But in the interim, they may offer disincentives to encourage the child to act differently. For example, a parent may not expect his toddler to be able to sit still for significant periods of time, but may still express some degree of disapproval when she is unable to do so. In this sort of case, the parent is not actually holding the child responsible for her behavior (which would require holding the child to a norm to which the child is actually subject) but the parent may be acting *as if* he is doing so. This does not mean that in general we only pretend to hold children responsible, but certainly pretense is one mechanism by which we introduce children to what will be expected of them later on. Stated again for clarity, one should not take the fact that adults sometimes engage in this pretend responsibility to mean that this is the only way to conceive of responsibility for even very young children; children can quite rightfully be viewed as responsible in many instances.

Sometimes imposing disincentives in the absence of a norm violation can be a way of establishing norms. Consider, for example, how a teacher might say, "You are not in trouble this time, but next time I expect you to do better." There, she is indicating that a norm regarding the relevant behavior is forthcoming, but in the meantime, she is expressing disapproval that might move the child to do otherwise. In this case, as in the previous case, disincentives play an aspirational or hopeful role. But unlike the case involving the parent who expresses disapproval at his toddler who will not sit still, there is clearly an expectation that the child is already sensitive to norms and can be receptive to the teacher's attempt to create one in this case.

As these examples suggest, the boundaries between holding children responsible, merely disincentivizing, and punishing them are somewhat fuzzy. In practice, we should not expect to be able to neatly divide cases into these categories, especially if we are not directly involved in these cases. From the outside, punishment can look similar to disincentives and negative consequences that are not imposed as punishment. This is particularly true for young children, who are and should be shielded from a lot of the harsh treatment that constitutes punishment more generally—in other words, the punishment of young children ought to be particularly mild as punishment goes. But, in my view, punishment both intends to disincentivize and aims to communicate about wrongdoing. When one punishes, one aims to communicate that the one being punished has acted wrongly and has reason not to do so in future.

The fuzzy boundaries between child punishment and other forms of holding children responsible give rise to the following objection: if child punishment can be indistinguishable from other forms of holding children responsible, and yet punishment stands in need of distinctive moral justification, (1) how can one ever be sure whether one is, in fact, punishing children, and (2) whether such punishment is justified? I am less concerned with this first question—it seems to me that it only matters whether we are punishing children or merely disincentivizing their behavior in some other way when there is a question about whether punishment is justified. I find the second question more pressing and want to offer two initial responses. First, some instances of child punishment are very clearly punishment—that is, clearly distinguishable from other forms of holding children responsible. Though there can be many different mechanisms for achieving these ends, clear cases of child punishment explicitly reflect that the child has engaged in wrongdoing and communicate this to the child. Second, in cases where child punishment more closely resembles other forms of holding responsible, there should be less concern that punishment is unjustified. Adults should not demand too much of children and should not want children to feel guilt and shame for their behavior on occasions when they have, in fact, done nothing wrong. But, as I have suggested earlier, holding children responsible (even for things that are difficult for them to do) can be a hopeful gesture, one that shows that we see them as capable. When it comes to evaluating the appropriateness of holding children to a norm, and especially punishing them for violations of that norm, there is a certain amount of risk involved and, as they say, the devil is in the details.

Uncertainty and risk

The justification for punishing children depends on whether children engage in wrongdoing. Moreover, there are certain features of children's psychology and their participation in our responsibility practices that make it difficult for us to discern this with any degree of certainty. In particular, there are difficulties in discerning what is reasonable to expect of children and by whom. It is also important to consider that children are called into the responsibility community in their close relationships, beginning with their relationships with caregivers, and so it matters significantly whether and in what ways those relationships are sites of punishment as well as care.

First, though "children" is colloquially used to refer to people of a certain age, children are also individuals and have wildly different strengths, vulnerabilities, and levels of maturity. What comes easily to one child may be a tremendous struggle for another, and vice versa. In addition, as a matter of course, development is nonlinear, meaning that children do not simply progress from being less capable to being more capable. Tamar Schapiro, who characterizes childhood as a normative predicament that children have to be guided out of in order to become autonomous, suggests that this guidance involves sensitivity to the limitations of children's present capacities, as well as an understanding that those capacities will develop over time.

As she writes,

> Some readers have worried that the view I am putting forth implies that we ought to force children to take on adult responsibilities as early as possible, to "throw them in the deep end," as it were. But when a child (or any person, for that matter) is forced to perform tasks which are overly demanding given her abilities, this tends merely to reinforce her sense of her own dependence and powerlessness. Children should be given tasks which are challenging yet tractable, tasks which allow them to feel pleasure in their own achievement of mastery. (Schapiro 1999, 737)

To make matters still more complicated, determining what a person is responsible for is not a simple matter of discerning what they are capable of on their own. For all people, but particularly for developing agents, capacities are dynamic and can shift in response to what others, in fact, expect of us.

All persons are called into the responsibility community by those with whom they are in close relationships.[7] In general, people begin the broad practice of creating and being subject to norms in the relationships they have with their parents or other caregivers, eventually expanding that circle to include their teachers, siblings, and friends. At some point, developing people begin to understand themselves as owing things to strangers and acquaintances, and more generally, to others qua members of the moral community. As children mature and this transition takes place (i.e., they are no longer *only* subject to relationship-based norms), it can be unclear who exactly bears the authority to hold children responsible. As discussed before, relationship-based norms can have content that overlaps with general norms and so it can be unclear whether having a relationship with a particular child is required in order for it to be appropriate to hold that child responsible.

It can also be unclear whether it is reasonable to expect a child to behave in a certain way, even in the context of a close interpersonal relationship. When parents or teachers attempt to create norms that are unreasonably demanding, this runs the risk of not only overwhelming the child but undermining their authority to hold the child responsible. Though it is natural to think of raising and educating children as something hierarchical, and certainly there are power differentials in these contexts, children also create norms with their caregivers and play an active role in determining the relationship-based norms to which they are subject. This has the implication that determining whether children are deserving of punishment will be partially up to them—that is, the norms children are subject to are partly a function of past negotiations with those close to them. Punishment is only appropriate in response to norm violations that constitute wrongdoing, and children can have a say in (though not unilaterally determine) the expectations others are entitled to hold of them. Because these negotiations are often not explicit, different parties in a relationship may come to different understandings of which norms exist, which can pose problems for determining when punishment is appropriate, and also, potentially, pose challenges in the relationship in question more generally.

Given that young children are primarily subject to norms whose source is their close interpersonal relationships, judgments that children engage in wrongdoing are typically made by those with specific forms of influence upon which children are tremendously vulnerable and on whom they depend for their basic needs. As people mature, they are less vulnerable to the influences of others. They are able to think more independently about what is right and wrong and are able to get their basic needs met outside of the context of a few close relationships. As adults, they also have more recourse if they feel they are being punished though they have done no wrong. These considerations raise the stakes regarding whether punishment is the appropriate response to children. This is not to say that child punishment is never appropriate, but rather that the importance of caregiving relationships in shaping how well children's lives go makes it matter significantly whether and to what extent those relationships are sites of punishment.

The prospect of punishing children

It may seem problematic that it is hard to tell from the outside whether a particular person is punishing a child or not. If punishment stands in need of its own moral justification, one that is more demanding than the justification required for holding children responsible more broadly, this suggests it would be good to know when child punishment is occurring. While I recognize this concern (that children are vulnerable and deserve special moral consideration), I think this is a feature rather than a bug of my account, because it is reflective of the actual social practices of holding children responsible. Part of what I have tried to bring out in my analysis is the tremendous amount of uncertainty involved in those practices. This uncertainty, however, does not entail or even suggest that we should stop holding children responsible. Some moral risks are worth taking. But the account I have offered suggests that the moral risks of punishment are greater than the risks of holding children responsible in general, and punishment is not the only available response to undesirable behavior. It is not even the only available response to wrongdoing. Though punishment can importantly communicate that someone has violated norms that ought to be respected, one can also respond to wrongdoing by expressing a more diffuse disappointment or saying that one expects more of that person in the future.

There are some cases where it is of particular importance, however, to communicate to children that they *have* done something wrong (i.e., have violated particular norms). Where the stakes are high enough, and the norm violation is clear enough, punishment can be a vital way of steering children in the right direction. The plasticity of children's minds makes the risks of punishment higher, but may also make them more susceptible to the potential positive moral effects of punishment. Punishment can also communicate to third parties, such as the children's peers, that this sort of wrongdoing is taken seriously. If, for example, a child is bullying a classmate, it can be valuable for all parties involved to acknowledge this as wrongdoing, an achievement beyond merely disincentivizing the bullying behavior. Claiming that one should be cautious about punishing children is not to say that when punishment is warranted, it should always be the last possible resort. But, if I have correctly described the uncertainties involved in child punishment, the cases where it is clear that a child has engaged in wrongdoing, and that a potential punisher has the requisite authority to punish, will be few and far between.

Notes

1 For statements of these views, see, e.g., Vargas (2013), Wallace (1994), Darwall (2006), Coates and Swenson (2013), and Tiboris (2014).
2 This view is developed in more detail in Svirsky (2020). I also discuss how it applies to other so-called marginal agents, such as people with mental illness and addiction, and the continuities between these cases and those involving paradigm responsible agents.

3 By normative expectations, I mean expectations that someone should be or act in a particular way, rather than predictions that they will in fact be or act that way.
4 As I understand them, norms in general have five important aspects: (1) their content, (2) their source, (3) who is entitled to enforce the norm, (4) the range of consequences (both emotional and behavioral) that will result when one upholds or violates the norm, and (5) a specification of the circumstances that would make it inappropriate to enforce the norm. Norms that differ in any of these aspects are distinct from each other.
5 See Svirsky (2020). On this view, children are not *only* subject to relationship-based norms, particularly as they mature, but relationships are an important source of the norms that children are responsible for upholding.
6 Though not all such norms are relationship-based in the sense under discussion. That is, not all norms that govern our relations with others have their source in token relationships and can only be enforced by the parties in those relationships.
7 This language about being called into responsible agency is influenced by Hilde Lindemann's discussion of being called into personhood in her book, *Holding and Letting Go: The Social Practice of Personal Identities*.

Bibliography

Coates, D. Justin and Swenson, Philip (2013) "Reasons-Responsiveness and Degrees of Responsibility." *Philosophical Studies* 165 (2): 629–45.

Darwall, Stephen L. (2006) *The Second-Person Standpoint: Morality, Respect, and Accountability*. Cambridge, MA: Harvard University Press.

Lindemann, Hilde (2014) *Holding and Letting Go: The Social Practice of Personal Identities*. Oxford: Oxford University Press.

Schapiro, Tamar (1999) "What Is a Child?" *Ethics* 109 (4): 715–38.

Svirsky, Larisa (2020) "Responsibility and the Problem of So-Called Marginal Agents." *Journal of the American Philosophical Association* 6 (2): 246–63.

Tiboris, Michael (2014) "Blaming the Kids: Children's Agency and Diminished Responsibility." *Journal of Applied Philosophy* 31 (1): 77–90.

Vargas, Manuel (2013) *Building Better Beings: A Theory of Moral Responsibility*. Oxford: Oxford University Press.

Wallace, R. Jay (1994) *Responsibility and the Moral Sentiments*. Cambridge, MA: Harvard University Press.

Part II

Punishment in Practice and at the Margins

4

Justice for Trans Youth

Imagining Education Without Cisgenderism

Jenna Scaramanga

As I write this in spring 2022, trans youth are actively targeted by a wave of state bills in the United States. Trans girls, in particular, are the subject of a moral panic. Tennessee and Arkansas banned transition-related health care for minors in 2021 (Lavietes, 2022), with Arizona and Alabama following in April 2022 (Baska, 2022). Guidance from the Florida Department for Health seeks to ban not only medical but also social transition (Wakefield, 2022). This is in addition to a wave of bills targeting access to bathrooms and participation in sports (Turban, 2022). Utah, for example, banned trans girls from participation in girls' sports; it later emerged that of the state's 85,000 high school athletes, four were trans girls, of which only one competed in girls' sports (Whitehurst and Metz, 2022). All that noise and legislative effort had been leveraged to punish or otherwise restrict one child.

In this context, *justice* for trans youth feels distant. An end to active persecution would be a welcome start. Virtually all the recommendations for schools I will make at the conclusion of this chapter are either currently illegal in at least some US states or are the subject of proposed anti-trans legislation. But this only makes the need to support trans youth more urgent. Trans youth are being used as pawns in a culture war, and they are badly in need of advocates to speak on their behalf.

Media coverage of trans people centers on a handful of recycled talking points about pronouns, access to toilets and changing rooms, and trans women in sports. Shon Faye (2021, 14–15) argues "forcing trans people to involve themselves in these closed-loop debates ad infinitum is itself a tactic of those who wish to oppress us. Such debates are time-consuming, exhausting distractions from what we should really be focusing on: the material ways in which we are oppressed." The reason these talking points have been so effective in derailing conversations about arguably more pressing issues like housing, interpersonal violence, and access to health care, however, is that they cannot be ignored.

This is particularly true for trans youth, who are directly affected by anti-trans sports legislation, for whom changing rooms and toilets are frequently places where they experience physical and sexual violence (Wyss, 2004), and for whom the pronouns used at school are indicative of whether they are accepted and affirmed or rejected and othered. Faye is right to describe these debates as exhausting, as the questions are not asked in good faith. No matter how many times it is shown that trans people pose no threat in public bathrooms (Hasenbush, Flores and Herman, 2019), that trans girls can compete safely and fairly in sports, or that trans youth are indeed who they say they are (Gülgöz et al., 2019; Rae et al., 2019), the "concerns" will never be satisfied.

Terms

In this chapter, I use "trans" to refer to all those who do not identify with the gender they are assigned at birth, including nonbinary people. A trans boy is a boy who was assigned female at birth; a trans girl is a girl who was assigned male at birth. "Nonbinary" refers to all identities that are not adequately captured by "male" and "female," including agender, gender fluid, genderqueer, and two-spirit. "Social transition" refers to nonmedical changes, such as adopting the pronouns, name, and gender expression (clothing, hairstyles, etc.) of their gender identity. "Cisgender" people are those who are not trans and who do identify with their gender assigned at birth.

Why affirm trans kids?

Because of widespread misinformation about trans people, there are parents and teachers who have genuine misgivings about trans-inclusive school policies. Educators who wish to create safer nonpunitive environments for gender-diverse children must be ready to assuage such concerns without entertaining malicious anti-trans talking points.

Justice for trans youth has to begin with the acknowledgment that trans youth exist and are who they say they are. The implicit assumption behind laws like Florida's "Don't Say Gay" law (Phillips, 2022) is that there are no trans children, that being queer is a social contagion, and that if children do not hear about LGBTQ+ people, they will all grow up cisgender and heterosexual. This idea is far-fetched to those of us who grew up under Section 28, British laws in force from 1998 to 2000 (2003 in England and Wales) banning schools from "promoting homosexuality" (Lee, 2019). That law did not stop LGBTQ+ people of my generation from existing, but it has given us a plenty of material through which to work with our therapists. Anyone who thinks Section 28 failed only because it did not go far enough should consider conservative evangelical schools, which go a step further by tightly controlling students' social contact with those outside their religious community (Peshkin, 1986) but still produce LGBTQ+ graduates (Scaramanga, 2017). Trans students exist whether schools admit it or not.

Trans youth suffer greatly elevated rates of depression, self-harm, and suicidality, but evidence shows that when they are supported to live in the gender that feels most authentic, they have improved mental health outcomes (Turban and Ehrensaft, 2018). Strikingly, when they are supported to socially transition, trans youth report only marginally elevated anxiety, along with levels of depression and self-worth that do not differ from their cisgender peers (Olson et al., 2016; Durwood, McLaughlin and Olson, 2017; Gibson, Glazier and Olson, 2021). Adolescents who socially transition do experience negative mental health outcomes—but this effect disappears when controlling for K-12 harassment based on gender identity (Turban et al., 2021). It is bullying and lack of support, not transitioning, that is associated with depression and suicidality. Even if one takes the purpose of schooling solely to be producing good exam results and test scores, affirming trans youth is necessary because poor mental health is detrimental to academic performance (Agnafors, Barmark and Sydsjö, 2021).

Trans youth are at increased risk of experiencing sexual assault in schools where they are prevented from using the bathroom that aligns with their gender identity (Murchison et al., 2019). Trans youth have better mental health when those around them use their chosen names (Russell et al., 2018) and when they are able to participate in school sports on teams that align with their gender identity (Clark and Kosciw, 2022). Hostile school climates contribute to low self-esteem and poor academic results, but supportive policies help to offset those effects (Kosciw et al., 2013). Unsurprisingly, parents report better well-being for their trans children when school and peers are supportive of gender identity (Durwood et al., 2021), while unsupportive teachers make it more likely trans students will leave school (Jones et al., 2016). Simply put, schools have a duty to support trans children in precisely the ways that anti-trans legislation seeks to ban.

Some parents and teachers are concerned that affirming trans children's identities too quickly could be a mistake because in some cases the children might later prefer to return to an identity that matches their birth sex. This understandable concern is sometimes prompted by two misconceptions. One is the belief that it is common for trans children to desist at a later date, a view propagated by flawed research (Newhook et al., 2018; TransEssays, 2022). Another is the unevidenced claim that cisgender children can be made to transition by adult encouragement (Ashley, 2020). If trans children do later come to identify with their birth sex, the best response is the same as for any transition: love, support, and validation (Key and Vacatio, 2022).

The power of trans joy

In repeating statistics about bullying and victimization of trans children, I am at risk of conflating gender diversity with depression and suicide (Gilbert et al., 2018). One of the very real harms of erasing LGBTQ+ people from school curricula is that the ordinary and the joyous in our lives are made invisible. When queer youth hear about themselves, it is only as tragic figures. This creates a negative feedback loop that only furthers marginalization. Righting the wrongs against gender-diverse youth requires us to acknowledge that trans joy is real. I have been elated to discover my gender in adulthood, and the power of living authentically is captured by the appropriately titled *Gender Euphoria* (Dale, 2021). This is not a mere aside. Rates of depression and suicidality among trans youth are sometimes proffered as reasons to deny trans youth the opportunity to live authentically through social or medical transition. Justice demands that trans youth see role models leading lives that are as full, fulfilling, and happy as anyone else's.

Types of punishment

In this chapter, I consider four types of "punishment" of trans children that are conceptually distinct. The first is when trans students are directly punished for disobeying those rules which harm them, such as a trans girl being punished for wearing a skirt. The second is punishments that are routinely used on all students but which have disproportionate impacts on trans students. For instance, transgender students are more likely to miss school due to harassment and victimization (Pampati et al., 2020), and those who are medically transitioning may need to miss school for medical appointments, which are often unavailable locally. School policies that penalize absences therefore impact trans students disproportionately. The third is when ordinary school rules inflict disadvantage or suffering on trans students, such as a requirement for students to use the name on their birth certificate or other official documents. The fourth is when schools tolerate or implicitly encourage disrespect for trans identities or fail to foster respect for them. Teachers who misgender or otherwise disrespect trans students, or tolerate this from others, send a message that anyone mistreating trans students will suffer few negative consequences. This is a green light for bullying.

It might be considered that of these four types of "punishment," only the second and fourth are punishments in the usual sense. In the third case, unjust policies may harm some students, but they do not directly punish them. However, unjust policies carry punishments for noncompliance, creating double binds for affected students who either experience psychological harm while obeying the rules or are sanctioned for disobeying. In the fourth case, it is the students' peers who punish them for gender nonconformity. In the worst instances of this, it may be that a teacher cynically allows bullies to carry out punishments the teacher believes trans students deserve. In the best case, it may be that the school has merely responded inadequately to bullying. In any scenario, however, the trans student is punished merely for being themselves while at school.

Cisgenderism

Feminist scholarship has demonstrated how schools inculcate gender ideology, often through mechanisms of rules and punishment. Too often schools are sites where traditional gender roles are socialized and reproduced, particularly to the detriment of girls. Through the curriculum, teacher expectations and practices, peer influences, and institutional policies, children are socialized into gender-role stereotypes and sexual scripts (Stromquist, 2007; Grose, Grabe and Kohfeldt, 2014). These gender ideologies presuppose masculine superiority and set out a limited range of acceptable behaviors for boys and girls. What is sometimes not illuminated is that these are *cis*gender ideologies. Schools are institutionally *cisgenderist* (Bower-Brown, Zadeh and Jadva, 2021)—that is, they are pervaded by the ideology that transgender identities are illegitimate and pathological.

Cisgenderism is the ideology that assumes being cisgender is healthy and ideal (Ansara and Hegerty, 2012); it is the system that classifies cis and trans people respectively as "Normal" and "Other." At a time when anti-trans activists accuse trans-inclusive education of bringing "gender ideology" into the classroom, it is valuable to highlight the unspoken ideological work done to normalize cisgenderism. *Cisnormativity* is the normative aspects of the cisgenderist system. For instance, when all toilets in a space are designated either male or female, it presumes that nonbinary people do not exist or will not use the space (Cavar and Baril, 2022). Cisnormativity creates hostile school environments for trans youth and governs the lives of all students (McBride, 2021). Where schools do recognize the harm of bullying, there is a tendency to see this as isolated individual action. The theory of cisgenderism requires us to consider ways schools are enablers of anti-trans bullying.

Gendered lessons are less common now that home economics classes for girls have fallen out of favor, but sports and sex education are two places where the expectations of the gender binary are instilled and enforced. It is not only that sports teams are divided by gender, but boys and girls are offered different sports because of assumptions about what are masculine or feminine activities: few English schools offer rugby to girls or netball to boys, for example. Messner (2011) argues contemporary youth sport's ascendant gender ideology is "soft essentialism," with ideas of "choice" for girls but unreconstructed views of boys and men.

By omitting LGBTQ+ sex education, schools prevent mutual understanding that might reduce bullying, send a message that LGBTQ+ students do not exist or do not matter—or worse, are shameful or dangerous—and deprive LGBTQ+ students of knowledge that can help them flourish. Schools further enable bullying through administrative policies that make it difficult for students to change their name and gender on documents (sometimes outing trans students in the process) and through opposition to LGBTQ+ societies and GSAs (Gender & Sexuality or Gay-Straight Alliances) (Gilbert et al., 2018). Ill-considered accommodations for gender-diverse students can serve to make them into targets, such as when a nonbinary student becomes the only one in the school to use a staff changing room (Bower-Brown, Zadeh and Jadva, 2021). Speaking only of bullying in terms of individual students' behavior hides the degree to which the mistreatment of trans students is an institutional problem.

Cisgenderist ideology rewards those who conform to the gender binary and punishes those who defy it. A review of the literature on trans youth (e.g., McBride, 2021) shows bullying and peer violence as the most pervasive problem. Trans youth experience bullying and violence at disproportionate rates (Day, Perez-Brumer and Russell, 2018; Witcomb et al., 2019; Kosciw et al., 2020). The seriousness with which schools take bullying can signal which forms of it are more or less acceptable. A school that does not use the chosen names and pronouns of its trans students sends the message that they are not worthy of this and other forms of respect. In recent qualitative research, trans youth have reported finding teachers unhelpful or even tacitly approving of this type of bullying:

> I was jumped in the locker area, and the only person that got suspended was me for using profanity at school. And nobody in the video who was seen attacking me was suspended. And that was a trend. In high school, I was again beaten in front of a large crowd of onlookers. In one hand, they had a phone and the other they were pointing, laughing, as I was bleeding. The boy that hit me said, "It don't matter because that's a man." And nobody in that moment stood up and took any sort of stand against that violence. And so from school to school a norm was set that violence against her is okay. (Logo, 2022, 8:33)

> "My school is so lenient with the usage of slurs like 'faggot' and 'tranny' that students feel comfortable enough to use them in their regular vocabulary, even in lessons to answer questions" (magiboy, aged 13). (Bower-Brown, Zadeh and Jadva, 2021)

> "When I complain about being insulted by staff to other teachers they say that everyone's entitled to their own opinions" (trans boy, aged 14). (Bower-Brown, Zadeh and Jadva, 2021)

Schools effectively outsource punishment for defying the gender binary by complicit silence and inaction regarding the bullying of trans students.

Dress codes

Schools with gendered uniform or dress codes explicitly enforce the gender binary. Some schools punish dress-code infractions by sending students home. When trans youth are forced to wear the uniform associated with their assigned gender at birth, they are effectively punished simply for being who they are. It places them in a double bind where they cannot avoid punishment: they either wear clothes that make them alienated and dysphoric, or they face school discipline. For nonbinary students, such binary uniform lists frequently give them no good options. Some schools refuse to respect trans students' requested pronouns and do not challenge students who misgender trans peers, but do punish trans students for uniform infractions. For trans students in such schools, there could hardly be a clearer message that the gender binary is more important than the student's well-being.

Schools that do not adopt affirming policies offer trans students a series of similar lose-lose situations. Trans athletes face abuse regardless of which team they play for, as illustrated by Mack Beggs, a trans boy who was forced to wrestle in the girls' division and faced boos when he won championships (Schilken, 2018). Trans students may face punishment, from either authorities or their peers, regardless of which toilets they use. If the school offers a solution at all, it may be a single inconveniently located gender neutral toilet, forcing students to choose between physical discomfort and missing lessons or break time. Anecdotally, many trans students do not use the toilet at all at school because there are none suitable available. This can result in urinary tract infections and other health complications. If these students then receive an after-school detention, they experience it as a vastly crueller punishment than it is for other students. Schools do not need to single out trans students for particular punishments; the system punishes them for being who they are.

Conversion therapy

It is illuminating to compare the assumptions of conversion therapy with the gender ideologies implicit in many school policies. Conversion therapy is the attempt to "cure" gay and trans people, making them heterosexual and cisgender.

Much of the classic literature on conversion therapy does not distinguish clearly between sexual orientation and gender identity—and in many cases the subjects of such efforts were too young to have expressed any sexual attraction. Researchers opposing "gender deviance" referred to children who defied their gender roles variously as "prehomosexual, gender-conflicted, gender-confused, and gender-disturbed" (Nicolosi, 2017, p. 13), "effeminate" or "feminoid boys" (Ansara and Hegerty, 2012, p. 139) or as "sissies" (TransEssays, 2022). The treatment for this condition was simply the rigid enforcement of traditional gender norms and roles:

> [T]he child must be sensitized to when he is walking, sitting, or using his hands "like a girl." Parents should be instructed to consistently point out to the

boy when such behavior occurs. (Green, Newman, and Stoller, 1972, cited in TransEssays, 2022)

I can see where not every kid wants to play ball, but at the same time he doesn't have to do girlish things. . . . He was playing with a doll while I was saying it. He got a little upset and put the doll away . . . I told him that as he grows up, and if he continues to do sissy things, that he won't have many friends, and people will make fun of him, and that he'll be very unhappy. (Green, 1972, cited in TransEssays, 2022)

Spiegel (2008) recounts how the conversion therapist Ken Zucker treated a five-year-old boy who had been playing with dolls: "Bradley would no longer be allowed to spend time with girls. He would no longer be allowed to play with girlish toys or pretend that he was a female character." While opponents of trans rights accuse trans people of perpetuating gender stereotypes (Women's Declaration International, 2022), we have historically been punished for defying them, and efforts to "cure" us have always consisted of rigid enforcement of gender stereotypes. Policing of gender presentation and gender expression are central to conversion therapy for gay and trans youth. To the extent that schools restrict certain activities or toys to girls or boys only, have gendered dress codes, and/or instill gendered expectations of behavior, they are performing a form of conversion therapy.

Peer groups often do much of the policing of gendered behavior, although teachers may also do this (McBride, 2021). The previous quotation from Green sounds uncannily like school bullies I have been unfortunate to know. Peer pressure and peer hazing can act to discourage boys and girls from having close platonic friendships and to enforce gender stereotypes. To the extent that schools condone or permit this, they again perpetuate "soft" conversion therapy. There is no evidence conversion therapy or any other repressive tactics can change a person's gender or sexuality, but those exposed to conversion therapy attempts are likely to experience lasting and severe psychological distress (Turban et al., 2020).

Taking nonbinary seriously

The existence of nonbinary children in many ways presents a bigger challenge to the existing order in schools than does the existence of trans boys and trans girls. It is tempting to think that the latter can be accommodated without major changes to school policy, simply by recognizing their genders and treating them accordingly. Taking seriously the existence of nonbinary and gender-fluid children requires dismantling binary assumptions wherever they appear. You can accommodate a trans girl, for example, by letting her play on the girls' sports team. Recognizing that there are more than two genders brings into question the entire logic of dividing sports into boys' and girls' categories.

Conclusion: Education beyond the binary

In a school that is focused on trans students' safety and comfort, students could experiment freely with their gender presentation with no expectation that changes be permanent or that anyone can infer your gender from your choice of clothes. Rather than boys' and girls' dress codes, there would simply be a list of acceptable attire from which all students can choose. We should think little of a student wearing a dress to school one day and a shirt and tie the next. It would be unremarkable for students to ask to be referred to temporarily by different pronouns, simply to see how they feel. Opponents of youth transition speak of being afraid of young people making irreversible changes they then regret. One way to minimize the chance of regret is to normalize gender exploration, such that there is no shame associated with reverting back to an earlier identity. Sports would be chosen by students' interests and teams selected by ability and desire to play. Sex education would, in an age-appropriate way, acknowledge the reality of trans bodies and ensure that all students learn about bodies of all kinds. All-gender toilets and changing rooms would be provided, with individual cubicles for privacy.

A nonpunitive education that is truly inclusive of trans youth is one that has greater opportunities for all students. Feminists have long argued against gendering toys because it can inculcate harmful stereotypes, and the right to wear trousers was symbolically important to the women's movement. Making it safe for boys to wear skirts to school means challenging beliefs that things coded as feminine are inherently lesser. Integrating sports means challenging stereotypes about girls as weak and accepting that girls can be muscular and athletic. A school that is safe for trans children is also one that is safer for LGB students. The same gender stereotypes have historically been weaponized equally as punishments against gay and trans students.

It is easy to talk about a world in which everyone is free to explore their gender without judgment. It is harder to talk about how to get there, particularly in a climate where wider society is engaged in a moral panic about trans youth (Faye, 2021). Affirming teachers may find themselves in decidedly non-affirming, gender-punitive schools. Schools that are trying to be affirming may find themselves navigating guidance or legislation that is decidedly anti-trans. Many resources contain lists of recommended steps schools can take to accommodate trans children (e.g., Kosciw et al., 2020; Bower-Brown, Zadeh and Jadva, 2021; Key and Vacatio, 2022). Common recommendations include:

- Creating and implementing trans-affirming policies, specifically naming gender identity and expression;
- Supporting the creation of LGBT and GSA societies;
- Seeking specific gender-inclusive training for all staff; and
- Providing all-gender toilets and changing rooms and allowing students to self-select which facilities to use based on their identity.

A major challenge exists in creating an adequately safe space for trans youth to come out. A global poll found that 4 percent of Generation Z are trans or nonbinary (Ipsos, 2021), so if any moderately large school has no out trans students, there has been a failure either in making them feel safe or in providing an education that allows them to explore and discover their own identity. The first priority of the school must be in making clear to all persons that trans students will be supported. Once students do come out, the next step is easier: namely, ask them what they need. Despite the fact that being transgender is not a mental illness, trans youth are still generally treated as unreliable narrators of their own lives and needs. Many countries require specialist psychiatric assessment before they can access health care and in media reports it is more common for medical experts to comment on their needs than it is to hear from young trans people themselves. Taking trans identity seriously, without visiting punishments upon them merely for their existence, involves believing trans students and listening to what they need.

References

Agnafors, Sara, Barmark, Mimmi, and Sydsjö, Gunilla (2021) "Mental Health and Academic Performance: A Study on Selection and Causation Effects from Childhood to Early Adulthood." *Social Psychiatry and Psychiatric Epidemiology* 56: 857–66.
Ansara, Y. Gavriel, and Hegarty, Peter (2012) "Cisgenderism in Psychology: Pathologising and Misgendering Children from 1999 to 2008." *Psychology & Sexuality* 3 (2): 137–60.
Ashley, Florence (2020) "Homophobia, Conversion Therapy, and Care Models for Trans Youth: Defending the Gender-Affirmative Approach." *Journal of LGBT Youth* 17 (4): 361–83.

Baska, Maggie (2022) "Families and Doctors Sue Alabama over Cruel Ban on 'Life-Saving' Trans Healthcare." Retrieved April 29, 2022. https://www.pinknews.co.uk/2022/04/12/alabama-trans-healthcare-ban-lawsuit/.

Bower-Brown, Susie, Zadeh, Sophie, and Jadva, Vasanti (2021) "Binary-trans, Non-binary and Gender-Questioning Adolescents' Experiences in UK Schools." *Journal of LGBT Youth*. doi:10.1080/19361653.2021.1873215

Cavar, Sarah and Baril, Alexandre (2022) "Disability." In L. Erickson-Schroth (ed.), *Trans Bodies, Trans Selves: A Resource by and for Transgender Communities*, 67–93. Oxford: Oxford University Press.

Clark, Caitlin M., and Kosciw, Joseph G. (2022) "Engaged or Excluded: LGBTQ Youth's Participation in School Sports and Their Relationship to Psychological Well-being." *Psychology in the Schools* 59 (1): 95–114.

Dale, Laura Kate (ed.). (2021) *Gender Euphoria: Stories of Joy from Trans, Non-binary and Intersex Writers*. London: Unbound.

Day, Jack K., Perez-Brumer, Amaya, and Russell, Stephen T. (2018) "Safe Schools? Transgender Youth's School Experiences and Perceptions of School Climate." *Journal of Youth and Adolescence* 47 (8): 1731–42.

Durwood, Lily, McLaughlin, Katie A., and Olson, Kristina R. (2017) "Mental Health and Self-Worth in Socially Transitioned Transgender Youth." *Journal of the American Academy of Child and Adolescent Psychiatry* 56 (2): 116–23.

Durwood, Lily, Eisner, Léïla, Fladeboe, Kaitlyn, Ji, Chonghui Gabriella, Barney, Samantha, McLaughlin, Katie A., and Olson, Kristina R. (2021) "Social Support and Internalizing Psychopathology in Transgender Youth." *Journal of Youth and Adolescence* 50 (5): 841–54.

Faye, Shon (2021) *The Transgender Issue*. London: Allen Lane.

Gibson, Dominic J., Glazier, Jessica J., and Olson, Kristina R. (2021) "Evaluation of Anxiety and Depression in a Community Sample of Transgender Youth." *JAMA Network Open* 4 (4): e214739. doi:10.1001/jamanetworkopen.2021.4739.

Gilbert, Jen, Fields, Jessica, Mamo, Laura, and Lesko, Nancy (2018) "Intimate Possibilities: The Beyond Bullying Project and Stories of LGBTQ Sexuality and Gender in US Schools." *Harvard Educational Review* 88 (2): 163–83.

Grose, Rose Grace, Grabe, Shelly, and Kohfeldt, Danielle (2014) "Sexual Education, Gender Ideology, and Youth Sexual Empowerment." *Journal of Sex Research* 51 (7): 742–53.

Gülgöz, Selin, Glazier, Jessica J., Enright, Elizabeth A., Alonso, Daniel J., Durwood, Lily J., Fast, Anne A., Lowe, Riley, Ji, Chonghui, Heer, Jeffrey, Martine, Carol Lynn, and Olson, Kristina R. (2019) "Similarity in Transgender and Cisgender Children's Gender Development." *Proceedings of the National Academy of Sciences* 116 (49): 24480–5.

Hasenbush, Amira, Flores, Andrew R., and Herman, Jody L. (2019) "Gender Identity Nondiscrimination Laws in Public Accommodations: A Review of Evidence Regarding Safety and Privacy in Public Restrooms, Locker Rooms, and Changing Rooms." *Sexuality Research and Social Policy* 16: 70–83.

Ipsos. (2021) *LGBT+ Pride 2021 Global Survey*. Retrieved May 4, 2022. https://www.ipsos.com/sites/default/files/ct/news/documents/2021-06/LGBT%20Pride%202021%20Global%20Survey%20Report%20-%20US%20Version%20-%20Rev%202.pdf.

Jones, Tiffany, Smith, Elizabeth, Ward, Ros, Dixon, Jennifer, Hillier, Lynne, and Mitchell, Anne (2016) "School Experiences of Transgender and Gender Diverse Students in Australia." *Sex Education* 16 (2): 156–71.

Key, Aidan, and Vacatio, Micah (2022) "Children." In Laura Erickson-Schroth (ed.), *Trans Bodies, Trans Selves: A Resource by and for Transgender Communities*, 499–529. Oxford: Oxford University Press.

Kosciw, Joseph G., Palmer, Neal A., Kull, Ryan M., and Greytak, Emily A. (2013) "The Effect of Negative School Climate on Academic Outcomes for LGBT Youth and the Role of In-school Supports." *Journal of School Violence* 12 (1): 45–63.

Kosciw, Joseph G., Clark, Caitlin M., Truong, Nhan L., and Zongrone, Adrian D. (2020) *The 2019 National School Climate Survey: The Experiences of Lesbian, Gay, Bisexual, Transgender, and Queer Youth in Our Nation's Schools*. New York: Gay, Lesbian and Straight Education Network (GLSEN). https://www.glsen.org/sites/default/files/2021-04/NSCS19-FullReport-032421-Web_0.pdf.

Lavietes, Matt (2022) "At Least 7 States Proposed Anti-Trans Bills in First Week of 2022." Retrieved April 29, 2022. https://www.nbcnews.com/nbc-out/out-politics-and-policy/least-7-states-proposed-anti-trans-bills-first-week-2022-rcna11205.

Lee, Catherine (2019) "Fifteen Years On: The Legacy of Section 28 for LGBT+ Teachers in English Schools." *Sex Education* 19 (6): 675–90.

Logo (2022) *Trans Youth Town Hall Part 2: Health & Safety*. Retrieved April 29, 2022. https://youtu.be/9tplXCNTjhw.

McBride, Ruari-Santiago (2021) "A Literature Review of the Secondary School Experiences of Trans Youth." *Journal of LGBT Youth* 18 (2): 103–34.

Messner, Michael (2011) "Gender Ideologies, Youth Sports, and the Production of Soft Essentialism." *Sociology of Sport Journal* 28: 151–70.

Murchison, Gabriel R., Agénor, Madina, Reisner, Sari L., and Watson, Ryan J. (2019) "School Restroom and Locker Room Restrictions and Sexual Assault Risk Among Transgender Youth." *Pediatrics* 143 (6).

Newhook, Julia Temple, Winters, Kelley, Pyne, Jake, Jamieson, Ally, Holmes, Cindy, Feder, Stephen, Pickett, Sarah, and Sinnott, Mari-Lynne (2018) "Teach Your Parents and Providers Well: Call for Refocus on the Health of Trans and Gender-Diverse Children." *Canadian Family Physician* 64 (5): 332–5.

Nicolosi, J. (2017) *A Parent's Guide to Preventing Homosexuality*. Unknown: Liberal Mind Publishers.

Olson, Kristina R., Durwood, Lily, DeMeules, Madeleine, and McLaughlin, Katie A. (2016) "Mental Health of Transgender Children Who Are Supported in Their Identities." *Pediatrics* 137 (3): e20153223.

Pampati, Sanjana, Andrzejewski, Jack, Sheremenko, Ganna, Johns, Michelle, Lesesne, Catherine A., and Rasberry, Catherine N. (2020) "School Climate Among Transgender

High School Students: An Exploration of School Connectedness, Perceived Safety, Bullying, and Absenteeism." *The Journal of School Nursing* 36 (4): 293–303.

Peshkin, Alan (1986) *God's Choice: The Total World of a Fundamentalist Christian School*. Chicago, IL: University of Chicago Press.

Phillips, Amber (2022) *Florida's Law Limiting LGBTQ Discussion in Schools, Explained*. Retrieved April 29, 2022. https://www.washingtonpost.com/politics/2022/04/01/what-is-florida-dont-say-gay-bill/.

Rae, James R., Gülgöz, Selin, Durwood, Lily, DeMeules, Madeleine, Lowe, Riley, Lindquist, Gabrielle, and Olson, Kristina R. (2019) "Predicting Early-Childhood Gender Transitions." *Psychological Science* 30 (5): 669–81.

Russell, Stephen T., Pollitt, Amanda M., Li, Gu, and Grossman, Arnold H. (2018) "Chosen Name Use Is Linked to Reduced Depressive Symptoms, Suicidal Ideation, and Suicidal Behavior Among Transgender Youth." *Journal of Adolescent Health* 63 (4): 503–5. doi:10.1016/j.jadohealth.2018.02.003.

Scaramanga, Jenna (2017) "Systems of Indoctrination: Accelerated Christian Education in England." PhD thesis. UCL.

Schilken, Chuck (2018) *Transgender Boy Wins Texas Girls Wrestling Championship for the Second Year in a Row*. Retrieved April 29, 2022. https://www.latimes.com/sports/sportsnow/la-sp-transgender-wrestler-texas-20180226-story.html.

Spiegel, Alix (2008) *Two Families Grapple with Sons' Gender Identity*. Retrieved April 29, 2022. https://www.npr.org/2008/05/07/90247842/two-families-grapple-with-sons-gender-preferences?t=1651198006183.

Stromquist, Nelly P. (2007) "The Gender Socialization Process in Schools: A Cross-National Comparison. Paper Commissioned for the EFA Global Monitoring Report 2008." *Education for All by 2015: Will We Make It?* Retrieved April 29, 2022. https://citeseerx.ist.psu.edu/viewdoc/download?doi=10.1.1.474.3306&rep=rep1&type=pdf.

TransEssays. (2022) *Conversion Therapy on Transgender Children*. Retrieved April 29, 2022. https://medium.com/@TransEssays/conversion-therapy-on-transgender-children-fdf23e4a4340.

Turban, Jack L. (2022) *Transgender Youth: Bringing Evidence to the Political Debates*. Retrieved April 29, 2022. https://www.mdedge.com/pediatrics/article/253620/transgender-health/transgender-youth-bringing-evidence-political-debates.

Turban, Jack L., and Ehrensaft, Diane (2018) "Research Review: Gender Identity in Youth: Treatment Paradigms and Controversies." *Journal of Child Psychology and Psychiatry* 59 (12): 1228–43.

Turban, Jack L., Beckwith, Noor, Reisner, Sari L., and Keuroghlian, Alex S. (2020) "Association Between Recalled Exposure to Gender Identity Conversion Efforts and Psychological Distress and Suicide Attempts Among Transgender Adults." *JAMA Psychiatry* 77 (1): 68–76.

Turban, Jack L., King, Dana, Li, Jason J., and Keuroghlian, Alex S. (2021) "Timing of Social Transition for Transgender and Gender Diverse Youth, K-12 Harassment, and Adult Mental Health Outcomes." *Journal of Adolescent Health* 69 (6): 991–8.

Wakefield, Lily (2022) *Florida's Health Department Makes Chilling Move to Block Social Transition and Healthcare for Trans Kids*. Retrieved April 29, 2022. https://www.pinknews.co.uk/2022/04/20/florida-trans-kids-health-department-social-transition-healthcare/.

Whitehurst, Lindsay, and Metz, Sam (2022) "Utah Governor Vetoes Transgender Sports Ban, Faces Override." *AP News*. Retrieved April 29, 2022. https://apnews.com/article/sports-health-legislature-mental-health-utah-f0e76dad68c1dd9986cee0be1b057cef.

Witcomb, Gemma L., Claes, Laurence, Bouman, Walter Pierre, Nixon, Elena, Motmans, Joz, and Arcelus, Jon (2019) "Experiences and Psychological Wellbeing Outcomes Associated with Bullying in Treatment-Seeking Transgender and Gender-Diverse Youth." *LGBT Health* 6: 216–26.

Women's Declaration International (2022) *Declaration on Women's Sex-Based Rights*. Retrieved April 29, 2022. https://www.womensdeclaration.com/en/declaration-womens-sex-based-rights-full-text/.

Wyss, Shannon E. (2004) "'This Was My Hell': The Violence Experienced by Gender Non-Conforming Youth in US High Schools." *International Journal of Qualitative Studies in Education* 17 (5): 709–30.

5

Racialized Childhoods, Educational Goods, and "No Excuses" Schools

In Defense of Play and Agency

Abigail Beneke

During the day, the teachers had been tasked with monitoring student behavior and taking note of the students who were not complying with the school's behavioral expectations. [. . .] As I listened to this discussion, I was struck by the degree to which students were watched and assessed. Though it was given gently and with encouragement, the message that students received was clear: they were under the school's watchful eye. There would be no twirling, jumping, or eating out of turn at Dream Academy. (Golann, 2021, 31)

The above excerpt from Joanne Golann's (2021) ethnographic study of a "No Excuses" school demonstrates how the school model diminishes low-income Black and Latinx students' access to play and agency for the promise of educational goods—namely, high standardized test scores and the potential of college acceptance and future economic productivity. Proponents of No Excuses schools argue that this type of discipline is necessary to close the racial opportunity gap. In this chapter, I analyze the No Excuses model and related claims in favor of limiting students' access to play and agency, offering a new perspective on the relationship among play, agency, and educational goods.

In my analysis of the No Excuses model, I do not intend to suggest that this is the only type of school that makes these trade-offs. Many types of schools, including traditional public schools, often make a similar calculus among students' opportunities for play, agency, and educational goods. Rather, I use the case of No Excuses schools because these trade-offs are transparently made and well-documented. Thus, this work is not limited to the No Excuses context but could be used to consider such trade-offs in schools, more broadly.

The chapter proceeds in six sections. I first situate the chapter in relevant literature from critical childhood studies and philosophical literature on childhood and educational goods. I then interpret the rationale for No Excuses schools, describing what I take to be the factors most salient for the purposes of this chapter. Next, I consider three perceived claims that seemingly necessitate the trade-off of children's play and agency for increased educational goods. Through analysis of these claims, I show that educators need not sacrifice play and agency for educational goods to this degree and that these goods may be mutually pursued. Moreover, given the troubling context of systemic racial injustice and the phenomenon of "adultification," schools have an added ethical obligation to protect Black students' access to play and agency.

Racialized childhoods and educational goods

Childhood is a relatively recent social construction. With rising rates of literacy and decreased infant mortality in the seventeenth century came new theories of human development, and with them, the notion of childhood as a formal life stage (Ariès, 1962). While Calvinists viewed children as inherently sinful and sexual, this image changed by the mid-nineteenth century, shifting to a view of children as innocent and capable of leading adults to salvation (Bernstein, 2011). By the nineteenth century, "sentimental culture had woven childhood and innocence together wholly" (Bernstein, 2011, 4). Childhood became understood as an embodiment of innocence rather than a symbol of it (Bernstein, 2011).

Childhood has been racialized as White since its inception and has not been equally available, historically or contemporarily, to non-Whites (Bernstein, 2011; Dumas and Nelson, 2016; Meiners, 2016). Beginning with chattel slavery, Black children "were rarely perceived as being worthy of playtime and were often put to work as young as two and three years old" (Dumas and Nelson, 2016, 33). Racialized conceptions of childhood persist today. "It is neither precisely clear who counts as a child or a youth, why benefits are attached to some childhoods and denied to others, and what the collateral consequences are when individuals and communities demand differential treatment either for or because of the children" (Meiners, 2016, 6). Scholars in the growing tradition of critical childhood studies have pointed to the constructed nature of childhood, the contradictions therein, and how children exhibit agency within this category

(Dumas and Nelson, 2016; James, 2004; Stephens, 1995; Wyness, 2012). As Meiners (2016) argues, the notion of "the child" has been selectively deployed to protect the innocence of mostly White children while being used to contain or limit non-White children. For example, Black children are eighteen times more likely to be tried as adults than White children (Williams, 2018). Alongside recognizing the harmful effects of racialized conceptions of childhood, like Dumas and Nelson (2016), I simultaneously acknowledge the unique features of childhood due to children's developing bodies and the social positions they occupy. Namely (1) children are more physically vulnerable than adults and (2) children occupy less powerful social positions (Dumas and Nelson, 2016). These two features of childhood are significant for my analysis.

Racialized conceptions of childhood affect the lived experiences of marginalized children. Black children are subject to "adultification," meaning they are perceived as "less innocent and more adult-like" than White children of the same age (Epstein, Blake and González, 2017, 1). Drawing on a survey of 325 adults from various racial and ethnic backgrounds, Epstein, Blake, and González (2017) found that compared to White girls of the same age, Black girls were perceived as needing less nurturing, protection, support, and comfort. Simultaneously, they were perceived as more independent and knowledgeable about "adult topics," including sex (Epstein, Blake and González, 2017). Black boys are also subject to adultification (Dancy, 2014; Ferguson, 2001; Goff et al., 2008; Goff, Jackson and Di Leone, 2014). Drawing on laboratory, field, and translational methods, Goff, Jackson, and Di Leone (2014) found that Black boys are perceived as "older and less innocent and that they prompt a less essential conception of childhood than do their White same-age peers" (p. 526). Adultification leads to "unequal childhoods" for Black children and their White peers (Lareau, 2011).

Adultification has far-ranging consequences for school punishment. In their mixed-methods study of Denver Public Schools, Annamma et al. (2016) found that Black girls were more likely to be punished for subjective reasons that relied on the judgment of school staff, such as "disobedience/defiance, detrimental behavior, and third-degree assault[1]" (p. 232). Moreover, Black girls were subject to harsher punishments than their White peers, even when they were referred for the same behaviors (Anamma et al., 2016). A much larger corpus of data on the punishment of Black boys has shown they are more severely punished than their White and Asian peers (Ferguson, 2001; Gregory, 1997; Wallace et al., 2008). Wallace et al. (2008) found that though the rate at which Black boys are referred to the office is fairly consistent with that of other racial and ethnic groups, they were significantly more likely to be suspended or expelled. Between 1991 and 2005, 56 percent of Black boys were suspended or expelled compared to 19 percent to 43 percent of boys in other racial/ethnic groups (Wallace et al., 2008). Evidence does not support the theory that students from certain racial and ethnic groups "misbehave" more than others (Gregory et al., 2010). And though there is less literature on the adultification of children in other racial/ethnic groups, school punishment is also harsh and unequal for Latinx and Native American children when compared to their White and Asian peers (DeVoe and Darling-Churchill, 2008; Gordon et al., 2000; Rios, 2011; Skiba and Losen, 2015–16; Wallace et al., 2008), as well as for students with disabilities (Vincent and Tobin, 2010).

Philosophical literature has raised a broad range of questions about whether there are special childhood "goods" (i.e., as opposed to "bads") that apply to all children, how they should be weighed against other goods, and what is owed to children (see, e.g., Gheaus, 2018; Hannan, 2018; Macloud, 2018; Schapiro, 1999; Tomlin, 2016). Shapiro (1999) argues that because children have not formed fixed identities and do not yet have clear values and aims, adults are within their rights to paternalize them while adults simultaneously have a duty to help children reach adulthood. Tomlin (2016) suggests that under the "caterpillar/butterfly" view, childhood and adulthood should not be assessed using the same criteria because they are different kinds of human beings. Hannan (2018) contends that many of the "goods" of childhood are actually bads, pointing to four bads specific to childhood: (1) children's impaired capacity for practical reasoning, (2) children's lack of an established practical identity, (3) subjugation by adults, and (4) asymmetry between children's and adult's vulnerability.

Others have expanded upon Shapiro's (1999) distinction between childhood and adulthood to argue that there are special goods associated with childhood that make it valuable. Gheaus (2018) adopts a developmental view of childhood to argue that rather than lacking the capacities of adults, children possess many valuable capacities lost in adulthood. Specifically, drawing on research primarily from developmental psychology, Gheaus (2018) reasons that due to their brain development, children up to their early teens demonstrate capacities for philosophical, artistic, and scientific inquiry that are superior to adults' capacities. Gheaus suggests that a judgment of "whether the best human life contains no childhood, perpetual childhood or a combination of childhood and adulthood" will require an evaluation of relevant weighty goods (Gheaus, 2018). Macleod (2018) offers a nondevelopmental view of childhood, arguing that childhood is valuable, independent of its contribution to children's development into future adults. Macleod (2018) contends that schools ought to distribute the childhood goods of play, imagination, and innocence in an egalitarian manner, and that such nonpreparatory dimensions of schooling should not be sacrificed for the preparatory dimensions of schooling (i.e., those that prepare children for adulthood).

Unlike Tomlin (2016) and Macleod (2018), I view goods such as play and joy as universal (i.e., not unique to childhood). Adults, too, benefit from play and imagination. For example, Brown (2009) shows that adult play ranging from board games to intramural leagues leads to our social well-being. People along multiple lines of difference (e.g., age, ability, culture) engage in play that may take diverse forms. I do not attempt here to develop a defense of such goods as instrumental or intrinsic; for the purposes of this chapter, I simply take them to be universal. The primary difference between adulthood and childhood, then, is that certain goods are *uniquely withheld* from children because of their low social power. Social power and access to these goods are even lower for students who are systemically marginalized (e.g., along lines of race, class, disability, gender).

Building upon the literature, I examine No Excuses schools through the lens of two goods that are commonly withheld from children in No Excuses schools: play and agency. Though there is not universal agreement on what counts as a "good," following Macleod (2018), I recognize that "like many claims about human flourishing, there is little one can offer by way of proof of their value beyond reflective consideration of our intuitive responses to various scenarios real and imagined" (p. 79). Certainly, these goods, like all goods, are culturally constructed and have been viewed differently across societies and over time (Archard, 2004). Nonetheless, it seems that most would agree play and agency are valuable, even if they would make different determinations about their relative weight and distribution.

One of the primary reasons that No Excuses schools offer for limiting students' access to play and agency is that doing so is necessary to increase students' access to "educational goods" by raising their academic achievement as represented by standardized test scores (Brighouse et al., 2018). Educational goods refer to the "knowledge, skills, attitudes, and dispositions" that children must develop for a flourishing life, for both themselves and others (p. 19). While Brighouse et al. (2018) do not attempt to develop a comprehensive list of educational goods, they name six capacities that are germane to all people living in a modern society, including the capacities for personal autonomy, economic productivity, healthy personal relationships, democratic competence, personal fulfillment, and treating others as equals. In what follows, I analyze the trade-offs between students' access to play, agency, and educational goods in No Excuses schools, with particular attention to the context of systemic racial injustice and, relatedly, adultification.

"No Excuses" rationale

The roots of the No Excuses school model are often traced to the Knowledge is Power Program (KIPP), now one of the largest charter networks in the United States (Sondel, 2015). The first KIPP school was founded in 1994 by two former Teach for America (TFA) teachers, Mike Feinberg and Dave Levin, in Houston, Texas (KIPP, 2016). Feinberg and Levin's school model rested on the "five pillars": high expectations, choice and commitment, more time, power to lead, and focus on results (KIPP, 2016). Student test scores in math and reading soared, but this was believed to have been possible only through the school's firm behavioral guidelines. At KIPP, "the standards for behavior are just as unrelenting as they are for academics. The goal is to keep students focused on learning all the time. Any distractions are met with swift intervention" (CBS News, 1999). KIPP schools have since proliferated and are now used as a model for charter schools that wish to replicate their success (Kretchmar, Sondel and Ferrare, 2014). These schools are most often located in urban areas and serve primarily low-income Black and Latinx students (Furgeson et al., 2012).

Punishments (e.g., demerits, detention) and reinforcements (e.g., cheers, praise, pretend money for class store) are frequently meted out at No Excuses schools (Goodman, 2013). The form of behavioral control at No Excuses schools can be accurately described as a form of discipline. As Golann (2021) argues, drawing on the work of social theorist Michael Foucault, discipline "is an expression of power that is insidious and more difficult to see than sheer force" (p. 29). Students at No Excuses schools are given specific guidelines for how to dress, sit, "track" (i.e., visually focus upon) the speaker, and express joy (Goodman, 2013). This form of control includes and exceeds punishment practices and is seen as necessary to conserve time best used for increasing student achievement on standardized tests and, ultimately, for college admittance (Goodman, 2013).

Evaluating the claims

In what follows, I evaluate three perceived claims often explicitly or implicitly invoked in support of increasing educational goods at the cost of students' access to play and agency:

- (C1) "No Excuses schools increase students' educational goods more than other types of schools serving similar student populations."

- (C2) "It is necessary to limit play and agency through strict discipline to produce educational goods."
- (C3) "No Excuses schools provide sufficient access to (a) play and (b) agency."

I begin with an evaluation of C1. Evidence to date uses standardized test scores as a proxy for learning. Though there are reasons to think that standardized tests are an inadequate measure of student learning and that No Excuses schools focus too narrowly on tested subjects (i.e., math and reading) to the exclusion of other subjects (Sondel, 2015), analysis of standardized test scores is one way to assess the degree to which No Excuses schools increase students' educational goods. Overall, charter schools in the United States perform no better than traditional public schools, but some No Excuses schools, including KIPP schools, have produced higher test scores than other charter schools (Ferrare, 2019). Several studies have compared the outcomes of students who were admitted to No Excuses schools versus those who were not, finding that No Excuses schools have positive effects on test scores, as well as high school graduation rates and college acceptance (Cheng et al., 2017; Tuttle et al., 2013, 2015). A smaller body of research has examined the long-term effects of a KIPP education. While college admittance is generally higher for KIPP students, there is less evidence that KIPP students persist in college (Coen, Nichols-Barrer and Gleason, 2019). Overall, the current evidence base suggests that some No Excuses schools increase educational goods as measured by standardized test scores, though test scores are a limited representation of student learning.

Next, I turn to C2. There is limited evidence that No Excuses schools' disciplinary system is responsible for the test score gains made by some No Excuses schools. Golann and Torres (2018) investigated the claim that No Excuses schools promote academic achievement and concluded that they found "no compelling evidence that school disciplinary policies are necessary for academic achievement, as measured by student performance on standardized test scores" (p. 5). In their study of thirty-five New York City charters, Dobbie and Fryer (2011) found no association between No Excuses behavioral practices and academic achievement. In sum, No Excuses-style discipline, which places severe limits on students' access to play and agency, is not requisite to increasing educational goods as represented by standardized test scores.

Last, I turn to C3 and offer an extended analysis of its sub-arguments, significance, and its stakes. There is no easy proxy for measuring No Excuses schools' capacities for play and agency, and large-scale studies measuring the schools' capacity for these goods do not exist. Here, descriptive, qualitative studies of particular No Excuses schools are useful for understanding day-to-day school life. Consistent with a constructivist epistemology, these studies are not generalizable; rather, they offer an opportunity for nuanced examination of how play and agency might be fostered or limited under the No Excuses model. For the purposes of this chapter, I determine "adequacy" by assessing situations in which educators could reasonably increase access to play and agency in the context of schooling while not significantly undermining the other goods of schooling (e.g., educational goods, safety). I begin with an examination of play and follow with an examination of agency.

Play is a "voluntary, pleasurable experience" involving imagination and creativity (Yoon, 2014, 110). Though play can serve a productive role in helping students acquire educational goods such as literacy skills (Christie, 1998; Dyson, 2007; Vygotsky, 1978), others have argued for the intrinsic value of play—that is, purposeless play is a good in and of itself regardless of its benefits for children as future adults (Brennan, 2014; Brighouse et al., 2018; Macleod, 2010, 2018). As Macleod writes, "The unbridled and unselfconscious delight children can exhibit when they in engage in various forms of play provides strong evidence" of its value (2018, 79). No Excuses schools limit opportunities for spontaneous play through the highly regulated school day. Requirements for student comportment range from the way students enter the room to the way they sit in their seats and look at or "track" the speaker. Students at the school Golann (2021) studied could receive an infraction for having their head down on their desk, not looking at or "tracking" the speaker, twirling, or jumping.

A counterargument may be that the strict disciplinary code at No Excuses may engender predictability and feelings of safety that could be thought to give rise to play. However, evidence suggests these schools also heighten students' stress and anxiety, which seem to hinder the carefreeness needed for play. In his phenomenological case study of Black males who attended No Excuses schools, Griffin (2018) showed that in some cases, No Excuses schools retraumatized students who had experienced prior traumas. Golann's (2021) study echoes Griffin's (2018) findings. She found that students experienced stress and anxiety due to pressure to follow the school's strict disciplinary code. One Black girl told Golann (2021) that her hair fell out once she started attending a No Excuses school due to its strict discipline. Even "well-behaved" students at the school experienced stress due to pressure not to make a behavioral error (Golann, 2021).

Despite the limitations on time and space for play at No Excuses schools, there may be some occasions for play. For example, Golann (2020) recounts several field trips that students earned for following school rules, including a snow tubing trip and a visit to the aquarium. Golann recounts of the aquarium field trip, "It had been a fun field trip [. . .] Typical school rules were relaxed. There were no silent straight lines or hand signals, and students spent the day leisurely exploring exhibits in small groups" (Golann, 2020, 44–5). Such experiences may provide students with time, space, and an environment conducive to play. Yet, these instances are likely few and far between. More frequent are the call-and-response chants common in No Excuses schools. "Songs, choral responses, chants, and slogans" reinforce behavioral expectations and are common to the No Excuses model (Goodman, 2013, 92). These chants may be considered humorous or celebratory but could also be considered a "performance" of play or scripted play, rather than play itself. Overall, it seems that No Excuses schools limit students' opportunities for play through a strict behavioral code that regulates students' interactions and movements in such a way as to make play almost impossible for much of the day and creates stress and anxiety that make it difficult for students to engage in play at school. Therefore, the claim that No Excuses schools provide adequate access to play is uncompelling, because they could reasonably provide increased opportunities for play without significantly undermining other goods of schooling.

Finally, I turn to an examination of whether No Excuses schools provide students adequate access to agency. Agency is "the ability to act otherwise" (Lamboy, Taylor and Thompson, 2020, 63) and is crucial to even young children's ability to develop capabilities, knowledge, and skills (Adair, 2014). As I argued earlier, one unique feature of childhood is that adults withhold agency from children, because adults have greater social power than children. The behavioral control at No Excuses schools hinges upon withholding students' agency through monitoring and assessing their comportment. Educators "generally do not permit students to talk quietly in the hallway, enter and exit classrooms on their own, keep backpacks at their desk, wear jewelry, stare into space, slouch, put their head down, get out of their seat without permission, or refuse to track the teacher's eyes" (Golann, 2021, 5). In the middle school Golann (2021) studied, even students' facial expressions were monitored through explicit rules and punishments associated with eye-rolling and teeth-sucking. It seems that No Excuses schools could reasonably increase students' access to agency without significantly undermining the other goods of schooling.

An objection to this argument may be that students must exercise some agency in No Excuses schools, because agency can never be completely diminished. I agree that students do not passively accept No Excuses-style discipline. For example, Golann (2021) recounts examples of student resistance to school rules, such as "comb[ing] each other's hair," "eras[ing] names off the infraction list on the board," and "lean[ing] their chairs back on two legs" (pp. 84–5). However, children should be allowed more agency than the ability to skirt around school rules occasionally. Whatever the threshold for "adequate" agency in schools, these examples might intuitively seem to fall short.

One might think that No Excuses schools curb students' agency now for the promise of future agency. That is, if adults withhold agency from students now, students will have more agency as adults when they have completed college degrees and secured well-paying jobs. Some might think this is a just trade-off, particularly because the population of students who attend No Excuses schools (predominantly low-income Black and Latinx students) are more likely to experience diminished economic opportunity and mobility in adulthood than their more privileged peers (middle- and high-income White students) due to intersecting effects of racial and economic oppression (Kocchar and Fry, 2014). However, this view needlessly positions children's agency in opposition to educational goods and future economic productivity. Agency is instrumental to learning at all ages and increased student agency does not equate to lower test scores (Adair, 2014).

Additionally, one could argue that children can access agency outside of school and therefore schools are not obligated to provide it. However, the obligation to provide access to agency is especially important in No Excuses schools within the context of systemic racial oppression. Black children are adultified, or perceived to be more responsible and culpable for their actions than their White peers, and experience misattributions of agency both in and out of schools (Lamboy, Taylor and Thompson, 2020). In other words, adults perceive Black students as possessing an "excess of agency" and therefore restrict their behavior, and subsequently, their access to actual agency (Lamboy, Taylor and Thompson, 2020, 65). This phenomenon occurs not only in schools but out of schools as well, as evidenced by Black students' overrepresentation in juvenile justice institutions (Bahena et al., 2012). This misattribution follows Black children into adulthood; Black adults are also considered more culpable than Whites (The Sentencing Project, 2018) and are overrepresented in adult prisons (Advancement Project, 2010). Relatedly, Black boys' play is too often socially constructed as "criminal, dangerous, and monstrous," a phenomenon that further contributes to the patterned punishment of Black boys and men (Bryan, 2020, 673). Given broad patterns of unequal distribution across and beyond these contexts, schools are under an even greater obligation to provide access to agency and play.

To be sure, goods other than educational goods might inform the weight and distribution of play and agency. For example, some have argued that Black and Latinx parents who choose No Excuses schools prioritize a desire for school safety and therefore select No Excuses schools because of their strict discipline (Decker, Darville and Snyder, 2015). Indeed, Golann, Debs, and Weiss (2019) found that Black and Latinx parents they interviewed chose No Excuses schools out of concern for school safety, order, self-discipline, and academic rigor. However, the authors suggest "Black and Latinx parents' preference for discipline does not equate to behavioral discipline focused on rules, rewards, and punishment" characteristic of No Excuses schools (Golann, Debs, and Weiss, 2019, 1898). In other words, there is a mismatch between the style of discipline and punishment at No Excuses schools and what parents envision for their children.

Brighouse et al. (2018) contend that No Excuses schools should not be evaluated in contrast to an unrealistic version of traditional public school, wherein students experience a plethora of childhood goods. Indeed, the authors argue that students in traditional public schools might also experience a loss of childhood goods due to "disruptive classroom behavior and lax discipline in the hallways" (Brighouse et al., 2018, 148). I agree that students in traditional public schools may also experience diminished access to play and agency, and believe these schools, too, should seek to develop a balanced interplay between childhood and educational goods in addition to other weighty values, such as safety.

To be clear, I am not arguing that schools should never limit students' access to play and agency. For example, a teacher may rightfully ask young children to lower their volume, so they can get directions for a learning activity or hear a story. I take seriously Delpit's (2006) argument that progressive pedagogues too often undermine marginalized students' need for basic skills in favor of more loosely structured activities. Rather, I recognize the value of play and agency and contend that these goods can be simultaneously pursued alongside other learning aims, including skill acquisition. Indeed, there are many instances where children's play and agency are instrumental to increasing educational goods. However, if No Excuses schools were to provide increased opportunities for play and agency, the question remains whether they would continue to be distinct from traditional public schools or other charter schools, since strict discipline is so core to this model. Some KIPP schools have attempted to shift away from strict discipline and have begun to implement restorative justice (Sadler, 2021); this transition may provide possibilities for increased student play and agency.

Discussion

I have shown here that No Excuses schools withhold low-income Black and Latinx students' access to play and agency for the perceived purpose of increasing their educational goods. Through tight behavioral control, these schools trade-off students' play and agency for high test scores, in the hopes that students will later obtain college degrees and well-paying jobs. However, I have argued that play and agency need not be viewed in opposition to educational goods because (a) access to play and agency could reasonably be increased in the context of No Excuses schools without undermining other goods of schooling, and (b) play and agency are instrumental to the acquisition of educational goods.

I have argued that schools face an additional obligation to provide access to agency to Black students from whom such agency is disproportionally withheld outside of school and as adults in the context of systemic racial oppression. This does not mean that schools should neglect their obligations to provide students with basic knowledge and skills. Rather, schools should prioritize activities that harness students' agency and capacity for play for learning purposes. Furthermore, they should not withhold play and agency from students in cases where they could reasonably still pursue educational aims.

Note

1 This form of assault can include actions which are interpreted as causing fear of imminent bodily harm.

References

Adair, Jennifer K. (2014) "Agency and Expanding Capabilities in Early Grade Classrooms: What It Could Mean for Young Children." *Harvard Educational Review* 84 (2): 217–41.

Advancement Project. (2010) *Test, Punish, and Push Out: How "Zero Tolerance" and High Stakes Testing Funnel Youth into the School-to-Prison Pipeline*. Washington, DC: The Advancement Project. http://www.advancementproject.org/sites/default/files/publications/rev_fin.pdf.

Annamma, Subini A., Anyon, Yolanda, Joseph, Nicole M., Farrar, Jordan, Greer, Eldridge, Downing, Barbara and Simmons, John (2016) "Black Girls and School Discipline: The Complexities of Being Overrepresented and Understudied." *Urban Education* 54 (2): 211–42.

Archard, David (2004) *Children: Right and Childhood*. New York: Routledge.

Ariès, Philippe (1962) *Centuries of Childhood: A Social History of Family Life*. New York: Random House.

Bahena, Sofía, Cooc, North, Currie-Rubin, Rachel, Kuttner, Paul and Ng, Monica (eds.). (2012) *Disrupting the School-to-Prison Pipeline*. Cambridge, MA: Harvard Education Press.

Bernstein, R. (2011) *Racial Innocence: Performing American Childhood from Slavery to Civil Rights*. New York: New York University Press.

Brennan, Samantha (2014) "The Goods of Childhood, Children's Rights, and the Role of Parents as Advocates and Interpreters." In F. Baylis and C. McLeod (eds.), *Family-Making: Contemporary Ethical Challenges*, 29–48. Oxford: Oxford University Press.

Brighouse, Harry, Ladd, Helen F., Loeb, Susanna and Swift, Adam (2018) *Educational Goods: Values, Evidence, and Decision-Making*. Chicago, IL: The University of Chicago Press.

Bryan, Nathaniel (2020) "Shaking the *Bad Boys*: Troubling the Criminalization of Black Boys' Childhood Play, Hegemonic White Masculinity and Femininity, and the School Playground-to-Prison Pipeline." *Race Ethnicity and Education* 23 (5): 673–92.

CBS News. (1999) *Mike & Dave on 60 Minutes* [Vimeo]. https://vimeo.com/91447154.

Cheng, Albert, Hitt, Collin, Kisida, Brian and Mills, Jonathan N. (2017) "No Excuses Charter Schools: A Meta-Analysis of the Experimental Evidence on Student Achievement." *Journal of School Choice* 11 (2): 209–38.

Christy, James F. (1998) "Play as a Medium for Literacy Development." In Doris Pronin Fromberg and Doris Bergent (eds.), *Play from Birth to Twelve and Beyond: Contexts, Perspectives, and Meaning*, 50–5. New York: Garland.

Coen, Thomas, Nichols-Barrer, Ira and Gleason, Philip (2019) *Long-Term Impacts of KIPP Middle Schools on College Enrollment and Early College Persistence*. Cambridge, MA: Mathematica Policy Research.

Dancy, T. Elon, III. (2014) "The Adultification of Black Boys: What Educational Settings Can Learn from Trayvon Martin." In Kenneth J. Fasching-Varner and Rema E. Reynolds (eds.), *Trayvon Martin, Race, and American Justice*, 49–55. New York: Springer.

Decker, Geoff, Snyder, Stephanie and Darville, Sarah. (2015) "Suspensions at City Charter Schools Far Outpace Those at District Schools, Data Show." *Chalkbeat*. https://ny.chalkbeat.org/2015/2/23/21092194/suspensions-at-city-charter-schools-far-outpace-those-at-district-schools-data-show

DeVoe, Jill Fleury, Darling-Churchill, Kristen E. and Snyder, Thomas D. (2008) *Status and Trends in the Education of American Indians and Alaska Natives: 2008 (NCES 2008-084)*. Washington, DC: National Center for Education Statistics, Institute of Education Sciences, US Department of Education.

Dobbie, Will and Fryer, Roland G. (2011) *Getting Beneath the Veil of Effective Schools: Evidence from New York City* (Working Paper No. 17632). Washington, DC: National Bureau of Economic Research. http://www.nber.org/ papers/w17632.

Dumas, Michael J. and Nelson, Joseph D. (2016) "(Re)imagining Black Boyhood: Toward a Critical Framework for Educational Research." *Harvard Educational Review* 86 (1): 27–47.

Dyson, Anne H. (2007) "School Literacy and the Development of a Child Culture: Written Remnants of the 'Gusto of Life.'" In D. Thiessen and A. Cook-Sander (eds.), *International Handbook of Student Experiences in Elementary and Secondary School*, 115–42. Dordrecht: Springer.

Epstein, Rebecca, Blake, Jamilia J. and González, Thalia. (2017) *Girlhood Interrupted: The Erasure of Black Girls' Childhood*. The Center on Poverty and Inequality. Washington, DC: Georgetown Law.

Ferguson, Ann A. (2001) *Bad Boys: Public Schools in the Making of Black Masculinity*. Ann Arbor, MI: University of Michigan Press.

Ferrare, Joseph J. (2019) "Charter School Outcomes." In Mark Berends, Ann Primus and Matthew G. Springer (eds.), *Handbook of Research on School Choice*, 160–73. New York: Routledge.

Furgeson, Joshua, Gill, Brian, Haimson, Joshua, Killewald, Alexandra, McCullough, Moira, Nichols-Barrer, Ira, The, Bing-ru, et al. (2012) *Charter-school Management Organizations: Diverse Strategies and Diverse Student Impacts*. Bothell, WA: Mathematica Policy Research.

Gheaus, Anca. (2018) "Children's Vulnerability and Legitimate Authority over Children." *Journal of Applied Philosophy* 35 (1): 60–75.

Goff, Phillip Atiba, Eberhardt, Jennifer L., Williams, Melissa J. and Jackson, Matthew Christian. (2008) "Not Yet Human: Implicit Knowledge, Historical Dehumanization, and Contemporary Consequences." *Journal of Personality and Social Psychology* 94 (2): 292–306.

Goff, Phillip Atiba, Jackson, Matthew Christian,

Di Leone, Brooke, Culotta, Carmen M., and DiTomasso, Natalie A. (2014) "The Essence of Innocence: Consequences of Dehumanizing Black Children." *Journal of Personality and Social Psychology* 106 (4): 526–45.

Golann, Joanne W. (2021) *Scripting the Moves: Culture and Control in a "No-Excuses" Charter School*. Princeton, NJ and Oxford: Princeton University Press.

Golann, Joanne W. and Torres, A. Chris (2020) "Do No-Excuses Disciplinary Practices Promote Success?" *Journal of Urban Affairs* 42 (4): 617–33.

Golann, Joanne W., Debs, Mira and Weiss, Anna L. (2019) "'To Be Strict on Your Own': Black and Latinx Parents Evaluate Discipline in Urban Choice Schools." *American Educational Research Journal* 26 (5): 1896–929.

Goodman, Joan F. (2013) "Charter Management Organizations and the Regulated Environment: Is It Worth the Price?" *Educational Researcher* 42 (2): 89–96.

Gordon, Rebecca, Della Piana, Libero and Keleher, Terry (2000). *Facing the Consequences: An Examination of Racial Discrimination in U.S. Public Schools*, March. Oakland, CA: Applied Research Center.

Gregory, Anne, Skiba, Russell J., and Noguera, Pedro A. (2010). "The Achievement Gap and the Discipline Gap: Two Sides of the Same Coin?" *Educational Researcher* 39 (1): 59–68.

Gregory, James F. (1997) "Three Strikes and They're Out: African American Boys and American Schools' Responses to Misbehavior." *International Journal of Adolescence and Youth* 7: 25–34.

Griffin, Ramon (2018) *A Phenomenological Case Study of Four Black Males Exposed to Cumulative Trauma That Attended a "No Excuses" Charter School*. Doctoral Dissertation, Michigan State University.

Hannan, Sarah (2018) "Why Childhood Is Bad for Children." *Journal of Applied Philosophy* 35 (1): 11–28.

James, Allison (2004) "Understanding Childhood from an Interdisciplinary Perspective: Problems and Potentials." In P. B. Pufall and R. P. Unsworth (eds.), *Rethinking Childhood*, 25–37. New Brunswick, NJ: Rutgers University.

KIPP (2016) "KIPP History." http://www.kipp.org/about/history/.

Kochhar, Rakesh and Fry, Richard (2014) *Wealth Inequality Has Widened Along Racial, Ethnic Lines Since End of Great Recession*. Pew Research Center. https://www.pewresearch.org/fact-tank/2014/12/12/racial-wealth-gaps-great-recession/.

Kretchmar, Kerry, Sondel, Beth and Ferrare, Joseph J. (2014) "Mapping the Terrain: Teach for America, Charter School Reform, and Corporate Sponsorship." *Journal of Education Policy* 29: 742–59.

Lamboy, Lily Taylor, Ashley and Thompson, Winston C. (2020) "Paternalistic Aims and (mis)attributions of Agency: What the Over-punishment of Black Girls in US Classrooms Teaches Us about Just School Discipline." *Theory and Research in Education* 18 (1): 59–77.

Laureau, Annette (2011) *Unequal Childhoods: Class, Race, and Family Life*. Berkeley and Los Angeles, CA: University of California Press.

Macleod, Colin M. (2010) "Primary Goods, Capabilities, and Children." In Ingrid Robeyns and Harry Brighouse (eds.), *Measuring Justice: Primary Goods and Capabilities*, 174–92. Cambridge University Press.

Macleod, Colin M. (2018) "Just Schools and Good Childhoods: Non-Preparatory Dimensions of Educational Justice." *Journal of Applied Philosophy* 35 (1): 76–89.

Meiners, Erica R. (2016) *For the Children?: Protecting Innocence in a Carceral State*. Minneapolis and London: University of Minnesota Press.

Rios, Victor (2011) *Punished: Policing the Lives of Black and Latino Boys*. New York and London: New York University Press.

Sadler, James (2021) *No-excuses in Restorative Justice Clothing: The Effects of Adopting Restorative Justice in a No-excuses Setting*. [Doctoral dissertation, University of

North Carolina at Chapel Hill]. University of North Carolina at Chapel Hill Digital Repository.

Shapiro, Tamar (1999) "What Is a Child?" *Ethics* 109 (4): 715–38.

Skiba, Russell J. and Losen, Daniel J. (2015–16) "From Reaction to Prevention: Turning the Page on School Discipline." *American Educator*. https://files.eric.ed.gov/fulltext/EJ1086522.pdf.

Sondel, Beth (2015) "Raising Citizens or Raising Test Scores? Teach for America, 'No Excuses' Charters, and the Development of the Neoliberal Citizen." *Theory & Research in Social Education* 43: 289–313.

Stephens, Sharon (ed.). (1995) *Children and the Politics of Culture*. Princeton, NJ: Princeton University Press.

The Sentencing Project (2018) *Report to the United Nations on Racial Disparities in the U.S. Criminal Justice System*. https://www.sentencingproject.org/publications/un-report-on-racial-disparities/.

Tomlin, Patrick (2016) "Saplings or Caterpillars? Trying to Understand Children's Wellbeing." *Journal of Applied Philosophy* 35 (1): 29–46.

Tuttle, Christina C., Gill, Brian, Gleason, Philip, Knechtel, Virginia, Nichols-Barrer, Ira and Resch, Alexandra (2013) *KIPP Middle Schools: Impacts on Achievement and Other Outcomes*. Final Report. Mathematica Policy Research.

Tuttle, Christina C., Gleason, Philip, Knechtel, Virginia, Nichols-Barrer, Ira, Booker, Kevin, Chojnacki, Gregory, Coen, Thomas and Goble, Lisbeth (2015) *Understanding the Effect of KIPP as It Scales: Vol. 1, Impacts on Achievement and Other Outcomes*. Washington, DC: Mathematica Policy Research.

Vincent, Claudia G. and Tobin, Tary J. (2010) "The Relationship between Implementation of School-wide Positive Behavior Support (SWPBS) and Disciplinary Exclusion of Students from Various Ethnic Backgrounds with and without Disabilities." *Journal of Emotional and Behavioral Disorders* 19 (4): 217–32. doi:10.1177%2F1063426610377329.

Vygotsky, Lev S. (1978) *Mind in Society*. Cambridge, MA: Harvard University Press.

Wallace, John M., Jr., Goodkind, Sara, Wallace, Cynthia M. and Bachman, Jerald G. (2008) "Racial, Ethnic, and Gender Differences in School Discipline among U.S. High School Students: 1991–2005." *Negro Educational Review* 59: 47–62.

Williams, Vanessa (2018) "Innocence Erased: How Society Keeps Black Boys from Being Boys." *The Washington Post*, September 21. https://www.washingtonpost.com/nation/2018/09/21/innocence-denied-black-boys-who-face-harsher-scrutiny-consequences-than-their-White-peers/.

Wyness, Michael (2012) *Childhood and Society: An Introduction to the Sociology of Childhood*. New York: Palgrave Macmillan.

Yoon, Haeny S. (2014) "Can I Play with You? The Intersection of Play and Writing in a Kindergarten Classroom." *Contemporary Issues in Early Childhood* 15 (2): 109–21.

6

Punishment in Early Childhood

Do Exclusionary Practices Threaten Children's Moral Rights?

Joy Dangora Erickson

Seclusion punishments typically involve involuntarily removing a child from their classroom and placing them in an isolated alternate space. The child is forced to remain unaccompanied in the space for an amount of time deemed appropriate by school staff (Scheuermann et al., 2016). In the United States and elsewhere (e.g., England), recent reports of children as young as five years old being placed in seclusion spaces, sometimes referred to as isolation rooms or quiet rooms, to curb disruptive behaviors have gained national attention. Reports suggest that the punishment may be more prevalent than once thought (Richards, Cohen and Chavis 2019; Staufenberg, 2018).

Psychological harm is one potential consequence of secluding young children (NDRN, 2009). Children who are placed in isolation rooms and/or separated in other ways from their classroom community can experience harmful levels of stress and trauma.[1] This is particularly concerning for very young children; during the early childhood period, trauma can have a range of negative effects on children's development. For example, trauma can interrupt the maturation of the brain's frontal lobes which develop rapidly during the first six years of life. When this developmental process is interrupted, children's self-regulation skills (e.g., ability to focus on a task) and executive function skills (e.g., ability to stop and think before reacting to stimuli) can be delayed or impaired.[2] Because these skills are considered vital for setting and meeting goals, experts including those at the Center for the Developing Child at Harvard University, recommend that young children be supportively coached (e.g., communicate messages of safety) by a nurturing adult through highly stressful situations (Nicholson, Perez and Kurtz, 2019). Given the possibility for seclusion punishments to negatively impact children's development, it seems reasonable for nations to enforce some form of wide-reaching legal protections to deter adults from secluding young children. In the United States, federal law has yet to regulate school seclusion punishments despite congressional efforts to do so, and in many states, seclusion is legal so long as school officials believe the secluded child to be a threat to themself and/or others. As is the case in other Western nations (e.g., England), not all children in the United States are equally likely to be secluded. Black and Hispanic children and children identified as having one or more disabilities tend to be secluded at rates higher than those of their White and nondisabled peers (US Department of Education, 2019); seclusion punishments appear to be discriminatory in many cases.

In 2019 ProPublica Illinois and the *Chicago Tribune* together looked more closely at school seclusion records across the state of Illinois. They found that schools had administered seclusion punishments over 20,000 times during a period spanning the 2017–18 academic year and into the first half of the 2018–19 academic year (Richards, Cohen and Chavis, 2019). Some of the secluded students were reported to have committed what might be considered violent acts (e.g., kicking, biting); however, many others were placed in isolation rooms for minor infractions (e.g., not doing homework, cussing).

One case stemming from this investigation that received much attention is that of Isaiah Knipe. From kindergarten to third grade, Isaiah, a young student of color with special needs, was repeatedly placed alone in his school's quiet room for what the school deemed inappropriate behavior (e.g., pushing over a desk). Frustrated by being locked inside alone, Isaiah began banging his head against the room's plywood and concrete walls; the school's nurse noted the potential for concussion in her reports. Isaiah told his mother that he explained to school officials that he banged his head against the room's walls because he did not want to be locked inside of it (Jensen, 2019). School officials continued to isolate him for some time afterwards.

Based on investigative reporting, it is reasonable to arrive at the conclusion that being forced into the seclusion space caused Isaiah physical (e.g., observed head injury) and emotional harms (e.g., self-reported high levels of frustration). He also likely lost critical learning time and opportunities for advancing his social development while secluded. Locked in the isolation room alone, Isaiah was denied the opportunity to be coached by a nurturing adult in self-regulation strategies or anything else. This case along with thousands of others reported by ProPublica and the *Chicago Tribune* sparked Illinois lawmakers in 2020 to support a bill banning seclusion punishments in Illinois schools (Richards and

Cohen, 2021a). As of this writing, Illinois just recently (August 2021) barred schools from locking children in isolation rooms alone and has required schools to limit isolation punishments and physical restraint to instances in which employees perceive there to be "imminent danger of physical harm" (Richards and Cohen, 2021b). Though this is a step forward in that fewer young children are likely to be placed in isolation rooms alone, it is unclear how children who are placed in isolation will be supported, if at all, by the adults now required to accompany them.

Placing young children in quiet rooms when they should be learning and socializing seems unjust, and yet many do not have a *legal right* to be free of this practice—one recognized within the legal system and "backed by the force of law" (Noggle, 2019, 101). But the absence of one or more legal rights does not necessarily deny children related moral rights. It is not uncommon for moral rights to be recognized before legal rights. For some, the egregiousness of placing young children in quiet rooms may stem from a fundamental moral responsibility to protect them from various harms (e.g., physical, emotional, academic).

Despite not having a legal right to be free from seclusion punishments, I argue in the sections that follow that all children, including very young children, have moral rights that exclusionary practices more broadly construed (e.g., expulsions, suspensions, and time-outs) stand to violate. Additionally, I argue that (1) adults have an obligation to exhaust all other potential options before isolating children from their schools, classrooms, community members, and/or learning experiences, and (2) if a child must be isolated, adults have an obligation to honor that child's moral rights to the fullest extent possible.

Young children as holders of moral rights

The language of children's rights has wide currency as a powerful tool for moral persuasion and social protection. Specifically, the view that children hold moral rights has influenced major early childhood pedagogical frameworks and program guidelines for decades. The integrated network of early learning centers in Reggio Emilia, Italy, from which the Reggio Approach was born shortly after the Second World War, was founded on "the principle of children's right to education" as well as the rights of children, families, and teachers to "maximize well-being for all involved" (Piccinini and Giudici, 2012, 95). Today, early childhood education settings across the globe have embraced a Reggio-inspired approach to teaching that encourages and appreciates children's efforts to exercise control over their learning.

Similarly, the National Association for the Education of Young Children (NAEYC), a professional organization that regularly publishes and updates standards for early childhood providers, indirectly recognizes young children as moral rights holders in their "Code of Ethical Conduct and Statement of Commitment" (NAEYC, 2011). Within the overview of Section I: Ethical Responsibilities to Children, the organization states that they are "committed to promoting children's self-awareness, competence, self-worth, resiliency, and physical well-being" (NAEYC, 2011, 2). Bulleted underneath the overview is responsibility I-1.5: "To create and maintain safe and healthy settings that foster children's social, emotional, cognitive, and physical development and that respect their dignity and their contributions (NAEYC, 2011, 2)." These responsibilities of educators might reasonably be interpreted as guaranteeing the children in their care (1) the right to develop socially, emotionally, cognitively, and physically, (2) the right to be treated with dignity, and (3) the right to make respected contributions to the educational space.

Though both the guiding principles of the Reggio Approach and the NAEYC position statement can be interpreted as implying that young children have a number of moral rights that adults charged with their care are obligated to honor, a strong argument in support of children as holders of moral rights is not offered. To buttress claims that young children have moral rights, early childhood stakeholders might consider arguments articulated in educational philosophy.

Children's morally significant status

One way moral rights are described within educational philosophy is as those rights in which something is due to someone on the basis of their "morally significant status" as a person (Noggle, 2019, 102). This conception of morally significant status may be better comprehended by contrasting an individual destroying property with an individual physically damaging another human. Both can reasonably be considered violations of acceptable behavior; however, damaging a person usually results in far stiffer legal and social penalties. People arguably hold higher moral value than nonliving things and nonhuman animals[3] for the primary reason that they are human (Brennan and Noggle, 1997; Noggle, 2019). When a person holds a basic moral right, one or more people typically[4] have an obligation to either do something or abstain from doing something to honor that right (Noggle, 2019).

- An example illustrating a responsibility to act might be a young child has a moral right to be educated, and therefore, the adults charged with the child's care (and potentially others) have a responsibility to provide the child with an education.
- Another example illustrating a responsibility to act might be a young child has a right to be free from a variety of harms (e.g., physical, emotional, psychological), and any adult who suspects a child might be harmed in a particular environment has a responsibility to determine whether the environment is safe and protect the child from harm if necessary.
- An example illustrating a responsibility to abstain from acting might be a young child has a moral right to be free from a variety of types of harm, and therefore, adults charged with caring for the child (and potentially other adults) have an obligation to abstain from knowingly harming the child directly or indirectly.

It is largely uncontested among educational philosophers that children hold some fundamental moral rights (i.e., basic human rights). These often include a right to an education and a right to be free from deliberate harm. Some philosophers (e.g., rights theorists) maintain that in certain instances fundamental moral rights that protect one's human dignity should be honored even when denying them is in the interest of the common good (Dworkin, 1977). Others (e.g., will/choice theorists; Goodwin and Gibson, 1977; Hart, 1955) argue that children cannot hold the fullest cache of moral rights because of their less-developed (compared to many adults) capacities for autonomy (i.e., abilities to make competent choices). To be clear, my position here does not claim that children's and potentially others' (e.g., people with profound cognitive disabilities) basic human rights hinge on their age and/or capacities for autonomy (i.e., informed self-direction). To the contrary, in my view all humans should be guaranteed a set of fundamental moral rights; however, I recognize that it might be reasonable for people with substantially less mature capacities for autonomy, including children, to be granted fewer rights beyond the most basic ones. There are justifiable reasons not to grant children the rights to drive and vote, for example.

When considering the moral rights of children, it is worth highlighting their *potential* for informed self-direction (e.g., Brighouse, 2002; Tillson and Oxley, 2020). Though this potential in and of itself does not necessarily guarantee children any additional moral rights, the maturation of children's capacities for autonomy is dependent in part on how those capacities are nurtured early on (Noggle, 2019). Children's health, well-being, and education, for example, can influence the degree to which they are able to make informed choices in adulthood. Therefore, it seems reasonable to posit, based on the theories of Vygotsky and others, that supported practice thinking critically about and making decisions for oneself can nurture one's developing capacity for self-direction and that being guaranteed opportunities to provide feedback on and make some decisions about participation in mandatory daily events (e.g., school) might be a right worth affording children who are able to do so. All this is to say that in light of children's potential for self-direction being influenced by how such capacities are nurtured, it may be advantageous to prioritize moral rights that some might argue lie outside a set of basic human rights.

Most children undoubtedly have a weighty interest in becoming competent self-directed adults, and competent adults contribute to the health of nations. Considering children's moral rights related to their developing autonomy can support educational institutions (e.g., schools) in recognizing their obligations to children (Brighouse and McAvoy, 2010). It is for these reasons that although the United States has yet to ratify the United Nations Convention on the Rights of the Child, upholding the moral rights of children outlined in this document—which, some might argue, includes rights beyond the scope of basic human rights—is likely to benefit individual children and also influence the prosperity of countries including the United States (Tilson and Oxley, 2020).

The United Nations Convention on the Rights of the Child

The United Nations Convention on the Rights of the Child (UNCRC) (1981) is the most widely ratified children's rights treaty in the world to date; much of the world appears committed to protecting children's rights. Though not legally binding in the United States, the UNCRC can be described as a mutually agreed-upon decree of children's moral rights (Tillson and Oxley, 2020). According to the UNCRC (e.g., Preamble), it is the moral standing of children, or their inherent human dignity, that dictates what those charged with their care should or should not do to/for them. The UNCRC's fifty-four articles span a wide range of rights. Many may prove helpful in better understanding how young children's rights could be threatened by exclusionary practices. Here I highlight four in particular; it seems highly plausible that one or more exclusionary practices could violate the rights outlined in Articles 28, 19, 12, and 37.

Article 28

Article 28 guarantees every child a "compulsory free primary education." Article 28 includes a stipulation specific to school discipline: children's human dignity must be preserved in all instances in which disciplinary action is taken. Given young children's developing brains and specifically their developing capacities for self-regulation and executive functioning, ensuring them a compulsory education that preserves their dignity seems imperative for short-term and long-term well-being.

Article 19

Article 19 guarantees children protection from all forms of violence, abuse, neglect, maltreatment, and/or exploitation; all people caring for children are obligated to protect them from such harms. Given the possibility for stress and trauma to result from subjecting young children to seclusion punishments and the lasting impacts stress and trauma can have on the young child's rapidly developing brain, this article also seems especially relevant to consider in relation to other exclusionary behavior management practices.

Article 12

Article 12 guarantees to all children capable of doing so the right to form and openly express their individual opinions on all matters impacting them. Additionally, Article 12 maintains that children's views should be seriously considered; however, according to the UNCRC, the amount of weight children's views are afforded should take into consideration their age and maturity. This article promotes children's developing capacities for autonomy by encouraging them to think critically and share their opinions about all that occurs inside and outside of schools; children are encouraged to exercise and defend their right to be heard.

Article 37

Article 37 guarantees children the right to be free from any form of cruel or dehumanizing treatment. Additionally, the article specifies that children cannot be deprived of their liberty unlawfully or arbitrarily and that their arrest, detention, or imprisonment should only occur as a last resort and for the shortest appropriate amount of time. Article 37 guarantees all children deprived of their liberty the right to be treated humanely, with respect, and in accordance with their age-specific needs. Finally, it guarantees those deprived of their liberty the rights to legal assistance and to challenge the legality of their deprivation of liberty.

Might exclusionary practices violate children's moral rights?

It is fairly straightforward to imagine how placing children in isolation rooms might threaten their moral rights as they are outlined in the four articles just described. Isaiah Knipe's rights, for example, were arguably violated in at least the following ways:

- While in the quiet room Isaiah was deprived of a free compulsory education (Article 28); he was repeatedly left alone in the room from kindergarten through grade three without a teacher to guide and support his learning and development. It is important to note that Developmentally Appropriate Practice, the early childhood education framework endorsed by the National Association for the Education of Young Children (NAEYC), strives to foster multiple forms of early development (e.g., cognitive, linguistic, social, emotional, physical) via intentionally integrated learning experiences. Being locked in an isolation room where he was unable to engage in such experiences may have deprived Isaiah of a wide range of developmental opportunities.
- Isaiah was arguably physically (e.g., head trauma) and emotionally (e.g., self-reported extreme frustration) harmed by his repeated visits to the isolation room. Because he was alone in the room, no one was present to protect him from these harms or coach him through his stress. Additionally, according to investigative reporting, the person outside the room did not immediately remove him from harm (Article 19).
- Though Isaiah attempted to defend his rights by expressing his discomfort with the seclusion punishment to school staff (it is not known whether he was invited to do so), it does not appear that staff took his concerns seriously, as he was repeatedly placed in the room thereafter (Article 12).
- It is justifiable to describe Isaiah as being deprived of various liberties (e.g., freedom of movement, freedom to self-select academic activities, freedom to socialize with others) while inside the isolation room. Given that this child with special needs also banged his head against the walls of the room on

multiple occasions (without a previous history of doing so), the punishment might also be reasonably described as cruel and dehumanizing (Article 37).

Isaiah's case arguably offers an example of a child's basic moral rights being violated by a school seclusion punishment. However, the rights of the other children (and potentially those of the adults) in Isaiah's learning environment[5] cannot be discounted. Is it possible that the repeated isolation of Isaiah is justifiable? According to Tillson and Oxley (2020), there may be instances in which exclusion from the classroom community is morally justified. Specifically, nonpunitive exclusion—exclusion that does not aim to produce suffering and is intended to prevent harming others—might be acceptable so long as (1) all other strategies have been exhausted; (2) the detriment to the secluded child is not disproportionate to the protected interests of the other children; (3) losses to the learner caused by the isolation are as minimal as affordable or offset; and (4) it is administered not for its own sake but to protect the weighty interests of others. Though some forms of school seclusions (e.g., certain forms of time-out) might meet these criteria for nonpunitive exclusion, the form Isaiah was subject to does not appear to do so. And, even if it had, the school, according to Tillson and Oxley, has an additional obligation to honor Isaiah's basic moral rights (e.g., his right to remain free of harm) to the greatest extent possible. Investigative reports suggest that this was largely not happening. Hopefully, the attention brought to Isaiah's case and others will discourage adults from placing children in quiet rooms, but what about less severe exclusionary practices commonly employed in early childhood settings in the United States and elsewhere? Might expulsions, suspensions, and traditional time-outs, for example, also threaten children's rights? In the sections that follow, I examine each of these common practices in greater detail.

Expulsions

Approximately half of the states in the United States either explicitly allow early childhood expulsion or permit local governments to regulate school expulsions (Stegelin, 2018). Expulsions from early childhood programs typically involve permanently removing a child from a day care or school on the basis of undesirable behavior(s) (National Center for Pyramid Model Innovations, n.d.). In the first nationally representative survey of private and public preschool discipline, the Center for American Progress found that approximately 17,000 US students were expelled in 2016; Black children were more likely to be expelled than White children, and boys were more likely to be expelled than girls (Kearns, 2017). Expulsions can have a host of negative immediate and long-term effects on children. In addition to disrupting learning and causing children and their families extreme stress, expulsions are associated with academic failure, future expulsion from school, dropping out of school, and incarceration (Stegelin, 2018; US Department of Health and Human Services, 2016).

In relation to UNCRC articles 28, 19, 12, and 37, expulsions stand to threaten young children's moral rights in at least the following ways:

- When expelled, children may be denied their right to a free compulsory public education (Article 28). Though the UNCRC does not stipulate whether preschool comprises a part of primary education, it serves to reason that the existence of free (public) preschools in the United States and elsewhere suggests preschool is a valued component of primary education. If children are not being comparably educated in the space where they are serving their expulsion, their right to a free compulsory education is arguably being violated. It is important to note that even if the academic education provided during the expulsion is comparable, young children's right to a free compulsory public education may still be violated if the expulsion does not sufficiently support growth across developmental domains (e.g., social, emotional, linguistic, physical); recall that early childhood is a time of rapid brain development making young children especially vulnerable to gaps in their education. In many learning centers around the world, early childhood education involves addressing the needs of the whole child—academic advancement represents only one part of a whole-child approach to early education.
- Expelled children may incur physical and/or emotional harm (Article 19). Staying home with an abusive adult or no adult at all could result in physical harm. More likely in many cases may be the potential for emotional harm; emotionally, young children may struggle to understand why they are being punished and assume that they were removed from school/daycare for being "bad"; such thinking can lead to the development of a negative self-concept (Jones and Levin, 2016). Stress and trauma incurred in response to expulsion can have long-term effects on young children's physical and mental health; at a minimum expulsion threatens children's sense of security (Stegelin, 2018). Additionally, expulsion may interfere with the identification and support of other underlying issues (e.g., learning

disability, health concern). A delay in identification and/or support for underlying issues could lead to additional harm(s).
- Many young children do not have a say in whether they are expelled from school (Article 12). When children's views around their expulsion(s) are not invited and/or considered, their right to form and express opinions on all matters impacting them and their right to be taken seriously are violated.
- Violations to children's rights to be free of cruel and dehumanizing punishment and free from deprivation of their liberty (Article 37) are also possible. Children's home conditions vary. It is possible that some children may be subject to cruelty and dehumanizing treatment. Perhaps more plausible, expelled children may be deprived of opportunities for self-direction (e.g., children cannot participate in school activities including art or music class).

Suspensions

Suspensions in early childhood education settings in the United States and elsewhere often involve temporarily removing a child from the classroom in response to one or more undesirable behaviors. Children may be isolated within the school, sent home, or sent to another education facility (e.g., behavior center) (National Center for Pyramid Model Innovations, n.d.). In the United States, parameters for early childhood suspension vary from state to state. Some states regulate the number of days a child can be suspended; laws range from three to twenty days. Some states permit children to be suspended up to a full semester, while others leave suspension decisions to the discretion of the local government (Stegelin, 2018). The Center for American Progress found that approximately 50,000 US preschool students were suspended at least one time in 2016. Again, Black children were more likely to be suspended than White children, and boys were suspended more often than girls (Kearns, 2017). Suspensions can result in maladaptive immediate and long-term outcomes similar to those associated with expulsions.

Though potentially less severe in terms of the amount of missed school time, the ways in which young children's rights might be violated when forced to serve out-of-school suspensions largely mirror those previously outlined specific to expulsions. In-school suspensions and suspensions that involve moving a child to another formal education setting could threaten children's rights specific to UNCRC articles 28, 19, 12, and 37 in at least the following ways:

- Suspensions, both in-school and out-of-school, stand to violate children's right to a free compulsory public education in largely the same ways as expulsion (Article 28). Assuming children are receiving some form of comparable academic instruction while suspended, they may not be permitted to attend special classes (e.g., art, physical education, music) or interact with other children. This could impact a variety of types of development (e.g., social, emotional, physical, cognitive). Children's right to a free compulsory public education is violated if their growth across developmental domains is not adequately nurtured.
- Assuming suspended children are physically safe in their learning environment, they may still incur emotional harms similar to those potentially resulting from being expelled (Article 19). Children's sense of security may be threatened and delays in the identification and support of other underlying issues are possible.
- As is the case with expulsion, many young children do not have a say in whether they are suspended from school (Article 12); when children's views around their suspension(s) are not invited and considered, their right to form and express opinions on matters impacting them and their right to be taken seriously are violated.
- Suspension may violate children's rights to be free of cruel and dehumanizing punishment and free from deprivation of liberty (Article 37) in many of the ways expulsion can. Assuming imposed suspensions are not cruel and/or dehumanizing, they limit or deny children opportunities for self-direction.

Time-Outs

Time-out is a third exclusionary practice commonly utilized in schools in the United States and around the globe. Time-out is endorsed by the American Academy of Pediatrics and regularly recommended by pediatricians as a way to curb aggression, foster compliance, and/or promote self-regulation (Jenco, 2019). Time-outs take a variety of forms. More precisely, the term refers to a procedure called "time-out from positive reinforcement"; a consequence is administered immediately after a child exhibits an undesirable behavior to deny the child access to reinforcement with the goal of stopping and/or decreasing incidences of the problematic behavior (Cooper, Heron and Heward, 2007). However, the degree to which children are excluded across the range of time-out practices varies widely. Time-out does not require the removal of a child

Table 6.1 Time-Out and Articles 28, 19, 12, and 37

Article	Planned Ignoring	Contingent Observation
28	The potential exists for children to be denied components of a compulsory public education when their teacher intentionally ignores them. The amount of time the teacher ignores the child may influence the extent to which this right is violated; turning away from a child for only a few seconds may pose less of a risk than repeatedly ignoring a child or turning away for longer periods.	The potential exists for children to be denied components of a free compulsory education when they watch activities from the sidelines instead of actively participating in them. UDL (https://udlguidelines.cast.org/engagement) posits that children learn best when able to engage with information in a variety of ways. Denying physical involvement in one or more activities may substantially impede some children's learning (e.g., children with disabilities, children learning the language relied upon in the classroom) and in doing so, violate their right to an education.
19	The amount of time a teacher spends ignoring a child may be pertinent when considering the potential for emotional harm. It seems less likely that a child would incur significant emotional harm as a result of being briefly ignored by a teacher. However, it also seems reasonable to suspect that repeated and/or prolonged instances of planned ignoring could disrupt child-teacher relationships and, in turn, influence children's emotional well-being and/or learning.	When separated inside or outside the classroom from peers, children may incur short-term emotional harm (e.g., thinking they are "bad"). However, studies (e.g., Knight et al., 2020) examining the impact of time-outs administered to young children in the home suggest the risk for long-term negative psychological and behavioral effects is low.
12	Planned ignoring stands to violate children's rights to express their opinion(s) about the practice and have their views taken seriously in the same ways expulsion and suspension do.	Contingent observation stands to violate children's rights to express their opinion(s) about the practice and have their views taken seriously in the same ways expulsion and suspension do.
37	In most instances, it seems unlikely that ignoring a child for a short period of time would amount to cruel or dehumanizing punishment. Similarly, a short period of ignoring seems unlikely to constitute a deprivation of liberty. Longer and/or excessive instances might pose a greater threat to children's liberties.	Though in most cases, removing a child from an activity seems unlikely to constitute cruel or dehumanizing punishment, doing so is likely to infringe upon the child's liberty (e.g., freedom to direct their own behavior as they normally would). Children forced into time-out spots, for example, are not free to move about the classroom and/or engage in activities or with peers as they normally would.

from their classroom. Forms of time-out that do not remove children from their classrooms are referred to as non-exclusion time-outs (APSEA, 2016). This term is a bit of a misnomer; though children are not physically removed from the classroom space per se, they are prevented from interacting with other members of the classroom community (e.g., teachers, peers) and/or from fully engaging in classroom activities.

Here I consider two specific "non-exclusion" time-out practices commonly employed in the United States and Canada, namely planned ignoring and contingent observation. Planned ignoring involves a teacher denying a child attention (including verbal interaction and physical contact) for some time after an undesirable behavior is exhibited. Contingent observation involves moving a child to another part of the classroom where they can observe the activity they were removed from but not participate in it. Many early childhood classrooms have designated "quiet corners" or "cool-down spots" for contingent observation (APSEA, 2016).

Proponents of non-exclusion time-outs, which include physicians and researchers, claim these practices (when used appropriately) can keep children from inflicting self-harm and/or from harming others and can teach children how to regulate their bodies (APSEA, 2016; Martinelli n.d.). Research stemming mainly from the field of applied behavior analysis suggests time-outs can be effective in reducing undesirable behaviors in specific populations (e.g., children with autism, children with oppositional defiant disorder) (Campbell, 2003; Vegas, Jenson and Kircher, 2007). However, these potential benefits may come at a cost to young children's moral rights specific to UNCRC articles 28, 19, 12, and 37 in at least the ways discussed in Table 6.1.

The degree to which young children's rights are threatened by non-exclusion time-out practices appears dependent on the ways in which the teacher executes these time-outs. Though both planned ignoring and contingent observation could foreseeably threaten children's moral rights, it seems reasonable to assume that a short instance of planned ignoring presents fewer opportunities for doing so than contingent observation.

Conclusion

Isaiah Knipe's case of repeated seclusion offers an example of how a young child's basic moral rights were arguably violated during a sensitive developmental period specific to UNCRC articles 28, 19, 12, and 37. Particularly during his kindergarten year, any extreme stress and trauma Isaiah experienced as a result of being placed in the isolation room could have interfered with his brain development, and in turn, the development of other processes (e.g., the advancement of his self-regulation and/or executive function skills). Given these potential consequences, it does not seem unreasonable for governments to regulate the use of seclusion punishments in schools and especially in early childhood education settings.

The more common and less severe exclusionary practices of expulsion, suspension, and time-out may also threaten children's moral rights to varying degrees. Admittedly, there are likely instances in which such practices are justified (e.g., when adults cannot otherwise keep a child from harming themself and/or others). However, even in these instances, adults should be mindful of their responsibilities to nurture the isolated child's developing capacity for autonomy and all that that might entail. Put differently, if a young child must be subject to an exclusionary punishment, their moral rights should be respected to the fullest extent possible.

With the exception of occasional brief instances of planned ignoring, this recommendation has significant implications for the behavior management practices discussed. Adults charged with children's care—and perhaps especially those charged with the care of young children—in schools and elsewhere, for example, should do all they can to ensure isolated children are making the holistic developmental gains they would typically expect them to make. Developmental progress encompasses far more than merely meeting academic benchmarks; for young children in particular, social, emotional, physical, linguistic, and cognitive development—at a minimum—should all be considered and nurtured during this critical period of brain development.

Given the possibilities of violating children's moral rights and disrupting their development, decisions about when and how to use exclusionary practices should not be made lightly. Careful consideration of the well-being of the child or children who are disturbing classroom routines in relation to that of their peers is necessary. One strategy adults might attempt before carrying out these practices is to reframe their thinking in a way that involves answering one or more "could" questions. Rather than limiting potential solutions for curbing problem behaviors to exclusionary practices, adults might draw upon their own life experiences and the experiences of others to imagine what might be done outside of traditional behavior management techniques in each specific situation. Framing thinking in this way can yield a variety of options capable of better supporting individual children as well as the other members of the classroom community (Wakeham,

2016). Regardless of whether the adults in charge employ this strategy or others, it is vital that they seriously consider all viable options before excluding children from their schools, classrooms, peers, and/or learning experiences. Doing so stands to more fully honor children's personhood.

Notes

1. Macy and colleagues (2004) describe traumatic events as those that overburden the child's nervous system and render it unable to cope with stress. Traumatized children often feel "unsafe, vulnerable, and out of control" (Nicholson, Perez and Kurtz, 2019, 19).
2. For a synthesis of research describing the effects maltreatment can have on the developing brain, see the Child Welfare Information Gateway (2015) issue brief.
3. Acknowledging the moral personhood of nonhuman animals (Regan, 2004), I maintain that humans generally hold higher moral status.
4. There may be instances in which a thing (e.g., cure for a deadly disease) is deemed of greater value to society than an individual person; the potential value in saving multiple human lives may trump the loss of an individual life.
5. Commentaries (e.g., Wakeham, 2016) examining Levinson and Ben-Porath's (2016) case of child exclusion emphasize and weigh the rights of peers in relation to the excluded child.

References

APSEA. (2016) "Current Research Regarding Time-out." *The Atlantic Provinces Special Education Authority.* https://apsea.ca/assets/files/aie/talks/research-timeout/current-research-time-out.pdf (accessed July 30, 2021).

Brennan, Samantha and Noggle, Rovert (1997) "The Moral Status of Children: Children's Rights, Parents' Rights, and Family Justice." *Social Theory and Practice* 23 (1): 1–26.

Brighouse, Harry (2002) "What Rights (If Any) Do Children Have?" In D. Archard and C. Macleod (eds.), *The Moral and Political Status of Children*, 31–52. Oxford: Oxford University Press.

Brighouse, Harry and McAvoy, Paula (2010) "Do Children Have Any Rights?" In R. Bailey (ed.), *The Philosophy of Education: An Introduction*, 74–85. London: Continuum.

Campbell, Jonathan (2003) "Efficacy of Behavioral Interventions for Reducing Problem Behavior in Persons with Autism: A Quantitative Synthesis of Single-Subject Research." *Research in Developmental Disabilities* 24: 120–38.

CAST. (2018) "Provide Multiple Means of Engagement." *Universal Design for Learning Guidelines version 2.2*. http://udlguidelines.cast.orghttps://udlguidelines.cast.org/engagement (assessed July 30, 2021).

Child Welfare Information Gateway. (2015) "Understanding the Effects of Maltreatment on Brain Development." *US Department of Health and Human Services, Children's Bureau*, https://www.childwelfare.gov/pubs/issue-briefs/brain-development/ (accessed December 17, 2021).

Cooper, John, Heron, Timothy and Heward, William (2007) *Applied Behavior Analysis*. New York: Pearson Education Inc.

Dworkin, Ronald (1977) *Taking Rights Seriously*. Cambridge, MA: Harvard University Press.

Goodwin, Robert and Gibson, Diane (1977) "Rights: Young and Old." *Oxford Journal of Legal Studies* 17 (2): 186–203.

Hart, Herbert (1955) "Are There Any Natural Rights?" *Philosophical Review* 64 (2): 175–91.

Jenco, Melissa (2019) "Time-Outs Not Linked to Long-Term Problems." *AAP News & Journals*, November 6. https://www.aappublications.org/news/2019/11/06/healthbrief110619.

Jensen, Jennifer (2019) "Isolation Rooms Banned After Traumatizing Students." *WCIA.com*, November 27. https://www.wcia.com/local/isolation-rooms-banned-after-traumatizing-students (accessed July 30, 2021).

Jones, Denisha and Levin, Diane (2016) "Here's Why Preschool Suspensions Are Harmful." *Education Week*, February 23. https://www.edweek.org/teaching-learning/opinion-heres-why-preschool-suspensions-are-harmful/2016/02 (accessed July 30, 2021).

Kearns, Devon (2017) "RELEASE: Sobering Analysis Finds 250 Preschoolers Suspended or Expelled Every Day." *Center for American Progress*, November 6. https://www.americanprogress.org/press/release-sobering-analysis-finds-250-preschoolers-suspended-expelled-every-day/ (accessed July 30, 2021).

Knight, Rachel, Albright, Jeremy, Deling, Lindsay, Dorey-Stites, Dawn and Drayton, Amy (2020) "Longitudinal Relationship Between Time-out and Child Emotional and Behavioral Functioning." *Journal of Developmental & Behavioral Pediatrics* 41 (1): 31–7.

Macy, Robert, Behar, Lenore, Paulson, Robert, Delman, Jon, Schmid, Lisa and Smith, Stefanie F. (2004) "Community-based, Acute Posttraumatic Stress Management: A Description and Evaluation of a Psychosocial-Intervention Continuum." *Harvard Review of Psychiatry* 12 (4): 217–28.

Martinelli, Katherine (n.d.) "Are Time Outs Harmful to Children?" *Child Mind Institute*. https://childmind.org/article/are-time-outs-harmful-kids/ (accessed June 21, 2021).

NAEYC. (2011) "Code of Ethical Conduct and Statement of Commitment [Position Statement]." *National Association for the Education of Young Children*, May. https://www.naeyc.org/resources/position-statements/ethical-conduct (accessed December 14, 2021).

NCPMI (n.d.) "Suspension and Expulsion in Early Childhood." *National Center for Pyramid Model Innovations.* https://challengingbehavior.cbcs.usf.edu/Pyramid/suspension.html (accessed June 21, 2021).

NDRN. (2009) "School Is Not Supposed to Hurt: Investigative Report on Abusive Restraint and Seclusion in Schools." *National Disability Rights Network*, January. https://www.ndrn.org/wp-content/uploads/2019/03/SR-Report2009.pdf (accessed June 21, 2021).

Nicholson, Julie, Perez, Linda and Kurtz, Julie (2019) *Trauma-Informed Practices for Early Childhood Educators: Relationship-Based Approaches that Support Healing and Build Resilience in Young Children.* New York: Routledge.

Noggle, Robert (2019) "Children's Rights." In A. Gheaus, G. Calder and J. Wispelaere (eds.), *The Routledge Handbook of the Philosophy of Childhood and Children*, 101–11. New York: Routledge.

Piccinini, Sandra and Giudici, Claudia (2012) "Reggio Emilia: A Transforming City." In Carolyn. Edwards, Lella Gandini and George Forman (eds.), *The Hundred Languages of Children: The Reggio Emilia Experience in Transformation*, 89–99. Westport, CT: Praeger.

Regan, T. (2004). *The case for animal rights.* Berkeley, CA. University of California Press.

Richards, Jennifer and Cohen, Jodie (2021a) "Time Runs Out for Ban on Locked Seclusion and Face-down Restraints in Illinois Schools: Advocates Vow to Try Again." *Chicago Tribune*, January 13. https://www.chicagotribune.com/investigations/ct-seclusion-restraint-illinois-/ (accessed June 30, 2021).

Richards, Jennifer and Cohen, Jodie (2021b) "Illinois Dramatically Limits Use of Seclusion and Face-down Restraints in Schools." *Propublica*, August 13. https://www.propublica.org/article/illinois-dramatically-limits-use-of-seclusion-and-face-down-restraints-in-schools (accessed November 7, 2021).

Richards, Jennifer, Cohen, Jodie and Chavis, Lakeidra (2019) "The Quiet Rooms." *Chicago Tribune*, November 19. https://graphics.chicagotribune.com/illinois-seclusion/index.html (accessed November 7, 2021).

Scheuermann, Brenda, Peterson, Reece, Ryan, Joseph and Billingsley, Glenna (2016) "Professional Practice and Ethical Issues Related to Physical Restraint and Seclusion in Schools." *Journal of Disability Policy Studies* 27 (2): 86–95.

Staufenberg, Jess (2018) "Isolation Rooms: How Swathes of Schools Are Removing Pupils from Their Classrooms." *Schools Week*, October 19. https://schoolsweek.co.uk/isolation-rooms-how-schools-are-removing-pupils-from-classrooms/ (accessed November 7, 2021).

Stegelin, Dolores (2018) "Preschool Suspension and Expulsion: Defining the Issues." *Institute for Child Success*, December. https://www.instituteforchildsuccess.org/publication/preschool-suspension-and-expulsion-defining-the-issues/ (accessed November 7, 2021).

Tillson, John and Oxley, Laura (2020) "Children's Moral Rights and UK School Exclusions." *Theory and Research in Education* 18 (1): 40–58.

United Nations Convention on the Rights of the Child. (1981) https://www.unicef.org.uk/what-we-do/un-convention-child-rights/ (accessed July 30, 2021).

US Department of Education. (2019) "2015–16 Civil Rights Data Collection: School Climate and Safety." *US Department of Education*, Office for Civil Rights, May. https://www2.ed.gov/about/offices/list/ocr/docs/school-climate-and-safety.pdf (accessed July 30, 2021).

US Department of Health and Human Services. (2016) "Policy Statement on Expulsion and Suspension Policies in Early Childhood Settings." *Administration for Children and Families*, November 7. https://www.acf.hhs.gov/sites/default/files/documents/ecd/expulsion_ps_numbered.pdf (accessed July 30, 2021).

Vegas, Kristopher, Jenson, William and Kircher, John (2007) "A Single-subject Meta-analysis of the Effectiveness of Time-out in Reducing Disruptive Classroom Behavior." *Behavioral Disorders* 32 (2): 109–21.

Wakeham, Joshua (2016) "Navigating Rocky Choices with Practical Wisdom." In Meira Levinson and Jacob Fay (eds.), *Dilemmas of Educational Ethics: Cases and Commentaries*, 44–8, Cambridge, MA: Harvard Education Press.

7

A New Look at Shaming in Schools

Clio Stearns and Peter Stearns

When educators think about punishing or disciplining students, a range of emotional dimensions may come to mind. Punishment can elicit anger, fear, and sadness. The emotional experience of a punishment is sometimes part of the punisher's motivation, for a variety of reasons, though some disciplinary measures may provoke emotions in unintended ways. One common emotion associated with punishment is shame. For the purposes of this chapter, shame is defined as a painful, humiliated feeling associated with a strong sense of wrongdoing and group disapproval (Tanger and Dearing, 2002). To be sure, there are massive cultural and temperamental differences in what causes a person to feel shame, as well as how shame is expressed and how outsiders respond to it. A child might feel shame in school for performing poorly on a test whose scores are publicized, for causing a peer group to fall behind on a project, for disappointing a teacher, or, in some US contexts, even for needing to take advantage of school meals (Fleischhaker and Campbell, 2020).

Somewhat separate from the internal experience of shame is the act of intentionally or inadvertently shaming someone else. To shame someone is to cause them to experience shame. Historically, some school punishments, like the proverbial dunce cap, have relied heavily on shaming; the entire purpose and function of the punishment is to inculcate shame (Weaver, 2012). Practices like these continue, though usually in less egregious and ostentatious fashion. Calling out a student for misbehavior or weak academic performance in front of the class, sending them out of the room or away from the group, or posting the names of students who have not accomplished a particular task are some instances of the kinds of shaming that go on in schools. Publicizing names of students who owe money or materials back to the school is another quite common contemporary example of shaming used in US schools. But the feeling of shame in schools, distinct from purposeful shaming, can also occur unintentionally, through measures that call students to the attention of their peers or others.

Intentional shaming has historically been, and is currently, used in schools in a variety of ways. Indignant public outcries, and anger within educational communities, tend to respond to shaming when it appears to be used exclusively with intent to punish. However, shaming is also sometimes used pedagogically, with the articulated intent (and sometime success) of dissuading students from engaging in patterns perceived as problematic or educationally detrimental. We argue that a historical and cross-cultural lens shows that the kind of shaming associated with setting an example and establishing behavioral norms is more common than shaming as a punitive approach and that it is also more ethically complicated. Because we believe that both the feeling of shame and the acts that might cause another person shame are inevitable aspects of education, we avoid claiming a normative stance regarding shame or shaming per se. Instead, we argue that educators should accept the omnipresence of shame and shaming in schools and keep a focus on recuperating and reintegrating students who experience shame as part of their education.

Whether or not it is ethical for educators to rely on shaming as a punishment is a complex question, one that incorporates assumptions about how much one person can ever take responsibility for the emotional experience of another. Throughout this chapter, we emphasize that the internal experience of shame is both related to and separate from the practice of shaming, especially intentional and purposeful shaming. Some shame as part of educational processes and, indeed, of development is unavoidable, even for teachers who have no conscious intention of shaming explicitly.

Commensurately, questioning the ethics of shaming as a punitive measure is ultimately less relevant than considering how shaming might occur in schools more justly. One important, and often neglected, aspect of shame and shaming as educational phenomena is recovery subsequent to the shaming experience, and we discuss this from a few different angles. American educators have been told more about shame's harmful effects than about options in the ways shame is administered (Perry, 2019). This leads to a problematic denial of shame's inevitability and, in turn, to an avoidance of discussion regarding how to reintegrate students who have experienced shame or shaming. A different balance may be helpful, including the possibility of paying more attention than is currently emphasized to assisting in restoration following shame, through deliberate efforts at reintegration into the community and the educational experience.

The remainder of this chapter considers the role of shame and shaming in schools in contemporary contexts but with a historical perspective. Throughout the chapter, we discuss shaming as both an individual and social experience, recognizing that it is in part this tension that complicates any discussion of the ethics of shame and shaming. We offer two contemporary case studies from US schools, both analyzed from historical perspectives. Then, we offer a distinct case study from Chinese education. Aspects of the study are distinctly US-centric, and that context has been our scholarly focus, but the implications particularly for the significance of restoration are more broadly relevant. We close with a discussion of shaming that looks past its pitfalls and benefits toward understanding what it means from the perspective of educational justice to leverage student emotions toward education in social behaviors, norms, and community functioning, and how it may be possible to handle shame and shaming somewhat more constructively than is now the case.

Success Academy and shaming

In February 2016, the New York City-based charter school network, Success Academy, made national headlines over a shaming scandal. An assistant teacher recorded the third-grade teacher she worked with yelling at a child who got the wrong answer to a math problem. "There's nothing that infuriates me more than when you don't do what's on your paper," said the teacher to the girl loudly, in front of all of her classmates, before sending her away from the group. The teacher then had another student answer the question and proceeded to chastise the original student multiple times (Taylor, 2016).

When the video was leaked to *The New York Times*, school leaders immediately responded with firm declarations that this teacher's behavior was an anomaly and did not represent the schools' policy or typical approach. Eva Moskowitz, the charter network leader, was quoted saying that teachers should never "give consequences intended to shame children" or "speak to a child in a way they wouldn't in front of the child's parents." Almost immediately, multiple former Success Academy teachers and parents came forward refuting Moskowitz's proclamations. One teacher said, "It's this culture of, 'If you've made them cry, you've succeeded in getting your point across'" (The New York Times, 2016).

The volley that followed was nuanced. Increasing numbers of teachers and parents came forward with anger about the charter network's techniques, and educational journalists weighed in copiously, largely with the argument that this incident spoke to the problems with unregulated discipline practices at charter schools overall. The educational consensus seemed to be that the teacher had engaged in shaming and that shaming was bad: excessively punitive, psychologically damaging, and ethically problematic (Allen, 2016). Then, school community members and social media followers argued back that this was one more example of the mainstream news media itself engaging in shaming, particularly of families of color for opting to send their children to this allegedly dubious set of schools (The New York Times, 2016). One parent was quoted saying, "I don't understand why *The New York Times* thinks it has to educate me as a parent about the school that I choose to send my children to." A Twitter post pointed out, "The easy thing to do is fault #SuccessAcademy for faulty pedagogy. The hard thing to do is analyze our relationship with children of color" (Prothero, 2020).

This specific scandal eventually ran its course; the teacher in question took a temporary leave and then returned to the classroom. Since then, the charter network has repeatedly been embroiled in similar disputes, though, including about the racialized shaming of students who protested against the George Floyd murder in 2020, and the shaming and exclusion of special education students whose families were trying to get them spots in the schools (New York One, 2020). How to make sense of the shaming practices that these and other teachers and school administrators use? Conversely, what to do with the accusation that calling out these practices in schools primarily serving low-income students of color is also shaming and is in some ways a public iteration of the very practice it pretends to critique?

The controversy over the Success Academy incident highlights how much confusion there is over shame in contemporary US educational culture. On the one hand, we see an educator shaming her student. The student is visibly upset by this; so, too, are many spectators, both during and after the episode. Moskowitz's defensiveness indicates a general awareness that there is a level of punitive shaming that the public will not tolerate or at least will not admit to tolerating. On the other hand, though, why is it necessarily bad for a teacher to have personal stake in a child's performance, and to make this known, even at the risk of bad feelings on the part of the child? Teachers are routinely coached to form close relationships with students and to take their successes and struggles to heart (Owen, 2015). Why, then, is the public expression of this, and its fallout, the root of such a scandal?

Further, what the episode and its coverage neglect to show us is what the actual educational consequences of this kind of shaming are. Success Academy and similar charter school networks are known for their high standardized test scores; they consistently outperform other schools in similar demographic areas (Russakoff, 2019). This, too, has been a source of ongoing criticism; the schools, it is said, overemphasize testing, teach to the test, and problematically de-emphasize subject areas and educational domains that are not tested (DiCarlo, 2012). Unlike most US public schools, they exclude from admission or counsel out children who are unlikely to perform up to their precise standards.

These are all legitimate critiques, but the question remains: Is it possible that the shaming that happens within these schools is in fact helpful to some students or to the broader community? This is where the distinction between shaming as a purely punitive practice and one with potential pedagogical intent and impact is important. It ties, also, to the parental backlash against the public critiques of the network. Whose place is it to decide if children are getting shamed excessively in schools, particularly when perhaps the achievements that grow out of these practices may seem, because of the tremendous educational and systemic barriers the children face, otherwise largely inaccessible?

The purpose here is not to weigh in on the ethical rectitude of this teacher's practices or those of any other charter school practitioner. Instead, the point is simply that shame is not an easy punishment to control, to practice intentionally, or to rule against. Public outcry around shaming will almost always call on individualized experiences with the emotion and its related practices, and will as a result be fraught and sometimes contradictory. Unlike punishments rooted more obviously in behavior or actions, shame deals with emotion and emotional relationships, and it probably has elements that are both right and wrong, educationally positive, and incredibly negative all at once.

Since the ethical nature of shaming in schools is genuinely ambiguous, it might become more relevant not to ask, "Should this teacher have engaged in shaming? Should *The New York Times* have shamed the teacher?" but, instead, "Now that a lot of educational stakeholders, including an 8-year-old child, have been shamed and experienced shame, what ought to happen next?" What are some ways that shame in the context of school might be leveraged in the name of justice and education? Here, it might be useful to consider what happens to the child who is shamed by their teacher, to help them recover and reenter the group. The entire episode might read differently if the child, chastened perhaps egregiously, has a scaffolded, public opportunity to recover and to gain strong recognition from their peers for doing so. Similarly, it is worth asking what becomes of the teacher and school whose practices are publicly shamed and what their options are or ought to be for rejoining the educational system and the good graces of society.

Historical perspective

A history of shaming in the schools suggests three points that are worth considering in dealing with shaming as a contemporary option and dilemma. This form of emotional discipline has an extensive history, which does not validate it but does require some assessment of its long utility. It has been seriously questioned in Western culture for over two centuries, opening the second issue of why something so long accepted now elicits especially wide concern. Finally, after what is now a long campaign to purge shame from schools, with notable success against some of the most blatant forms of shaming, the emotion remains deeply lodged in many classroom procedures, as the Success Academy episode and its fallout demonstrate. Therefore, the third question is why shame is so hard to get rid of and whether it can be approached more constructively.

Shaming students seems to be as old as schools are. Evidence from ancient Egypt, where a minority of boys were trained to be scribes, suggests that misbehaving or poorly performing students were exposed to general scorn, displayed in public stocks (Trigger, 1983). Traditional Islamic schools relied heavily on shaming, and the same was true in the expanding educational system of Tokugawa Japan (Dore, 1984). In colonial America, particularly in the Puritan strongholds, a variety of shaming methods were employed, ranging from isolating a student in the classroom to endure the stares of his peers to administering whippings in the same public setting (Demos, 1988). In these examples, the shame was frequently more keenly registered than the physical pain.

McGuffey's Reader, that staple in American schools through the nineteenth century, invoked shame frequently: "Oh, how dreadful must be the confusion and shame, with which the deceitful child will be overcome." "Shame, shame on the child who had not magnanimity enough to tell the truth" (McGuffey, 1876). Shame was thought a desirable educational practice, both to inhibit bad behavior and to promote ethical social practices. More prosaically, again in many nineteenth-century American classrooms, misbehaving boys might be shamed by assignments to sit among the girls. Tom Sawyer was deliberately shamed for his poor schoolwork by having to repeat himself over and over in front of mocking classmates (Weaver, 2012).

Obviously, school shaming was the kind of tradition that easily perpetuated itself, without much formal reconsideration. It may (though historians use this notion cautiously) have seemed natural. Children experience shame and learn shaming in their toddler years, one and a half to three, with some variation depending on culture, often, for example, as part of toilet training. They become skilled at shaming each other, as a matter of building group cohesion. Utilizing such a ubiquitous disciplinary emotion doubtless seemed normal to many societies (Lewis, 2000).

Shame has the further distinction and sometime advantage of both punishing individual misbehavior and setting an example for others; its cautionary role deserves careful attention. In some cultures, like Puritan New England, shaming was further called for because of deep beliefs in children's sinfulness, though this specific religious motivation is not the main point (Brady, 2013). School and shaming have long been wed. Even John Locke, the philosopher who famously began to undo the belief in original sin and highlighted the virtues of education, assumed that shame, unlike not physical chastisement and injury, remained a vital disciplinary tool (Demos, 1988).

Simultaneous to this and ongoing throughout the eighteenth and nineteenth centuries, boarding schools for indigenous students in the United States and Canada relied on overt shaming as a means for cultural indoctrination. The White colonialist sense that shame was an appropriate method for schooling indigenous children was largely immune to subsequent sociological and psychological literature cautioning against shame (Hinton, Woolford and Benvenuto, 2014).

However, shame began to be seriously revisited in mainstream and now colonialist Western culture by the later eighteenth century. A new culture, placing even greater value on the individual than Locke did, now saw shame as an inexcusable affront to human dignity. Attacks on shame became part of the general movement to revisit traditional punishments and their frequent cruelty. Leading US thinkers actively participated in this revised approach. As US founding father Benjamin West put it, shaming "is universally acknowledged to be a worse punishment than death." By the nineteenth century, when traditional shaming venues like the public stocks were closed by law, newspapers railed against shame for its damage to self-respect (Rush, 1787; Stearns, 2017).

This was a major cultural about-face, and it has been elaborated substantially in recent decades by the uptake of psychological research that sees shame, as opposed to guilt, as deeply damaging, frequently prompting even worse behavior by people who lose their sense of worth (Tangney et al., 2011). Efforts to apply the new wisdom to children and school settings clearly date to the nineteenth century in the United States. Childrearing experts by the 1830s noted that children subject to ridicule would be "tortured into . . . misanthropy." "A sense of degradation is not healthy for character" (Child, 1831; Beecher, 1842).

As early as the 1870s, experts began urging the importance, but also the fragility, of self-esteem: shame should not be allowed to jeopardize it (Adler, 1892). It is crucial to point out that there is not enough known about shaming practices, or their absence, in segregated schools for African American children, though hooks (1994) and others suggest that an emphasis on cultural pride, community, and indeed reintegration of misbehaving students took precedence over shame in these environments. The increasing psychological literature of the time, though, focused largely on the dignity and developmental needs and rights of White children and the cultural norms associated with White families.

Obviously, ongoing concerns about shame today reflect this revolutionary revision of children's putative nature and conceptions of what constitutes appropriate treatment, heightened by warnings from contemporary psychologists. American culture differs in this respect from its counterparts in places like East Asia, where a comparable reassessment has simply not occurred (Stearns, 2017). The contemporary discursive approach has teeth: some of the most blatant forms of school shaming, like the dunce cap, have completely ended in the United States. Teachers who relapse meet severe consequences, like the Idaho fourth-grade instructor in 2012, who allowed kids to paint the faces of students who had done badly in reading and who was summarily fired. Any discussion of shame today must take the widespread, if very modern, Western aversion into account (Leibowitz, 2012).

However, this brings up a third point: American teachers have been pressed to minimize shame for upwards of a century and a half, in keeping with this modern psychological wisdom. Teacher training manuals began to inveigh against shame in the 1880s and 1890s, urging, for example, that, instead, "the great ruling power in a school, the essential power, should be Love." John Dewey and other leading educations explicitly warned against the damage done by shame. This pressure has of course led to change, including the high sensitivity of many parents, especially racially and socioeconomically privileged ones, to any evidence that their children have been subjected to shame (Brownell, 1854; Shook, 2014).

Yet shaming persists, if usually in a more controlled fashion than was traditionally the case. In the nineteenth century, many teachers were being told to avoid both physical discipline and shaming, but as a matter of practice they could not abandon both weapons equally. They continued some shaming techniques. (It seemed more important to stop caning.) (Kaestle, 1978; Middleton, 2008). New problems unexpectedly created new temptations to shame: for example, the big hygiene push in the 1920s and 1930s, often exacerbated by ethnic prejudices (Vinikas, 1992). Indeed, growing classroom diversity has raised important new issues around shaming from that point forward. Increased American emphasis on school sports performance created another new venue for shaming (Stearns, 2017, 86–8). Even the preferred disciplinary approach, awarding good behavior with praise and prizes, has its shaming counterpart: the kid who does not get the gold star and whose classmates and parents are often fully aware of the fact.

So, for clear historical, psychodynamic, and sociological reasons, a disciplinary emotion persists, despite a widespread belief that it should not. The tension does help curb shaming practices that most Americans find particularly damaging. But in other respects, the modern American reproval of shaming may not be optimal, among other things because, short of excess, it remains unclear what the boundary lines are between appropriate and inappropriate levels. Most obviously, the official aversion to shame, apart from its incomplete impact, makes it difficult to discuss whether some kinds of shaming are more constructive than others.

For students themselves, who have found in social media yet another way to shame quite flagrantly, we do not model good shaming practices. Our modern historical experiment, of trying to reverse an age-old emotional practice, need not be discarded, but it might well be readjusted. For example, one feature of American culture when shaming was more accepted has largely slipped from sight: the reacceptance of the shamed individual after a period of time. Thus, while we are justly appalled at the shaming of Hester Prynne in the *Scarlet Letter*, we should also remember that eventually, her community explicitly tried to welcome her back.

Going to the corner

The dunce cap example of shaming might seem so antiquated as to be laughable. As shown via the Success Academy episode and its fallout, there is a general cultural sense in the United States that children should not be shamed in schools. In fact, there is a general sense among parents and the media that children mostly *are not* shamed in US schools. However, it is common practice for contemporary elementary teachers to publicly remove students from the group when they are behaving in ways the teacher finds disruptive. Teachers might try to remove the implications of shame from this disciplinary move by using something that they might call a "Calm Down Corner," a "Comfort Corner," or a "Peace Corner" (Action for Healthy Kids, 2021). Many contemporary behavior management systems and SEL (social and emotional learning) programs promote the use of one area of the classroom for this purpose, as "a quiet place for rough moments" (Responsive Classroom, 2017).

At first blush, the Calm Down Corner seems to have little to do with shaming; its title indicates that it is a place to generate positive emotions in its attendees. However, observations of how teachers use these corners in practice reveal that they are in many ways not particularly different from giving a child a dunce cap or having them sit on a shaming stool.

The following vignette comes from a first-grade classroom in a US public school, and it is emblematic of how many of the teachers we have studied make use of these classroom spaces.

It is the middle of morning meeting, and Ms. C. is visibly frustrated with Tonya, a student who cannot seem to stop fiddling with the math materials on the shelf in front of her. "Tonya," says Ms. C., "We do not just grab materials in this classroom." Tonya stops for a moment, then starts again. Ms. C. looks around at her other students. Then she looks directly at Tonya and says loudly and calmly, "My goodness, I love how some of the students in the class are keeping their hands folded in their laps. I love how Eli's hands are folded, and Jazzy has her hands under her body to keep them still."

Tonya looks at her teacher and puts her hands in her lap again. Then, as Ms. C. turns back to the lesson, Tonya starts playing with manipulatives again. "Tonya," Ms. C. says firmly, "if you cannot keep your hands to yourself, you need to go to the Calm Down Corner." Tonya stares at her and then continues playing. Ms. C.'s voice grows louder, "Tonya, I need you to go to the corner right now." Tonya gets up and walks slowly toward the corner. The class is quiet for a full minute, and several of her classmates watch her as she parks herself on the chair in the corner and puts her head in her hands.

What Ms. C. does in this anecdote is not too different from what most elementary and early childhood teachers do with some regularity. They pinpoint a student who is behaving in a way they find irksome and/or disruptive, and they remove them from the group as a way of stopping the distraction or disruption. This removal allows them to proceed with the lesson as planned while they also make an example of the student who has caused the ostensible problem. They do so publicly; everyone sees Tonya's removal, and in fact, it is not really possible to have a Calm Down Corner in the classroom and keep it private. Tonya's putting her head in her hands does seem to indicate that she is experiencing shame or at least something unpleasant, and her classmates watching her shows that there is something very public in this transaction.

Is it wrong on an ethical level for Ms. C. to send Tonya to the corner? Certainly there are other ways to handle the behavior: ignoring it, perhaps, or waiting until later to discuss it with her, or giving her something less distracting and communal to fiddle with. At the same time, it is understandable that a first-grade teacher juggling so many different things would resort to this kind of disciplinary practice. What gets tangled, though, is the language used to describe this kind of practice. Calling the corner the "Calm Down Corner" indicates that Tonya wanted or needed a break or to calm down. She did not; Tonya would have been perfectly satisfied to spend the rest of the lesson fiddling with classroom materials. In fact, this corner, which exists in most elementary classrooms in some form or another, is an example of shaming. It is indicative about cultural norms that we refuse to name it as such. Why do we pretend that shaming in schools is over? Why are we ashamed of shaming?

Again, it is possible that the answers to these questions lie partially in the distinction between shaming as a punitive practice, which would be socially frowned upon, and shaming as potentially educational. Would Ms. C. be able to talk more honestly with Tonya about what is happening with her, if she could frame it as "I am sending you away because I want the other students to understand I do not want them to play with classroom materials while I am teaching?" At the same time, though, maybe this is not actually true. Arguably, Ms. C. really is responding to an impulse to punish Tonya, and it is precisely the latent awareness of this that prevents the contemporary American teacher from calling shaming what it is. Unfortunately, this generates confusion in many children; it is strange, at best, to be told you are given comfort and calm when in fact what you are handed is something closer to, albeit brief, humiliation. Further, because there is no acknowledgment that what has happened to Tonya might constitute shaming, Ms. C. pays no heed to how she might best be returned to the group and be given a chance to regain face in front of her watchful peers.

The role of reintegration

The aforementioned case studies emphasize above all else the ambivalence toward shaming that characterizes the contemporary US educational context.

Given difficulties in the modern national approach to handling shame, some comparative insights may be helpful. These examples show how different cultural contexts offer insight into other possible ways that shame might play out educationally. Above all, they highlight the extent to which a more intentional approach to shame may help limit excessive emotional impact.

There is no question that East Asian cultures have preserved a more favorable estimation of shame than is true in the West. Contemporary polls of parents show that about half of East Asian parents, presenting with a shaming scenario, regard it as normal, whereas none of the American respondents does (Wong and Tsai, 2007).

A clear result is not only a greater use of shame in schools but, at least sometimes, a more careful calibration of the ways it is administered. Here is a case in point from 2006: a Chinese student who misbehaves at school is made to wear an intentionally shabby, school-issued sweater for the rest of the day. The overt purpose of the sweater is to shame the child, so all of the other kids and teachers in the school know of his indiscretions and the child is fully aware of their knowledge. However, at the end of the day, and equally publicly, the child removes the sweater. This, too, is overt and intentional. It is meant to indicate that the shame is now officially over and that it is time for everyone to reintegrate the child into the community (Frevert, 2015).

There are many contrasting points between this example and the US examples offered earlier. The first is that in the Chinese school, shame is seen as both purposeful and acceptable. While shaming this student is obviously punitive, and the lasting impact on the child wearing the sweater might be dire indeed when it comes to social acceptance and sense of self, the overarching purpose of the sweater is pedagogical. All day, wearing the sweater, the punished student functions as a reminder to others of what might happen if they engage in whatever the misbehavior was. The Success Academy story and its fallout show us how a US audience might react to this kind of shaming, largely due to concerns about the psychological impact on the individual being shamed. In the Chinese context, though, the focus is perhaps more on the rest of the community, and the pedagogical dimensions of the shaming take precedence over its punitive aspects.

At least as important, though, is the emphasis on reintegration that comes only as a result of the lack of shame or embarrassment on the part of the school associated with the shaming in the first place. It is because the school is overt and intentional about the shaming that they are able to make a public act out of ending the punishment as well. When the student removes the sweater, this is also pedagogical: now, it is the job of the community to reintegrate him into their fray (Braithwaite, 1989). With Tonya in Ms. C.'s class, this kind of reintegration is harder largely because no one is willing to admit that she is being shamed in the first place. When the school frames the shaming as somehow for the good of the child being shamed, so that she can "calm down" or achieve comfort, the onus for reintegration becomes obscured.

The point here is not that China is doing something right that the United States is doing wrong; indeed, there are also important Chinese classroom stories about the ways shaming in front of classmates prepares for acceptance of authoritarian politics (Xuecun, 2015). Rather, the point is that this kind of cross-cultural examination of shaming practices in schools highlights the ethical and the educational complexities of leveraging emotion for punishment and pedagogy. Just as the history of shaming puts current dilemmas into clearer perspective, so comparative work may highlight some options that could be adapted into American practice without opening the way to a wider embrace of shaming.

Conclusion and future directions

Historical data juxtaposed with contemporary examples demonstrate that shame is not a simple punishment to understand, and in fact, its ambiguity is probably connected with both its utility and its intractability. One of the things that becomes clearest is that Western educators have held, and continue to hold, a truly ambivalent relationship to shame. On the one hand, we practice it; on the other, we abhor it. On the one hand, we recognize its interiority; on the other, we rail against its intentional infliction.

As is the case with Western approaches to so many emotions with negative valence, the cultural ambivalence toward shame, particularly as an educational tool, gets in the way of discussion about how we might work with it more justly. We are so tempted by outcries against shame, and by pretending that it is possible to eliminate, that we neglect to focus on how we might work with this emotion once we have acknowledged its inevitability and its sometime genuine pedagogical utility.

Probably the most obvious and pragmatic approach to this is to focus on reintegration and restoration, similar to what we see in East Asian contexts and connected with broader frameworks focused on restorative justice in schools. If we can hit pause on claiming that education is possible without shame, we can instead spend time considering what might be the most sensible approach—or set of approaches—once a student has been shamed. How can such a student, or teacher for that matter, be helped to face and rejoin the community? How can other students learn to work through what they have witnessed and facilitate the reintegration (and realize the need to accept this in other shame contexts)? How can the broader culture come to understand that schools will undoubtedly elicit negative emotions in children and that children, like Tonya, require support in making sense of that?

On the other hand, how can we reasonably evaluate when and whether teacher actions that lead to shame are in fact excessive, as may be the case in some of the Success Academy anecdotes? Only by first achieving clarity about shaming practices and how they have evolved and how their narratives have been sometimes repressed over history can we start to move these conversations forward.

There are a number of possible directions for future research on shame as a punitive and educational practice. First, it is important to form a more solid, historically informed understanding of the racial dimensions of shame and how these have been historically, and are currently, perceived. Are shaming practices regarded differently by the public depending on the extent of the racial differential between the teaching corps and the student population? Future research might also focus on teachers' internalized sense of shame about using other forms of discipline, like yelling and other forms of aggression. How does teacher shame develop across cultures and societies, and how does it impact teachers' use of shame with students? Finally, though, and perhaps most importantly, there is a need for research into what it really means and involves to reintegrate students who have experienced shaming.

Bibliography

Action for Healthy Kids. Calm Down Corner. (2021) https://www.actionforhealthykids.org/activity/calm-down-corner/.

Adler, Felix (1892) *The Moral Instruction of Children*. New York: D. Appleton, 96.

Allen, Megan M. (2016) "What Happened at Success Academy: Race, Poverty, and the Shame Spotlight (Opinion)." *Education Week*, February 12. https://www.edweek.org/education/opinion-what-happened-at-success-academy-race-poverty-and-the-shame-spotlight/2016/02.

Beecher, Catharine (1842) *Treatise on Domestic Economy*. Boston: T.H. Webb, 220–33.

Brady, Michelle E. (2013) "Locke's *Thoughts* on Reputation." *The Review of Politics* 75: 335–56.

Braithwaite, John (1989) *Crime, Shame and Reintegration*. Cambridge: Cambridge University Press.

Brownell, Franklin C. (1854) "Ends and Means in Teaching." *Connecticut Common School Journal and Annals of Education* 9: 388.

Child, Lydia (1831) *The Mother's Book*. Boston: Carter, Hendee and Babcock, 6–10.

Demos, John (1988) "Shame and Guilt in Early New England." In Carol Z. Stearns and Peter N. Stearns (eds.), *Emotion and Social Change: Toward a New Psychohistory*, 69–86. New York: Holmes and Meier.

DiCarlo, Matthew (2012) "The Evidence on Charter Schools and Test Scores." *The Huffington Post*, January 23. https://www.huffpost.com/entry/charter-schools_b_1110503.

Dore, Ronald (1984) *Education in Tokugawa Japan*. London: Routledge and Kegan Paul.

Fleischhacker, Sheila and Campbell, Elizabeth (2020) "Ensuring Equitable Access to School Meals." *Journal of the Academy of Nutrition and Dietetics* 120 (5): 893–7. doi:10.1016/j.jand.2020.03.006.

Frevert, Ute (2015) "Shame and Humiliation." *History of Emotions: Insights into Research*, October, doi:10, 14280/08241.47.

Hinton, Alexander (2014) "Laban, Andrew Woolfod, and Jeff Benvenuto." In *Colonial Genocide in Indigenous North America*. New York: Duke University Press. doi:10.1515/9780822376149.

Hooks, bell (1994) *Teaching to Transgress: Education as the Practice of Freedom*. New York: Routledge.

Kaestle, Carl (1978) "Social Change, Discipline, and the Common School in Early Nineteenth-Century America." *Journal of Interdisciplinary History* 9: 1–17.

Leibowitz, Barry (2012) "Punishment by Idaho Teacher Gets Poor Marks from Parents." CBS News, November 21. www.cbsnews.com.

Lewis, Michael (2000) "The Self-Conscious Emotions: Embarrassment, Pride, Shame, and Guilt." In M. Lewis and Jeannette Haviland-Jones (eds.), *Handbook of Emotions*, 623–36. New York: Guilford Press.

McGuffey, William Holmes (1876) *McGuffey's Third Eclectic Reader*. New York: American Book, 43.

Middleton, Jacob (2008) "The Experience of Corporal Punishment in Schools, 1890–1940." *History of Education* 37: 253–75.

New York One. (2020) "Success Academy Faces Fierce Criticism Over Its Handling of Racial Issues." June 18. https://www.ny1.com/nyc/all-boroughs/news/2020/06/18/success-academy-faces-fierce-criticism-over-its-handling-of-racial-issues.

The New York Times. (2016) "Readers Respond to Video of Success Academy Teacher's Frustration With Student." *The New York Times*, February 13, https://www.nytimes.com/2016/02/13/nyregion/readers-respond-to-video-of-success-academy-teachers-frustration-with-student.html?

Owen, Lauren (2015) "Empathy in the Classroom: Why Should I Care?" *Edutopia*, November 11. https://www.edutopia.org/blog/empathy-classroom-why-should-i-care-lauren-owen.

Perry, Andre M. (2019) "Shaming Students Is Keeping Schools from Teaching Them." *Brookings*, January 17. https://www.brookings.edu/blog/brown-center-chalkboard/2019/01/17/shaming-students-is-keeping-schools-from-teaching-them/.

Prothero, Arianna (2020) "Success Academy Teacher Disciplines Student in Video Leaked to N.Y. Times." *Education Week*, November 18. https://www.edweek.org/policy-politics/success-academy-teacher-disciplines-student-in-video-leaked-to-n-y-times/2016/02.

Responsive Classroom (2017) "A Quiet Place for Rough Moments." February 22. https://www.responsiveclassroom.org/a-quiet-place-for-rough-moments/.

Rush, Benjamin (1787) *An Enquiry into the Effects of Public Punishments Upon Criminals, and Upon Society, Read in the Society for Promoting Political Enquiries.* Philadelphia: Joseph James. accessed September 18, 2016, at Readex, a Division of Newsbank Database.

Russakoff, Dale (2019) "The Secret to Success Academy's Top-Notch Test Scores." *The New York Times*, September 10. https://www.nytimes.com/2019/09/10/books/review/how-the-other-half-learns-robert-pondiscio.html.

Shook, John R. (2014) *Dewey's Social Philosophy: Democracy in Education*. New York: Palgrave MacMillan.

Stearns, Peter N. (2017) *Shame: A Brief History*. Urbana: University of Illinois Press, Chapter 4.

Tangney, June Price, et al. (2011) "Assessing Jail Inmates' Proneness to Shame and Guilt: Feeling Bad about the Behavior or the Self?" *Criminal Justice and Behavior* 38: 710–74.

Tangney, June Price and Dearing, Ronda L. (2002) *Shame and Guilt*. New York: Guilford Press.

Taylor, Kate (2016) "At Success Academy School, a Stumble in Math and a Teacher's Anger on Video." *The New York Times*, February 12. https://www.nytimes.com/2016/02/13/nyregion/success-academy-teacher-rips-up-student-paper.html.

Trigger, Bruce (1983) *Ancient Egypt: A Social History*. New York: Cambridge University Press, 81.

Vinikas, Vincent (1992) *Soft Soap, Hard Sell: American Hygiene in an Age of Advertisement*. Ames: Iowa State University Press.

Weaver, Heather A. (2012) "Object Lessons: A Cultural Genealogy of the Dunce Cap and the Apple as Visual Tropes of American Education." *Paedagogica Historica* 48 (2): 215–41. doi:10.1080/00309230.2011.560856.

Wong, Ying and Tsai, Jeanne (2007) "Cultural Models of Shame and Guilt." In J. Tracy, R. Robins and J. Tangney (eds.), *Handbook of Self-Conscious Emotions*, 210–23. New York: Guilford Press.

Xuecun, Murong (2015) "China's Tradition of Public Shaming Thrives." *New York Times*, March 20.

Part III

Due Process, Standing, and the Authority to Punish

8

Due Process

Fairness in Procedure and Substance in the Public Schools

Todd A. DeMitchell

Introduction

This chapter explores the application of the Fourteenth Amendment right of due process to students who face discipline that negatively impacts their access to a public education. The US Supreme Court described due process as the "touchstone" protecting "the individual against the arbitrary action of Government" (*County of Sacramento v. Lewis*, 845). The chapter first frames the issue of the relationship between ethics and discipline. A discussion of the major US Supreme Court decision *Goss v. Lopez* that defined the due process rights of students follows. Next, it explores the contours of American procedural due process (i.e., a fair notice and hearing) and substantive due process (i.e., fair laws) as applied to public school students.

This chapter is written from my perspective as a former teacher, principal, and superintendent. It reflects the belief that educators are granted great power over the minor children in their care. Educators must protect the legal rights of students as part of their professional responsibilities. Law is necessary to protect rights, but it is often not sufficient. The purpose of the law must also be served—"How small, of all that human hearts endure, that part which laws and kings can cure" (Goldsmith, 1764, line 429). We treat students fairly, not just because it is their legal right but because it is right.

The US Constitution, education, ethics, and discipline

The US Supreme Court has consistently announced the importance of an educated populace and the critical role of government in the support of its educational system. For example, the High Court wrote in the influential *Brown v. Board of Education* case, "Today, education is perhaps the most important function of state and local governments" (1954, 491). And again twenty-eight years later, the court declared,

> The American people have always regarded education and the acquisition of knowledge as matters of extreme importance. We have recognized the public schools as a most vital civic institution for the preservation of a democratic system of government and as the primary vehicle for transmitting the values on which our society rests. (*Plyler v. Doe*, 1982, 221)

An enduring American tradition is the idea of a commonwealth or community comprised of educated public citizens capable of enlightened, democratic self-government. As political philosopher Michael Sandel observed, "good citizens are made, not found" (1996, 319). For this reason, public education is perhaps the state's most important function. Justice Brennan's concurring opinion in *Abington Township, Pennsylvania v. Schemp* (1963) echoed this conclusion writing, "Americans regard the public schools as a most vital civic institution for the preservation of a democratic system of government" (p. 230).

Since public education is regarded as a most important federal interest, state responsibility, and local function, it stands to reason that not only how the public schools choose to educate their students is important, but it is also important how school officials may take away that educational opportunity from students through disciplinary action. Can an important activity for the good of society as well as for the good of the individual be easily withheld because the recipient is a minor? Or, should minors, like adults in our society, have some recourse to potentially arbitrary, capricious, or discriminatory decisions made by education officials that limit or remove educational opportunities?

When school administrators are involved in disciplinary meetings with a student they must treat the student fairly. Students deserve to be treated with dignity even when we must discipline them. As theologian and pastor Dietrich Bonhoeffer stated, "The test of the morality of a society is what it does for its children."

The school's culture embodies what is valued and who is valued. Adults and students need to feel connected by relationships and want to be embraced by a caring institution (Beck, 1992). Being cared for is important for all members of the organization, students, teachers, and administrators.

As a principal I placed the following quote on the front piece of the Faculty Handbook. This guided my interactions with students and informed my decisions regarding a student's constitutionally protected due process rights when considering suspending their access to a state-compelled education.

> I have come to a frightening conclusion. I am the decisive element in the classroom. It is my personal approach that creates the climate. It is my daily mood that makes the weather. As a teacher I possess tremendous power to make a child's life miserable or joyous. I can be a tool of torture or an instrument of inspiration. I can humiliate or humor, hurt or heal. In all situations it is my response that decides whether a crisis will be escalated or de-escalated, and a child humanized or de-humanized. (Haim G. Ginott 1972, 13)

As captured in the previous quote, educators can wield great power over students, much like that of parents, except they are backed by the authority of the public school. Educators have the common law obligation and the legal responsibility to their students to act in the place of the parent (*in loco parentis*)[1] when attending a public school. The hierarchical juxtapositions between educator and student create an ethical imperative in which educators must act with the best interests of the student centrally placed for pedagogical decisions as well as decisions which involve discipline and punishment.

The next section explores the intersection of ethics and the law in relation to the discipline of students. The US Supreme Court's watershed decision *Goss v. Lopez*, in which the protection of the individual against arbitrary punishment became a federal constitutional right for students.

Goss v. Lopez: The Supreme Court recognizes student due process rights

During February and March of 1971, students in the Columbus Public School System were involved in widespread unrest including disruption, disobedience, and damage to school property breaking windows and overturning lunch tables. Students, estimated from 75 to 150, were suspended without a hearing which would have allowed them to present their side of the incident giving rise to their suspension. Twelfth grade student Dwight Lopez was one of those students suspended without the opportunity to present his side of the story that he was an innocent bystander in the cafeteria and did not take part in the protest; he was in the wrong place at the wrong time.

Nine students, including Dwight Lopez, brought a class-action suit on behalf of all students at the Columbus Public Schools who were suspended on or after February 1971, against the school district and specific school administrators, including Norval Goss, the Director of Pupil Personnel. The suit sought a declaration that the Ohio statute authorizing the suspension was unconstitutional. The students' complaint alleged that their suspension, although consistent with Ohio Rev. Code Ann. § 3313.66 (1972) allowing principals to suspend a student for up to ten days without any type of hearing, violated their Fourteenth Amendment due process rights. The students argued that the disciplinary procedure "deprived them of both property (their statutory right to an education) and liberty (their reputation as reflected in school records) without due process of law" (Swem, 2017, 2). In addition, the plaintiffs also sought an expungement of their suspensions from their school record.

A three-judge panel of the federal district court heard the complaint following an evidentiary hearing which established the facts of the case. On September 12, 1973, the district court held that the students' right to due process was denied when they were "suspended without a hearing prior to suspension or within a reasonable time thereafter" (*Lopez v. Williams*, 1973, 1302). The court found the Ohio law on student suspensions to be unconstitutional. It also directed the school district to remove all references to the suspensions from student records. Furthermore, the district was directed to adopt fair suspension procedures, which required a notice of charges and a hearing before the student could be suspended or expelled. However, the order allowed for an immediate suspension in case of an emergency. The decision was appealed. The US Supreme Court heard oral arguments on October 16, 1974, and issued its opinion on January 22, 1975. This was the first student suspension case heard by the Supreme Court.

Justice Byron White writing for the High Court first responded to the Appellant school district administrators' contention that there was no constitutional right to a public education, thus the Due Process Clause does not protect against deprivations of an education through student disciplinary decisions. In response, Justice White identified two interests under the Due Process Clause that are implicated by the suspension of the students.

First, the students have a legal entitlement to an education in Ohio (also applicable to all states). The applicable state law requires that all residents between ages five and twenty-one years of age receive a free state-supported education. Ohio law also compelled attendance for not less than thirty-two weeks a year

(*Goss v. Lopez*, 1975, 573). Consequently, Ohio created a statutory "property interest which is protected by the Due Process Clause and which may not be taken away for misconduct without adherence to the minimum procedures required by that Clause" (*Goss v. Lopez*, 1975, 574). Students have the right to receive due process protections when faced with the loss of their property,[2] their public education, at the hands of the public school.

Next, the majority reviewed whether the students' liberty interests, in addition to their property interests, were also affected. A liberty interest, although the traditional concept provided freedom from physical restraint, includes the right to be free of official (government) stigmatization among other protections.[3] A person's good name and reputation can be at stake due to government action. The *Goss* Court wrote, "If sustained and recorded, those charges [of misconduct] could seriously damage the students' standing with their fellow pupils and their teachers as well as interfere with later opportunities for higher education and employment" (*Goss v. Lopez*, 1975, 574). A suspension from school may implicate a student's liberty interest in their good name, thus due process protections of notice and hearing are required.[4]

After establishing that the plaintiff students had a cognizable property right and a liberty interest, the court turned to what process is due. Justice White recognized that a short suspension is a mild deprivation, yet it is still a deprivation of the most important function, the delivery of education to the nation's children. "The risk of error is not at all trivial," he wrote (*Goss v. Lopez*, 1975, 580). Mindful of the difficulty of imposing restraints on our school systems which are "vast" and "complex," the court cautions that "care" and "restraint" must be used when fashioning the appropriate notice and hearing.

With the admonition that the student facing exclusion from the educational process must be heard, the court identified the essential elements of due process, while leaving flexibility for the nuances of the situation. The following is a recap of the court's major points for short suspension of ten days or less.

- "Longer suspensions or expulsions for the remainder of the school term, or permanently, may require more formal procedures" (*Goss v. Lopez*, 1975, 584).
- Due process applies to short-term suspensions of ten days or less. The student facing a suspension must receive an oral or written notice of the charges. For example, the majority acknowledges that there need not be a delay between the time of the notice and the hearing. The principal or assistant principal needs to explain the nature and facts of the infraction and afford the student

the opportunity to explain their version of the events (*Goss v. Lopez*, 1975, 582). This should alert the school administrator "to the existence of disputes about facts and argument" (*Goss v. Lopez*, 1975, 583). This additional information, the court asserted, is a "meaningful hedge" against error.
- Justice White wrote that construing the Due Process Clause in the public schools as affording the student the right to secure counsel, cross-examine witnesses, and to call witnesses is not required. He was concerned about overly formalizing and escalating the suspension process, as well as "destroying" the effectiveness of part of the teaching process.

The dissent: The "new thicket"

Justice Powell authored the dissent joined by Justices Blackmun and Rehnquist, and Chief Justice Burger. The dissent describes the majority ruling as entering a "new thicket," in which the courts may become ensnared with what has been formerly the "wide latitude" given to the educators to maintain discipline and good order. Imposing due process protections opens avenues for an unprecedented intrusion into the processes of elementary and secondary education" (*Goss v. Lopez*, 1975. (Powell, J. dissenting), 585). The role of the judiciary, he asserted, is limited given the unique nature of public education.[5]

The dissent disagrees with the premise of the majority's finding of the existence of property and liberty interests in short-term suspension, thus requiring due process protection for the student. If there are no related property or liberty interests associated with a suspension from a public school, the student is not, therefore, entitled to the Fourteenth Amendment protection of the Due Process Clause.

First, Justice Powell takes issue with the holding that an education is a property interest, whose loss for even a short period of time is a "severe detriment or grievous loss thus triggering due process protection." The right to an education under Ohio state law creates a property interest. However, the same statutory authority that creates the right also creates the process by which that right may be infringed; it is not an unqualified right. Justice Powell argues that due process only comes into play when the individual suffers a "severe detriment or grievous loss" which the plaintiffs did not experience. They went on to graduate.

Second, the dissent rejects the liberty interest argument asserted by the majority. Similar to their property right argument, Justice Powell asserts that there must be "serious damage" to one's reputation when suspended from school. Essentially, he dismisses the liberty interest with little analysis of the impact of suspension on the student. Justice Powell writes that the majority lost perspective and proportion, "For average, normal children—the vast majority—suspension for a few days is simply *not* a detriment; affects no reputations; indeed, it often may be viewed by the young as a badge of some distinction and a welcome holiday" (*Goss v. Lopez*, 1975, 598n 19, emphasis in original). Instead, the dissent visits the need for schools to maintain discipline and discusses the precedents that found that the rights of children are not coextensive with adults.

The dissent did not offer an alternative to suspension without giving a chance for the student to respond or offer an alternative explanation or unreported circumstances. The dissent apparently wanted no disturbance of the status quo. The voice of the student was not important enough to be heard.

The difference between the majority and the dissent is stark; either students have a protected interest in a state-supported education or they don't. If students do not have due process rights from an arbitrary loss of their statutory right to an education, then what vehicle is used to protect students from erroneous information which formed the basis for the discipline if the student cannot access a hearing to present accurate information. Furthermore, if there is no due process, would the courts be the only venue for the vindications of violations of their rights such as free speech and search and seizure which result in discipline. This is time-consuming, well beyond the time associated with a due process hearing, and it is expensive for families and schools.

The majority sought a balance between securing student rights and an efficient education. The Education Law Center captures this tension writing, which sets up the next section:

> To be both fair and effective, student discipline law and policy must balance two separate rights of students: the constitutional right to a public education, and the right to a safe and orderly learning environment. Procedures and laws to protect students from arbitrary and wrongful discipline are necessary, as are procedures and laws to allow schools to discipline disruptive and dangerous students. (2012, 7)

Fairness in student discipline. What is due process in the public schools?

Prior to the 1960s the rights of students "played an insignificant role" when disciplining students (Kubik, 1975, 302). Courts were reluctant to venture into matters of an educational nature claiming a lack of expertise. For example, the Arkansas Supreme Court, about 100 years ago, in a case of a student who was suspended for wearing face powder in violation of the school's rules, supported the school board. The court opined, "Courts have other more important functions to perform than that of hearing complaints of dissatisfied pupils of the public schools against rules and regulations promulgated by the school boards for the government of the schools" (*Pugsley v. Sellmeyer*, 1923, 539). As suggested by this and subsequent decisions, these early courts were reluctant to substitute their judgment for that of school boards, even if the court believed that the regulation was "unwise" or "inexpedient" (Edwards, 1931, 446).[6]

Due process is an important constraint on public school authorities seeking to discipline students. Its roots extend eight centuries to June 15, 1215, when King John of England signed the *Magna Carta Libertatum* (Great Charter of Freedoms), a charter of rights demanded by his subject lords. Due process is a constitutional protection for America's people against abuse by their government officials. Through *Goss v. Lopez*, it extends to public school students who face the possibility of suspension or expulsion from school.

The guarantee of due process: Fair treatment

Due process rights of the individual emerged from the roots of the guarantees of the Bill of Rights of the US Constitution. Due process is central to the relationship between the individual and her/his government. Fundamentally, due process is about fairness—how government treats the governed. "To a large extent, due process is an exercise in applied ethics: justice is, in the long run, intended to be fairness" (Scriven, 1997, 128).

As stated earlier due process is a right guaranteed in the US Constitution's Fifth and Fourteenth Amendments. When government seeks to deprive an individual of her/his life, liberty, or property it must afford the individual due process. Boiled down to its core, due process requires government to implement fair laws in a fair manner if it infringes upon a person's life, liberty, or property.

Of the three triggers for due process protection—deprivations of life, liberty, or property—life is not one that is found in the schools, complaints of boring students to death notwithstanding.[7] Due process in education involves issues of liberty deprivations, which occur when a person's good name, reputation, honor, or integrity is at stake in the schools' decisions. It is the property right, however, that is most often implicated in school due process proceedings. The amount of process that is due to the student is related to the extent of the deprivation that the student may suffer—the greater the deprivation, the more robust the procedure. As the Sixth Circuit Court of Appeals stated in a higher education due process case, "The more serious the deprivation, the more demanding the process" (*Doe v. University of Cincinnati*, 2017, 400).

The US Supreme Court in *Morrissey v. Brewer* opined, "Once it is determined that due process applies, the question remains what process is due" (1972, 481). The process remains flexible responding to the demands of the particular situation; it is not a "technical concept[] with fixed content" (*Cafeteria Workers v. McElroy*, 1961, 895).

Essentially, due process requires government to implement fair laws in a fair manner if it infringes upon a person's life, liberty, or property. There are two elements that comprise due process—procedural due process and substantive due process which are guaranteed in the US Constitution's Fifth and Fourteenth Amendments. These will be explored further.

Procedural due process

Procedural due process guarantees that a person who is deprived of her/his life, liberty, or property is entitled to a fair process. The procedures for possibly taking away a person's life, liberty, or property must meet the requirements of a fair *notice* of a fair *hearing*. "The fundamental requisite of due process of law is the opportunity to be heard" (*Grannis v. Ordean*, 1914, 394).

The notice must contain specific information about the day, time, and place of the hearing. It must also include, with a sufficient specificity, notice of the charges against the person so that he/she can prepare an adequate defense. The hearing must be held before a neutral tribunal with authority in the matter, typically a principal or assistant principal. It must be an orderly proceeding, and the "accused" must have the opportunity to offer a rebuttal and provide information to be considered by the decision-maker. The hearing, except in the matter of exigency of immediate harm, must be held prior to the implementation of discipline. The key is to provide the student with an opportunity to be heard in relation to the alleged offense.

These constitutional protections, however, are modified by the special characteristics of the public school with its compelling state interest in providing an efficient service to the public. Procedural due process is "tailored" according to the extent of the deprivation a person may suffer at the hands of government (*Goldberg v. Kelly*, 1970, 268–9). In other words, the greater the deprivation, the greater the procedural protections. For example, a first-grade student facing a one-day suspension is entitled to procedural due process protection (property interest) but that protection would not be as extensive if the student faced expulsion.

Substantive due process

Substantive due process is concerned with the substance of the law, rule, or regulation. The law, rule, or regulation that deprives an individual of their life, liberty, or property must be reasonable and consistent with the American sense of fairness. It must be clearly and rationally related to a lawful state function. The reasonable person test is used when the issue involves substantive due process. The test asks: "Would a reasonable person understand what to do or not do after reading the law, rule, or regulation?" Substantive due process challenges involve questions of vagueness or overbreadth as well as questions about fundamental fairness (conscious-shocking behavior).

Vague

Vague rules fail to provide adequate notice of what conduct is impermissible, and they invite uneven, biased, and variable application.

Examples of school regulations found to be vague include:

- "Gang related activities, such as display of 'colors, symbols, signals, signs, etc. will not be tolerated on school grounds.'" The term "gang-related activities" was not defined and left students unclear about what was allowed and gave school officials too much discretion to decide what constituted a gang symbol (*Stephenson v. Davenport Community School District*, 1997).
- Nonspecific regulations are often considered vague and thus violate substantive due process. For example, a federal district court held that such terms as "misconduct" (*Soglin v. Kauffman*, 1968, 295) and a Texas Court of Appeals found student regulations prohibiting "inappropriate actions" or "unacceptable behavior" are too vague for the reasonable student to know what not to do. (*Galveston Independent School District v. Boothe*, 1979). What actions are inappropriate or unacceptable? The end of the continuum of inappropriate or unacceptable behavior may be generally understood, such as stealing or a violent attack. However, as the behavior approaches the boundary of appropriate and acceptable behavior, that general understanding becomes more vague and fuzzy.

Overbroad

An overbroad rule does more than necessary to achieve the desired ends and in so doing infringes on constitutionally protected rights. Most overbreadth issues arise within the connection with the regulation of speech. Overbroad regulations prohibit types of conduct but unconstitutionally sweep constitutionally protected activities into its ambit.

Shocks the conscience

In *Rochin v. California*, the Supreme Court held that substantive due process is violated when government/public school, conduct "offend[s] those canons of decency and fairness" (1972, 169). Furthermore, due process is violated when government conduct reaches "a demonstrable level of outrageousness" (*Hampton v. United States*, 1976, 495 n. 7). Essentially, would the reasonable person believe that punishment is greatly disproportionate to the level of the infraction? The suspension of a student who attempts to eat a snack during a lesson (as a first infraction) could likely be considered shocking and fundamentally unfair.

This is a relatively high standard for the courts to meet. As stated earlier the courts eschew substituting their judgment for the judgment of school officials and school boards. Substantive due process protection is reserved not merely for unwise or erroneous governmental decisions but for egregious abuses of governmental power.

Examples of conscious-shocking allegations include a ten-day suspension for a student, who violated the prohibition against possessing/imbibing alcohol on a school trip to China did not shock the conscience of the court (*Sabol v. Walter Payton College Preparatory High School*, 2011). Similarly, a student was suspended for ten days when a student jokingly stated that a specifically named student, who brought baked goods to school for school events, had laced her brownies with marijuana. The student was tested for drugs with a negative finding. While the court was "dismayed" by the school officials' actions against her, it was not considered conscience shocking (*McDonald v. Sweetman*, 2004).

Student rules and due process

Due process for students is triggered by alleged violations of disciplinary rules. Therefore, student rules and their enforcement are the starting place for due process.

Rules are necessary to efficiently and effectively meet the educational goals of the school including providing a safe environment for all who enter the schoolhouse gate. Due to limited space we will only touch on a few challenges. The rules must comport with the due process requirements regarding vagueness and overbreadth.

Disciplinary rules are usually catalogued in a Student Code of Conduct that is distributed to all students in which they typically sign that they have received a copy of the code. The following are some suggested guidelines for reviewing whether the conduct code comports with due process. The guidelines include: (1) rules must be publicized to students and parents and must specifically and clearly state what behaviors are expected and what behaviors are prohibited; (2) rules must be consistently enforced and uniformly applied to all students without discrimination; (3) rules must be consistently enforced and uniformly applied to all students without discrimination; (4) punishments must be appropriate to the offense, taking into the student's circumstances; and (5) rules must not impair constitutionally protected rights unless there is an overriding public interest, such as a threat to the safety of others (McCarthy, Cambron-McCabe, & Eckes, 2014, 204.).

A second challenge is the effect of rules. An example is zero-tolerance rules. Zero-tolerance rules arose in the 1980s to combat the war on drugs but spread to the schools. It has been characterized as a no-nonsense, no-discretion, consistently applied response to certain offenses, most often weapons. Zero tolerance seeks to treat all violators the same without regard for the intent of the student and what constitutes a genuine threat. However, zero tolerance has been applied to such situations as bringing nail clippers to class, resulting in a ten-day suspension, and suspending a fifth-grade student for pointing his fingers like an imaginary gun and making laser noises (DeMitchell & Hambacher, 2016, 1).

However, there has been pushback against zero-tolerance policies. An American Bar Association's article discussed how some schools were replacing the rigidity with more creative approaches to discipline. The author wrote,

> There is no evidence, for instance, that zero tolerance policies—which mandate automatic punishment, such as suspension or expulsion, for infractions of a stated rule—have done anything to decrease school violence. Evidence is mounting, however, that extreme disciplinary reactions are resulting in higher rates of repeat offenses and dropout rates. (Ward, 2014)

Similarly, former US Attorney General Eric H. Holder in remarks at the Department of Justice and Department of Education joint rollout of the School Discipline Guidance stated,

Too often, so-called "zero-tolerance" policies—however well-intentioned—make students feel unwelcome in their own schools. They disrupt the learning process. And they can have significant and lasting negative effects on the long-term well-being of our young people—increasing their likelihood of future contact with juvenile and criminal justice systems. (Holder, 2014).

The failure of the policy to meet its asserted goal of making a safer place underscores the limits of due process hearings. They are contingent upon the adoption of fair policies that meet the goals of the law, rule, or regulation. Fourth Circuit judge Hamilton in a zero-tolerance case wrote that zero tolerance and the panic that gave rise to it have caused school officials to trade common sense that the punishment should fit the crime in favor of a single harsh punishment of mandatory suspension. "Such a policy has stripped away judgment and discretion on the part of those administering it; refuting the well established precept that judgment is the better part of wisdom" (*Ratner v. Loudon County Public Schools*, 2001, 143).[8]

Students learn more from the actions of adults than from their words. Law professor Justin Driver succinctly captures the importance of the synchronization of rule with the goal writing, "Students are invariably going to derive *some* lessons about justice (and injustice) from the treatment they and their classmates receive within the corridors of our nation's public schools. The only question is what the content of those lessons will be" (Driver, 2018, 155).

Student activities that are not considered property for purposes of due process protections

Not all actions and activities in which students engage at school constitute property for purposes of due process. Courts generally hold that students do not have a property right to participate in extracurricular activities, holding that "participation is a privilege rather than a right."[9] Therefore, due process protections are not triggered for extracurricular activities. Some school districts have clearly stated the proposition that participation in extracurricular activities is a privilege and not a right in their Code of Conduct for extracurricular activities.[10] For example, in *Young v. Price*, an Arkansas federal district court judge held that "[m]embership in the National Honor Society does not give rise to a property interest which entitles one to due process of law" (1983, 2). Thus, "[s]tudents do not possess a constitutionally protected interest in their participation in extracurricular activities" (*Spring Branch Independent School District v. Stamos*, 1985, 561).[11] Thus, *Goss v. Lopez* requirements do not apply if the student cannot demonstrate that their life, liberty, or property interests have been infringed upon by public school officials.

Due process: Ethics in discipline, legal rights, and responsibilities

Goss v. Lopez is an important court case. It recognizes that a public education is not only important but that it is a property right of students and that right cannot be taken away without the requirement of the over 800-year-old legal restraint upon the actions of government—due process. The identification of the constitutional right leads to a responsibility on the part of the schools to secure that right for students. *Goss* provides some guidance in fulfilling that responsibility.

Goss is also important for the cultural role that it plays in schools. "The ways in which schools punish misbehavior significantly shape the general feelings or environment of schools, a concept known as school climate" (Bower, 2021, 8). Bower's research further indicates that positive school climates are "characterized by consistent and fair disciplinary practices" (Bower, 2021, 8).

Schools exercise control over its students. The exercise of coercion communicates lessons about justice (or injustice) as well as worth. The connection between rules and discipline is important in establishing a culture in which "students and adults believe that they will be treated fairly by those tasked with maintaining a safe, respectful, and productive learning environment" (DeMitchell and Hambacher, 2016, 4). *Goss v. Lopez* supports a culture of listening to students, taking them seriously, and treating them ethically and with dignity. The core of due process is fair treatment by persons in authority. Students have a right to it, and educators have a responsibility to support that right. *Goss v. Lopez* serves an important legal role and cultural role in our public schools.

Notes

1 In 1769, Sir William Blackstone articulated the responsibility of schoolmaster to student in his doctrine of *in loco parentis*. He asserted that part of the authority of the parent is delegated to the schoolmaster/educator. For a discussion of Blackstone's *in loco parentis* doctrine and the sexual abuse of students, see Todd A. DeMitchell (2002).

2 The US Supreme Court in *Board of Education v. Roth*, 408 U.S. 564 (1972), quoted by the *Goss* Court, defined a property interest as one created not by the Constitution but by an independent source, such as state law (*Board of Education v. Roth*, 1972, 577). The Ohio statutes on public education and compulsory attendance established the right and the entitlement to the right.
3 For example, in education, the Supreme Court in *Ingraham v. Wright*, 430 U.S. 651 (1977), held that school children had a liberty interest to be free from wrongful or excessive corporal punishment.
4 Not all assertions of a liberty interest prevail in a due process case. For example, an eighth-grade student received a ten-day suspension for possession of drug-like powdery substance he was attempting to sell at school. The student, along with asserting that he had a due process right to cross-examine the student informant, which failed, claimed that his suspension for a drug-related offense "tarnished his reputation and restricted his employment opportunities" (*Paredes v. Curtis*, 864 F.2d 426, 429 (6th Cir. 1988)). The court disagreed that Paredes's relatively short ten-day suspension would forever taint his reputation.
5 The dissent finds that imposing due process protections upon the schools is most disturbing because of its indiscriminate reliance on an essentially adversarial process "as the means for resolving many of the most routine problems arising in the classroom" (*Paredes v. Curtis*, 1988, 594). The court, the dissent asserts, misapprehends the reality of the teacher-student relationship. "It is rarely adversary in nature except with respect to the chronically disruptive or insubordinate pupil whom the teacher must be free to discipline without frustrating formalities" (*Paredes v. Curtis*, 1988, 594).
6 For example, the US Supreme Court cautioned judges not "to substitute their own notions of sound educational policy for those of the authorities which they review." *Board of Education of the Hendrick Hudson Central School District v. Rowley*, 458 U.S. 176, 206 (1982).
7 Issues involving a student's death at school typically involve such torts of negligence as wrongful death and not the Due Process Clause. See Edward F. Dragan (September 11, 2013). Wrongful Death Lawsuits against Schools and Agencies. *Education Expert*, http://education-expert.com/2013/09/wrongful-death-lawsuits-schools-agencies/.
8 Teachers play a pivotal role in zero-tolerance discipline. They are often the initiators of the due process hearing with the school principal. For a discussion of focus group research with classroom teachers and how they handle the paradox of fair treatment under zero tolerance, see Fries and DeMitchell (2007).
9 Lunenburg (2011) (writing, "The reasoning of the courts is that extracurricular activities, as the name implies, are usually conducted outside the classroom before or after regular school hours, usually carry no credit, are generally supervised by school officials or others, are academically non-remedial, and are

of a voluntary nature for participants.") available at http://www.nationalforum.com/Electronic%20Journal%20Volumes/Lunenburg,%20Fred%20C.%20Students%20Property%20Right%20to%20and%20Education%20Extend%20to%20Participation%20in%20Extracurricular%20Activities%20FOCUS%20V5%20N1%202011.pdf.

10 See, e.g., Fayette County School System, *Athletic and Extracurricular Participation Code of Conduct*, "Participation in school athletic and extracurricular activities is a privilege and not a right. All students, parents, coaches, and sponsors understand that the top priority is academic achievement." Available at http://www.fcboe.org/files/athletics/codeofconductcontract.pdf. This exact same wording is found in the Rockdale County Public Schools in Georgia. Available at http://portal.rockdale.k12.ga.us/schools/shs/Athletics%20Documents/Code%20Of%20Conduct.pdf.

11 See also *Taylor v. Enumclaw School District No. 216*, 133 P.3d 492 (Wash. Ct. App. 2006), holding in a case of first impression that *Goss v. Lopez* does not apply to interscholastic sports; *Todd v. Rush County Schools*, 133 F.3d 984 (7th Cir. 1998), holding that playing football is a privilege and not a right.

Bibliography

Abington Township, Pennsylvania v. Schemp, 374 U.S. 203 (1963).

Author. (2012) *Student Discipline Rights and Procedures: A Guide for Advocates*. Newark, NJ: Education Law Center. https://edlawcenter.org/assets/files/pdfs/publications/StudentDisciplineRights_Guide_2012.pdf.

Beck, Lynn G. (1992) "The Place of a Caring Ethic in Educational Administration." *American Journal of Education* 100 (4): 454–96.

Bower, Erica Nicole (2021) *Is It Better to Be Tough, or Is Consistency Key? A Multilevel Analysis Examining the Effects of School Disciplinary Procedures on Perceptions of Climate and Safety Among Students and Teachers*. Unpublished doctoral (Ph.D.) dissertation Old Dominion University, Norfolk, VA.

Brown v. Board of Education, 347 U.S. 484 (1954).

Cafeteria Workers v. McElroy, 367 U.S. 886 (1961).

County of. Sacramento v. Lewis, 523 U.S. 833, 845 (1998).

DeMitchell, Todd A. (2002) "The Duty to Protect: Blackstone's Doctrine of In Loco Parentis: A Lens for Viewing the Sexual Abuse of Students." *Brigham Young University Education and Law Journal* 2002: 17–52.

DeMitchell, Todd A. and Hambacher, Elyse (2016) "Zero Tolerance, Threats of Harm, and the Imaginary Gun: 'Good Intentions Run Amuck.'" *Brigham Young University Education & Law Journal* 2016: 1–23.

Doe v. University of Cincinnati, 872 F.3d 393 (6th Cir. 2017).

Driver, Justin (2018) *The Public Schoolhouse Gate: Public Education, The Supreme Court, and the Battle for the American Mind*. New York: Pantheon Books.
Edwards, Newton (1931) "Legal Authority of Boards of Education to Enforce Rules and Regulations." *Elementary School Journal* 31: 446.
Fries, Kim and DeMitchell, Todd A. (2007) "Zero Tolerance and the Paradox of Fairness: Viewpoints from the Classroom." *Journal of Law & Education* 36: 211–29.
Galveston Independent School District v. Boothe, 590 S.W.2d 553 (Tex. Ct. App. 1979).
Ginott, Hiam G. (1972) *Teacher & Child: A Book for Teachers and Parents*. New York: HarperCollins, Publishers.
Goldberg v. Kelly, 397 U.S. 254 (1970).
Goldsmith, O. (1764) *The Traveler*, line 429.
Goss v. Lopez, 419 U.S. 565 (1975).
Grannis v. Ordean, 234 U.S. 385 (1914).
Hampton v. United States, 425 U.S. 484 (1976).
Ingraham v. Wright, 430 U.S. 651 (1977).
Joint Anti-Fascist Committee v. McGrath, 341 U.S. 123 (1951).
Kafka, Franz (1953) *The Trial*. New York: Alfred A Knopf.
Kubik, S. J. *Goss v. Lopez*, 95 S.Ct. 729 (1975). *Florida State University Law Review* 3 (1975): 301–13.
Lopez v. Williams, 372 F. Supp. 1279 (1973).
Lunenburg, Fred C. (2011) "Does a Student's Property Right to an Education Extend to Extracurricular Activities?" *Focus on Colleges, Universities, and Schools* 5: 1–3, 2
McCarthy, Martha M., Cambron-McCabe, Nelda H. and Eckes, Suzanne E. (2014) *Public School Law: Teachers' and Students' Rights*, 7th ed. Upper Saddle River, NJ: Pearson.
McDonald v. Sweetman, 2004 U.S. Dist. LEXIS 5558 (Dist. Ct. 2004).
Morrissey v. Brewer, 408 U.S. 471 (1972).
Plyler v. Doe, 457 U.S. 202 (1982).
Price v. Young, 580 F. Supp. 1 (E.D. Ark. 1983).
Pugsley v. Sellmeyer, 250 S.W. 538 (Ark. 1923).
Ratner v. Loudon County Public Schools, 16 F. App.x. 140 (4th Cir. 2001, cert. denied, 534 U.S. 1114 (2002) (Hamilton, J., concurring)).
Rochin v. California, 342 U.S. 165 (1972).
Sabol v. Walter Payton College Preparatory High School, 804 F.Supp.2d 747 (N.D. Ill. 2011).
Sandel, Michael J. (1996) *Democracy's Discontent: America in Search of a Public Philosophy*. Cambridge, MA: Harvard University Press.
Scriven, Michael (1997) "Due Process in Adverse Personnel Action." *Journal of Personnel Evaluation in Education* 11: 127–37, 128.
Shelton v. Tucker, 364 U.S. 479 (1960).
Soglin v. Kauffman, 295 F. Supp. 978 (W.D. Wis. 1968).
Spring Branch Independent School District v. Stamos, 695 S.W.2d 556 (Tex. 1985).

Stephenson v. Davenport Community Sch. Dist., 110 F.3d 1303 (8th Cir. 1997).

Swem, Lisa L. (2017) "*Goss v. Lopez* to Today: The Evolution of Student Discipline." *National School Boards Association, Council of School Attorneys*, Paper Presentation, 2017 School Law Seminar (March 23–25), Denver, Colorado.

U.S. Constitution Amendment XIV. § 1.

Ward, Stephanie Francis (2014) "Schools Start to Rethink Zero Tolerance Policies." *ABA Journal*, August 14. https://www.abajournal.com/magazine/article/schools_start_to_rethink_zero_tolerance_policies.

West Virginia Board of Education v. Barnette, 319 U.S. 624, 637 (1943).

Williams v. City of New York, 38 N.Y.S. 3d 528 (A.D. 1 Dept. 2016).

9

Taking Hypocrisy to School

Kartik Upadhyaya and John Tillson

Introduction

Many will recall frustration, from childhood and early adulthood, at being blamed by teachers for things that we witnessed them also doing. For example, a teacher might have criticized you for lashing out, wrongly, at a student, when you had seen the teacher similarly lashing out. It was right and appropriate that teachers blame students for these things. We will argue that despite this, it is sometimes wrong of teachers to blame students hypocritically. Indeed, interacting with students in a non-hypocritical way is part of effective education.

To begin, some qualifications on this chapter's analysis of both hypocritical and non-hypocritical blame in the context of schools. First, our aim is not to show that hostile attitudes, for example, resentment, indignation, or disdain, toward a person who has behaved wrongly are appropriately directed by teachers at schoolchildren.[1] We strongly doubt this is appropriate in general, let alone with children as the target, but in any event, such attitudes are not the form of blaming at the focal point of our chapter. Rather, by blaming a person, we mean "inviting that person to consider and discuss why what they did was wrong, what they ought to do to make things right, and why they ought to make things right in those ways." The tone of such discussions may be emphatic and serious enough to communicate the gravity and urgency of wrongdoing. In this way, schoolteacher sternness may be instrumental in ensuring that children receive the message of blame with the right communicative force. Second, even if it is often true that blame has to "sting" the blamed party in order to spur reflection and reform, we do not assume that an emotional sting, or the anger that causes it, is necessary for appropriate or valuable blaming, or indeed blaming tout court. We think it is wrong to inflict an emotional sting where this is unnecessary for reform, or counterproductive to it, or a greater disvalue than its value. Many disagree, holding that hostile attitudes and their sting are valuable; others think hostility is necessary for an activity to count as blaming.² But those who disagree can still accept the core of our argument by interpreting the term "blaming" in what follows as a process of *accurate and proportionate accountability*—accurate because it calls people to account for actual moral wrongs, proportionate because it does not respond too harshly or leniently.

Whatever we ultimately call it, though, is it not a good thing that children, teens, and young adults, when guilty of wrongdoing, are urged to partake in accountability practices of this sort? Is it not apt that teachers institute accountability, *even if* they are also morally at fault? Young people, after all, stand to learn much about how to reflect on, and respond to, wrongdoing. Teachers are supposed to be well-qualified to help students learn. It is difficult for teachers to avoid moral mistakes altogether and making moral mistakes does not necessarily undermine a person's pedagogic duties or abilities. Nonetheless, schoolteacher blaming can be undesirably hypocritical. In the following two sections, we make these claims and defend them against specific challenges.

In light of these benefits of hypocritical blaming, some might conclude that it is generally permissible for teachers to blame hypocritically.³ We respond to this in the third section by arguing that educational benefits often require teachers to blame students *non*-hypocritically rather than hypocritically. Sometimes, blaming a person in the best way possible means acknowledging our own faults, and teachers have strong—sometimes decisive—reason to blame students in this ideal way. In the final section, we respond to the potential objection that acknowledgment of wrongdoing is too professionally costly a demand to be placed on teachers. We explain that this is not always true.

At its core, the chapter's main lesson for educators is, perhaps, counterintuitive: sometimes, hypocrisy is not only a morally worse option but also a less prudent one. In our view, open self-scrutiny is not only noble but in the actor's own interests as well.

The value of accountability

Imagine the following case:

> *Tempers*: At school, student Ava gets angry at classmate Bea, and, as a result, directs abusive remarks against Ava. That wrong is witnessed by their form tutor, Clive. Clive also got angry at colleague Djamel yesterday, and directed similarly wrongful abusive remarks against Djamel. Clive blames Ava for the bad behaviour. In doing so, Clive does not acknowledge culpability for abusing Djamel.⁴

What should Clive have done in this case? Would it have been better to step back saying nothing? Or was it better to blame Ava? We think the latter.

In blaming, Clive gives Ava an opportunity to reflect on what she has done and to learn why it was wrong; this is a chance to understand what she must now do because of her actions, and how and why she must respond in that way. Ava may learn why and how to apologize to Bea, to make it up to her, and to better control her temper in order to avoid similar abusive behavior in future. That reflective opportunity has many valuable prospects. For example, it is clearly valuable for the victim, Bea, that Ava self-evaluates, apologizes in a way that shows an understanding of what she did, and perhaps explains herself in doing so—accountability is part of a victim getting what they are owed and it is, in itself, valuable that this happens.

If done in public, accountability also sets a positive example to other students of how to respond well to wrongdoing, as well as of what counts as wrongdoing. Clive blaming Ava is part of this. If the students rely on Clive's responses for moral guidance, silence on the issue of Ava's wrongdoing makes him a worse moral guide. If, on the other hand, the students know that Ava did wrong independently of Clive's responses to the episode, then observing Clive's failure to respond appropriately to the faults threatens their view of his moral credibility and, in turn, his future ability to guide the class on these matters.

Furthermore, it is good for Ava herself to partake in reform. Ava has an interest in avoiding future punishment for her mistakes. She also has an interest in knowing moral facts about herself. And, she has an interest in flourishing as a moral agent (albeit a developing one, as we will further discuss). Engaging Ava about her abusive behavior both respects and advances all these interests; if Clive keeps quiet, he fails to either respect or advance them. So, it is better, in normal circumstances at least, that Clive blame.[5]

Also plausible, however, is the hypocrisy of Clive's blaming Ava. Clive is guilty of the same thing, after all, and refuses to acknowledge this. But the fact, by itself, does not make it better for Clive to keep quiet. The fact that Clive has acted wrongly hardly means that it is *bad* for Ava and the others for Clive to blame her. Nor, indeed, does it eliminate the possibility of engaging Ava in a way that is good for her and others. The wrongness of Clive's conduct has no bearing at all on the wrongness of Ava's conduct and thus does nothing to undermine the stake that Ava and the others have in the right responses being made. In comparison to silence, hypocritical blaming is normally better.

Our ultimate task is to explain why, despite this fact, such hypocritical blaming can be wrong. But first, we will address two challenges to this account of the value of schoolteacher blame. One type of challenge denies the value of schoolteachers blaming students; another denies that Clive blaming Ava is in fact hypocritical.

Rules and responsibilities

Responsibilities

A key concern about the point of blaming children is that children are not fully fledged agents, capable of fully understanding and responding to moral issues.[6] For example, compared to adults, there are limits in the *uptake* that children experience upon being blamed: limits in the quality of reflection that moral interaction with a child can achieve. Because Ava's abilities to recognize, respond to, and apply normative reasons are not fully developed, the understanding she can gain of why it was wrong to abuse Bea as she did, and why she owes the corrective responses she does, might be relatively superficial. Furthermore, the strength of our duties to respond appropriately to wrongdoing is sensitive to how responsible we are for the wrongs we commit.[7]

This has implications for the value and stringency of corrective responses that children owe compared to adults. Because he is more normatively competent, Clive both committed a morally worse failure and is more capable of rectifying that failure for the right reasons. Similarly, Djamel, Clive's victim, may be more capable of recognizing these failures in Clive than Bea vis-à-vis Ava. Thus, it may be more meaningful for Djamel that Clive compensate and apologize to him than it would be for Bea that Ava compensates and apologizes to her. Given the pair's ability to achieve a deeper moral understanding, Clive's responses have greater import. Clive ought to bear more cost than Ava to deliver these responses.

We agree that certain reasons to blame are less weighty in the case of children. However, this does not warrant the conclusion that teachers' blame toward students is devoid of value or justification. For one thing, it is not as though Ava has *no* normative capacities—no ability to have behaved better, to reflect rationally, or to respond correctively—at all. This means that it is still somewhat accurate to hold that children could have known better and have means of addressing defects in their agency. So it is apt to engage the developing capacities of blameworthy children, provided they possess a high enough degree of competence.

Even in instances where it is not apt to engage children through blame, blaming them can produce good consequences which make it worthwhile—indeed, better consequences than blaming adults. Younger children, especially, seem more easily disposed than adults to listen to, and be motivated by, blaming responses to their behavior. For instance, as Clive's moral personality and agential habits are more molded than Ava's, he might find it more difficult than Ava to entertain reform and take appropriate steps to achieve it. Of course, children may struggle to achieve a deep understanding of their reasons to reform, but as they are more morally malleable, engaging them in moral reflection earlier on in life improves their chances of developing the right moral attitudes and dispositions in future. Teachers and the wider community owe students those chances.

In weighing the blaming consequences for children, one difficult task is to figure out what cost of blame would be too high on a child relative to their interest in a better moral future. As mentioned at the outset, blame can carry a sting, whether intentionally or not. Children will sometimes experience unavoidable distress in discussing their moral faults: anxiety about how others will regard them (e.g., Ava might worry over whether she will ever restore good relations with Bea); frustration at being unable to undo their actions; and disappointment in themselves. But recall our initial assumption that blame should be proportionate in the distress caused. It is plausible that many instances of blaming are proportionate in this sense, as the strength of our interests in moral flourishing tends to be weightier than interests in avoiding psychological discomfort. For example, many parents would prefer, for their children's sake, that their child suffers a broken leg,[8] or wrongful punishment,[9] over the child acting in a seriously immoral way. A broken leg and wrongful punishment are obviously costlier than the sting of typical instances of blame. Here, Ava's interests in self-knowledge and moral knowledge pull together with the interest others have against being wronged and in receiving rectification from wrongdoers.

Rules

The second challenge points out that school rules for teachers and students come apart. Some might wonder whether in breaking school rules, students generally act in ways that warrant blame, and thus whether teachers' bad behavior is comparable to that of students in a way that makes them vulnerable to hypocrisy.

We agree that much behavior identified as "bad" in class does not warrant blame at all, because it is not wrongful. For example, it is difficult to justify incredibly stringent uniform codes or certain rules based entirely on religious orthodoxy. Where rules are not justified, students are not blameworthy for flouting them, and blame is unwarranted as a response to something that is not blameworthy. Whether teachers morally ought to enforce unjustified rules via blame is likely to depend on the disastrousness of the consequences. If, say, the lack of blaming enforcement of religious norms is going to attract (unwarranted) complaints by parents, and a lack of parental trust in the school, then perhaps teachers ought to blame children for noncompliance. However, this relies on highly nonideal circumstances, and even these bad consequences are limited by our duties not to impose requirements on children that they may reasonably reject.[10]

However, none of this means that all school rules prohibit blameless acts. Note first that acts can be blameworthy even if they are not in themselves morally wrong. It is not in itself wrong to drive on the right-hand side of the road, but a person can be blameworthy for doing so if this is part of a wider system of just rules.[11] Similarly, while it is not in itself wrong to whisper during class, or to leave school premises at will, blame for infractions like these is warranted where children have strong moral reasons, or duties, not to undermine sets of rules that schools are justified in enforcing.

For many of these infractions, teachers are plausibly subject to both professional and moral duties to blame students, as they often agree to uphold these standards and benefit from everyone else's compliance. A practice of blaming helps to keep a just system of rules in place (and stably in place, where blaming advances understanding the point of these rules).[12] Failing to blame can involve a failure to do their fair share to maintain the practice.[13]

Some may grant that breaking school rules sometimes warrants blame but worry that because teachers and students are bound by different rules, schoolteacher blaming is not a practice that admits of hypocrisy. For example, teachers are permitted to whisper during class: it cannot then be hypocritical for a teacher who partakes in whispering to blame students for whispering.

A quick response to this idea is that some rules apply to both teachers and students. But the critic will point ought that even in these instances, the reasons why certain rules are justifiably enforced upon teachers are different from the reasons why they are justifiably enforced on students. For example, both teachers and students are prohibited from leaving the premises on a whim. But if a teacher breaks this rule, the wrongness of the teacher's infraction has a quite different moral explanation from that of a student breaking the same rule. This might raise doubts that schoolteacher blaming can be hypocritical, according to an intuitive view that blame is only hypocritical if the blamer does some wrong that is sufficiently similar in nature to that of the blamed. It is hard to isolate what makes wrongdoing sufficiently similar,[14] but more and less powerful cases are easy to distinguish. A shoplifter is not powerfully hypocritical in blaming someone for a racist comment. A racist commenter is more powerfully hypocritical in blaming someone for a casteist or sexist remark. And that person would be starkly hypocritical in blaming someone for prejudicially abusive behavior that they participated in together.[15]

But, again, this is no objection to the view that hypocrisy is a real phenomenon in schoolteaching. It only indicates certain limitations in its scope compared to other contexts. Sometimes rules that apply to teachers and students apply for the same reasons. This is so even where the rules do not prohibit something wrong in itself. For example, it is not wrong in itself for people to engage in consensual physical contact. But teachers and students both ought to limit physical contact during a pandemic. And their reasons to observe this rule—for example, to contribute to the safety of the community's most vulnerable—clearly overlap.

Of course, the clearest cases of the phenomenon are those like *Tempers*, where the failure on the part of both a teacher and student is not merely convention-based, or professional, but straightforwardly moral. Clive should not lose his temper and abuse Djamel, not simply because Djamel is a colleague but because he is a person with claims against that type of behavior. Ava should not lose her temper and abuse Bea not simply because they share a classroom but because Bea is a person with claims against that type of behavior. Whatever substantive story we tell about this, there is no reason why it cannot apply to both Clive's and Ava's wrongdoing. The reason is that most kinds of wrongdoing are in principle available to most agents, even agents in development. That point alone reveals that the possibilities of schoolteacher hypocrisy are ample.[16]

The pedagogic advantage of non-hypocritical blame

We have argued that schoolteachers who blame students are rightly accused of hypocrisy, but also that it is valuable for teachers to blame in these contexts. Why not then simply ignore schoolteacher hypocrisy or even encourage the practice? Our answer is that blaming a student *non-hypocritically* is a yet more valuable option and one that teachers often ought to take rather than blaming hypocritically. This section defends the first of these claims; the next section defends the latter.

Acknowledgment

What do we mean by the option of blaming non-hypocritically? One way teachers might blame non-hypocritically is by not committing similar fault. Recall, though, that we have in mind blamers who are already violating, or have violated, similar norms—avoiding similar fault is not an option. The question is how to blame a student *given* that the teacher is similarly faulty.

Suppose that in the course of blaming Ava, Clive openly and fully acknowledges his similar failure and the fact that he now faces demands similar to those faced by Ava. He says, sincerely, something along these lines: "I too should apologise to the victim, explain what happened, avoid similar actions in future, etc. I am ready to talk about this issue." Then Clive's blame is not hypocritical at all.

Not everyone shares this view. Some judge blame to be hypocritical purely because of the blamer's own bad behavior—as Clive has wrongly lashed out, there is no way for him avoid hypocrisy whenever he blames others for their lashing out.[17] This is not a plausible account of the wrongness of hypocrisy, at least when it comes to explaining why hypocritical blaming is wrong. Remember that Clive is engaging in accurate and proportionate accountability. If he fully and openly acknowledges similar fault, it is hard to see how Clive does something even pro tanto wrong.

Some might worry that the blame would be pro tanto wrong, and hypocritical, if Clive's future behavior fails to accord with the content of this acknowledgment: if, despite acknowledging his mistake, Clive later fails to make the relevant responses, of apology and rectification, to his wrongdoing while encouraging Ava to do the same. But, again, this is more plausible as a judgment about the quality of Clive's personality, rather than about the quality of the blaming interaction. Clive's character may be hypocritical in the sense that Clive later fails to practice what he preaches. That is a separate question from whether his blaming is hypocritical. Our interest is in the moral quality of certain practices of normative engagement, rather than of people. Assuming that Clive is sincere in his acknowledgment, we see no defect in the normative engagement.

In any event, most, we suspect, will concede that even if somewhat hypocritical, blaming is significantly less hypocritical when it involves open acknowledgment compared to blame (like *Tempers*) that involves no acknowledgment. It is that particular form of non-hypocrisy in blame—the non-hypocrisy that inheres in acknowledgment of similar wrongdoing—that we argue is morally preferable to hypocritical blame.

Mutual deliberation

Here is why we believe that non-hypocritical blame is a better option. If, in the course of blaming Ava, Clive acknowledges similar fault, a new avenue of conversation opens up. What is now possible is a process of *mutual deliberation*, in which Clive and Ava can reflect on both of their similar faults together. That new avenue morally improves the accountability process.[18]

To see how hypocrisy undermines mutual deliberation, consider what is and isn't possible to discuss when blame is hypocritical—that is, when Clive fails to acknowledge similar fault. It is possible for the pair to discuss Ava's fault together. It is also possible for Ava to discuss Clive's fault, if she knows about it already. But, if Clive won't acknowledge his fault, the pair cannot discuss Clive's fault together. Absent Clive's acknowledgment, then, they cannot achieve the ideal of discussing *both* of their similar faults together. Non-hypocrisy is necessary for that ideal.

One set of values of reasoning together about our similar faults are *agential*: these have to do with the value of recognizing and exercising co-agency. Mutual deliberation enables relations of solidarity, in which Clive and Ava openly and mutually recognize themselves as involved in the same normative endeavor. Mutual deliberation also involves a collaborative exercise of agency. Through the process of explaining, listening, and responding to one another about how we ought to address what we did, Clive and Ava jointly shape their moral identities and future actions in a reasons-responsive manner. We should value the opportunity to collaborate in this co-responsive way.

These agential values, it might seem, are less powerful in the context of teachers blaming students, given the limitations in children's agency alluded to earlier. While adults may be able to recognize one another as comembers of a community of normatively capable beings, children may not have a grasp of that concept and thus not belong to that community. However, as we also mentioned, beyond early infancy, children's agency falls along a continuum. Although their normative capacities (i.e., to know and do better) are limited, they are still capable of some rational reflection.

Furthermore, beyond agential value, mutual deliberation in the classroom also has *pedagogic* value. A classroom setting is an appropriate arena for students to begin learning the art of frank moral evaluation: the disposition to be ready to appraise not only other people's faults but also their own and to combine their capacities with others' to appraise both of these topics. Reasoning about similar wrongdoing is a way of practicing this skill.

Here is a simple reason why it is apt for teachers to familiarize children with the skill of combining self-evaluation with the evaluation of others: teachers have reason to teach students things that will morally benefit them and others in the future. While the value of mutual deliberation might be limited in early childhood, experiencing this ideal form of deliberation at that stage will help them realize better versions of it in later life than would otherwise be the case.

Moreover, cultivating the disposition to participate in mutual deliberation involves cultivating virtues that are valuable in themselves: the virtues of humility, modesty, and discursive open-mindedness, for example. It also protects against vices such as *grandstanding*, or using moral criticism as a means of acting as if, or showing off that, we are morally superior to others.[19] All of these character lessons are embodied in the willingness to reason about our faults with others.

Suppose we agree that mutual deliberation is valuable in the classroom. A critic might object that there are multiple ways of promoting mutual deliberation. Clive could promote mutual discussion between Ava and other students, for example. Why, then, does the value of mutual deliberation require Clive specifically to acknowledge *his* similar wrongdoing when blaming Ava? Because if Clive opts not to acknowledge and instead use other ways of teaching the virtues of non-hypocrisy, a core lesson about morality will be undermined. Let's call it:

Reasons-Uniformity: All reasons, in principle, apply uniformly to all agents.

It is vital, in building a sense of morality, to understand that it has this all-inclusive feature. When it comes to moral reasons and duties, no one is immune, no matter where they stand in the social or professional hierarchy. All agents are in it together. Clive's acknowledgment powerfully underscores this fact. In contrast, failing to acknowledge his wrongdoing expresses the corrosive idea that morality admits of arbitrary exceptions. Mere assertions of Reasons-Uniformity and adult fallibility are unlikely to teach this lesson as effectively.

Critics might also wonder whether the values sketched earlier prove too much. If the point of mutual deliberation is to exemplify certain virtues and lessons, it is unclear why this should only guide teachers who are actually similarly guilty. After all, a teacher could pretend to be similarly guilty in order to teach the relevant lessons. It may seem odd that the values we have sketched provide a reason to engage in such pretense.[20]

Note first that our view is meant to explain a deficiency in hypocritical blaming, rather than to advocate for a general duty to teach mutual deliberation. In our view, mutual deliberation explains why non-hypocritical blaming is a moral improvement on hypocritical blaming in the classroom. It does not follow that mutual deliberation is generally required. Indeed, the opposite seems true. It seems independently wrong to lie to children. And pretending to face shared moral demands runs the risk of undermining teacher credibility when the lie is exposed.

Second, as we understand mutual deliberation, its values are not ideally pursued by pretense. The solidaristic bond between similar wrongdoers that we have in mind depends on each showing the other recognition of a genuine shared need to respond to similar moral demand. That relationship cannot be instantiated by pretending to confront shared moral demands.

Another concern about the value of acknowledgment is that it is unprofessional. As we suggested earlier, being a teacher involves being a moral guide. If teachers acknowledge wrongdoing, they risk that students will take them less seriously as moral guides or begin to wonder whether the behavior at issue is ultimately acceptable. "If *Clive* loses his temper and abuses others," Ava might think, "then why can't I?"

We agree that acknowledgment is not always preferable, overall, to hypocrisy. Sometimes it will be better overall to postpone the cultivation of mutual deliberation for other occasions. However, in many instances, worries about professionalism and mixed messages have no force and indeed work in favor of non-hypocrisy. Consider:

> *Known Tempers*: As in *Tempers*, plus the fact that the whole class (Ava, Bea and co) witnessed Clive wrongly lashing out at colleague Djamel.

In *Known Tempers*, Clive's hypocrisy is not a failure to reveal wrongdoing, as the students witnessed what Clive did to Djamel. Instead, his hypocrisy is a failure to openly deliberate about his own wrongdoing and its similarity. For those students who already see the wrongness of what Clive behaved similarly, his failure to publicly recognize this fact about himself calls into question his credibility as a moral guide. For those who saw what Clive did and are unsure how to assess it, it also calls into question the lesson that this particular instance of blaming is meant to teach—that Ava acted wrongly. If Clive does not acknowledge his similar mistake, implicating that it is acceptable, it becomes less clear that Ava's behavior is not. In short, we need the unequivocal message that any such behavior is unacceptable for anyone. This is a strong reason for teachers to acknowledge.

The pedagogic duty of non-hypocritical blame

We have so far outlined the pedagogic values of non-hypocrisy, including lessons about co-agency, Reasons-Uniformity, and self-critique. We also noted, at the outset, that teachers owe pedagogic duties to children on the topic of morality. However, this does not establish that teachers have a duty to blame non-hypocritically, for the cost of acknowledgment might be unduly demanding. In this final section of the chapter, we now complete our argument by showing that acknowledgment is not as costly as it initially seems.

Overdetermined costs

Two possible costs of acknowledgment are as follows. First, teachers may lose their jobs or face other disciplinary action, if others discover their wrongdoing. This concern is particularly pressing since teaching is a morally delicate profession. For obvious reasons, standards of decent conduct in schooling—hence numbers of possible acts that warrant penalties—are quite extraordinarily high. Second, acknowledgment can hamper teacher-student relations, as students may be inclined to use information about what teachers have done as ammunition against them and fodder for gossip. Such ammunition can threaten a constructive classroom environment.

In response, not all instances of hypocrisy involve dismissible behavior.[21] In *Tempers*, the type of offense in question—lashing out at a colleague—though wrong, is rarely dismissible. Perhaps what Clive does, even if not dismissible, is an offense for which Clive nevertheless risks some appropriate disciplinary action.

More generally, worries about sanctions and gossip are relevant only if acknowledgment increases the chance of others knowing about a teacher's bad behavior. As *Known Tempers* shows, we cannot assume that this is always true. In *Known Tempers*, the costs of acknowledgment and revelation of wrongdoing come apart. The costs of revelation are sunk—penalties and possibilities of gossip are overdetermined—because what Clive did to Djamel is publicly known. Here, the costs that Clive confronts are just those of partaking in mutual deliberation during his blaming interaction with Ava. There may be some cost involved here, such as embarrassment or discomfort, in openly confronting his mistakes, but in the light of his responsibility as an educator, Clive ought to bear those costs. If he does not, his status as a moral guide will be undermined, as will the lessons of mutual deliberation. His failure to acknowledge would also impair rather than protect constructive teacher-student relations. As mentioned earlier, schoolteacher hypocrisy damages credibility in the eyes of students and can equally be used as ammunition against those in authority.

Encouraging the second-best

A final question about the argument in this chapter concerns the problem we discussed at the beginning. We started by arguing that there is positive value in teachers blaming, even if hypocritically. But we have now been arguing that in many cases, teachers do wrong to blame hypocritically, as they ought to blame non-hypocritically instead. This, some might worry, implies that teachers who will refuse to acknowledge wrongdoing ought to keep quiet, and let faults slide, rather than blaming the student in a manner that we have claimed is wrong.

We can formulate this point as a practical dilemma.[22] Suppose that for a particular infraction, a teacher is professionally or morally required to blame the student. Suppose also that this is an instance, like *Known Tempers*, where (we have argued) the teacher ought to blame the student non-hypocritically. But suppose we know for a fact that the teacher is stubborn: they are *not* ready and willing to acknowledge their similar mistake, and thus will blame the student hypocritically if they blame at all. On the one hand, according to our view, if the teacher keeps quiet about the student's infraction, they will fail in their duties to blame and fail to do something valuable for the students. On the other hand, if they blame, they fail in their duty to blame non-hypocritically. As both alternatives violate duties, there is a quandary about what to do. But, the critic might allege, this should be no quandary at all: the teacher clearly ought to blame! Therefore, our claim that teachers do wrong to blame non-hypocritically absurdly discourages them from doing something that is both valuable and part of their duty.

However, this is a mistaken reading of the argument we have given. Of course, we do believe that wrongful hypocrisy among schoolteachers should be discouraged. But we also believe that those who will refuse to blame non-hypocritically ought to do the second-best thing and blame hypocritically. Our view allows for this. Our view is that schoolteachers ought to blame non-hypocritically *rather than hypocritically*. This is compatible with saying that teachers ought to blame hypocritically *rather than not at all*.

To explain further: the reason why schoolteacher hypocrisy is wrong, on our account, depends on a comparison between the alternatives of hypocritical and non-hypocritical blaming. Where a teacher has stronger moral reason to blame a student in a mutually discursive manner, and can do this at low additional cost, it is wrong for that teacher, instead, to opt for the less good alternative of hypocritical blaming. As this does not involve any comparison between the alternatives of hypocritical blaming and silence, it is consistent with the claim that if non-hypocrisy won't be pursued, the teacher still has stronger moral reason to blame hypocritically than he does to let things slide.

Contrast the example of a stubborn teacher with a lifeguard, who can save one drowning swimmer or, at moderate extra cost, that swimmer plus another drowning swimmer nearby. The lifeguard saves only one, on the grounds that they wish to forgo the extra cost of saving both. This lifeguard acts wrongly in saving the one. But this is not because they are unjustified in saving the one swimmer rather than saving no one at all. It is because they are unjustified in failing to do something even better (saving both swimmers) than the second-best thing (saving the first swimmer). Likewise, given that a particular teacher is blaming a student, they can be unjustified in failing to blame them in the best way (non-hypocritically rather than hypocritically) even if they are justified in doing the second-best thing (blaming a student hypocritically rather than keeping quiet).

Overall, our youthful angst about our teachers' hypocrisy was sometimes on the mark. As children, we should have realized that the right response to this was not to object to the blaming we experienced. Teachers were right to blame us when we acted wrongly, even on pain of hypocrisy. Yet, at the same time, teachers ought to accept that the value of blaming students does not get them off the moral hook. When engaging in blame, they ought to pay attention to the benefits that non-hypocrisy can bring both to their pupils and to their own professional lives.

Notes

1 In this way, we can follow Pickard (2011, 218) in distinguishing between "affective" and "detached" blaming—that is, between blame that expresses blamers' hostile attitudes (and tends to cause a "sting") and blame that does not (and tends not to). However, we note that blame in our sense may be animated by and may express some relevant negative affect—like hurt and worry—while not being motivated by or expressing hostile attitudes and that blame may sometimes cause negative affect—like guilt and regret—which in turn stimulates moral growth.

2   There are myriad accounts of the value and necessity of hostility and other harmful responses to wrongdoing—a few examples are Owens (2012); Wolf (2011); Scanlon (2008); Bennett (2002); Wallace (1994); Strawson (1962).
3   Skeptics about the wrong of hypocritical blaming include Dover (2019), and Bell (2013).
4   Imagine further that Clive and Ava haven't done anything that expels them from the school but that neither is, as yet, fully reformed.
5   We don't here mean to be read as saying that blaming is valuable only if it causally contributes to reform. For example, it seems good to give someone a chance to respond appropriately to their wrongdoing even when they don't end up taking that chance. In addition, it is noninstrumentally valuable to treat the wrongdoer as a responsible agent and to express solidarity for victims of wrongdoing. Both of these values can be achieved in communicative blaming. Still, we take it that the most powerful reason to blame lies in encouraging the blame to comply with her corrective duties.
6   For a helpful survey of evidence on limited normative agency in children, see Chan and Clayton (2006).
7   There are different ways to explicate this idea. We might say that Ava's lashing out at Bea is not as grave a wrong as Clive's lashing out at a colleague. Or we might say that Ava's wrong is less of a moral failing than Clive's. Either way, Clive was better placed than Ava to act better than they did. That contrast makes Ava's moral need for reflection less urgent than Clive's.
8   Tadros (2019).
9   Tadros (2020).
10 Matthew Clayton (2006, forthcoming) gives an anti-perfectionist rationale for this kind of point, but equally perfectionist readings of the point are available. For instance, on some perfectionist views, coerced choices can lack the value that those same choices would have if they were made voluntarily. On these views, the value of students freely acting in some way can give schools a reason to make the option of so acting available without giving them a reason to make the action mandatory.
11 David Owens (2017) calls these *mala prohibita*. As he points out, mala prohibita might be both instrumentally and noninstrumentally justified.
12 Cf. Williams (1998).
13 See Simmons (1979) and Klosko (1987).
14 Cf. Lippert-Rasmussen (2013: 303–6).
15 Watson (2015) and Tadros (2009).
16 Admittedly, the nature of the particular duties at issue can give rise to further complications. For instance, even when duties fall on teachers and students alike, the duty is only enforceable for one of these groups. Consider that we may have duties to ourselves not to smoke, to eat healthily, and to participate in physical exercise. Where teachers blame students for violating these duties, it seems

hypocritical not to acknowledge their own failure to do so, given that teachers themselves have the same duties. However, in smoking, and not doing sports, adults may be doing bad things that they are entitled to do, whereas children are doing these things arguably without the same entitlements. Still, our view is that while hypocrisy is diminished in these contexts, it is not cancelled altogether.
17 This is how Dover characterizes the anti-hypocrisy norm (2019).
18 For detailed defense of this as a general account of hypocrisy, see Upadhyaya (2020).
19 For more on the problem of grandstanding, see Tosi and Warmke (2020).
20 We owe this question to Tom Douglas.
21 Perhaps for some wrongdoing, such as criminal offenses, it is impermissible for teachers to conceal the facts and perhaps incumbent on them to consider their position. In these cases, the question still remains as to whether teachers ought to acknowledge the relevant offenses *in the classroom*. At any rate, the issue of when and why a criminal ought to turn themselves in is beyond this chapter's scope.
22 A different kind of dilemma that is increasingly being discussed in moral philosophy is raised by the instance where not blaming the student is permissible—this might be true if the teacher has done her fair share of blaming already, for instance, or if the value of blaming is diminished since others have held the student accountable already. See, e.g., Pummer (2016) and Horton (2017). Cf. also Shelly Kagan's (1989, 16) telling example, in which it is impermissible to rescue a parrot from a house fire instead of a baby even when it is both permissible not to run in at all and better to save a parrot than to do nothing.

References

Bell, Macalester (2013) "The Standing to Blame: A Critique." In D. Justin Coates and Neal Tognazzini (eds.), *Blame: Its Nature and Norms*, 263–81. Oxford: Oxford University Press.

Bennett, Christopher (2002) "The Varieties of Retributive Experience." *The Philosophical Quarterly* 52: 145–63.

Chan, Tak Wing and Clayton, Matthew (2006) "Should the Voting Age be Lowered to Sixteen? Normative and Empirical Considerations." *Political Studies* 54: 533–58.

Clayton, Matthew (forthcoming) *Independence for Children*. Oxford: Oxford University Press.

Clayton, Matthew (2006) *Justice and Legitimacy in Upbringing*. Oxford: Oxford University Press.

Dover, Daniela (2019) "The Walk and the Talk." *Philosophical Review* 128 (4): 387–442.

Horton, Joe (2017) "The All or Nothing Problem." *Journal of Philosophy* 114: 94–104.

Kagan, Shelly (1989) *The Limits of Morality*. Oxford: Clarendon Press.
Klosko, George (1987) "The Principle of Fairness and Political Obligation." *Ethics* 97 (2): 353–62.
Lippert-Rasmussen, Kasper (2013) "Who can I Blame?" in Michael Kühler and Nadja Jelinek (eds.), *Autonomy and the Self*, 295–315. London: Springer.
Owens, David (2017) "Wrong by Convention." *Ethics* 127 (3): 553–75.
Owens, David (2012) *Shaping the Normative Landscape*. Oxford: Oxford University Press.
Pickard, Hanna (2011) "Responsibility Without Blame: Empathy and the Effective Treatment of Personality Disorder." *Philosophy, Psychiatry, Psychology* 18 (3): 209–24.
Pummer, Theron (2016) "Whether and Where to Give." *Philosophy & Public Affairs* 44 (1): 77–95.
Scanlon, Tim M. (2008) *Moral Dimensions: Permissibility, Meaning, Blame*. Cambridge, MA: Belknap Press.
Simmons, A. John (1979) "The Principle of Fair Play." *Philosophy & Public Affairs* 8 (4): 307–37.
Strawson, Peter F. (1962) "Freedom and Resentment." *Proceedings of the British Academy* 48: 1–25.
Tadros, Victor (2009) "Poverty and Criminal Responsibility." *Journal of Value Enquiry* 43 (3): 391–413.
Tadros, Victor (2019) *Wrongs and Crimes*. Oxford: Oxford University Press.
Tadros, Victor (2020) "Distributing Responsibility." *Philosophy & Public Affairs* 48 (3): 223–61.
Tosi, Justin and Warmke, Brandon (2020) *Grandstanding: The Use and Abuse of Moral Talk*. Oxford: Oxford University Press.
Upadhyaya, Kartik (2020) "What's Wrong with Hypocrisy." PhD thesis, University of Warwick.
Wallace, R. Jay (1994) *Responsibility and the Moral Sentiments*. Cambridge, MA: Harvard University Press.
Watson, Gary (2015) "A Moral Predicament in the Criminal Law." *Inquiry* 58 (2): 168–88.
Williams, Andrew (1998) "Incentives, Inequality, and Publicity." *Philosophy & Public Affairs* 27 (3): 225–47.
Wolf, Susan (2011) "Blame, Italian Style." In R. J. Wallace, R. Kumar and S. Freeman (eds.), *Reasons and Recognition: Essay on the Philosophy of T. M. Scanlon*, 332–47. New York: Oxford University Press.

10

The Punitive Classroom

Punishment and Punitive Feelings between Adults and Children

Ruth Cigman

Introduction

We are familiar with the thought that adults sometimes punish children. Maybe they should not do so, or should do so less often or less severely, but *that* they do so is not in question. We are also familiar with children's punitive feelings—anger, hostility, and so on. They say things like: "Why shouldn't I hurt her? She hurt me!"

What is less clear, or less discussed, is the reversal of these: the punishment of adults by children and the punitive feelings of adults toward children. Many philosophers deny that the former is logically possible. Children (they say) cannot punish adults, for they lack the authority that punishment logically requires. At most, they can "punish" adults or punish them in a metaphorical sense.

No one would deny that adults sometimes get angry with children; all teachers and parents feel this way at times. Why is this rarely discussed, and what might be the consequence of reticence around this topic? It may be argued that we should respect the professionalism of teachers: their capacity to hide their anger toward children in favor of kindness and a rational exercise of authority. And indeed, this is no doubt justified most of the time. However, the punishment of children raises ethical concerns. Some believe it can be cruel, disrespectful, inimical to learning, bad for self-confidence.[1] It is unclear how such concerns can be addressed if we do not reflect on adults' punitive feelings toward children. For it is *right* to suggest that anger sometimes motivates punishment—that it can spiral out of control, lose touch with reality, and even become, as Seneca said, a "short madness." It is also undeniable that children are occasionally bullied and even abused by adults. It is fair to ask: How might the anger of adults influence their punishment of children? How would we know, and how might we protect children from this?

This chapter explores authority, emotion, and conflict between adults and children. The emotion of anger in particular (with its cognates resentment, hostility, outrage, fury, vengefulness, etc.) will come under the spotlight as a motive for punishment that may be invisible or undeclared. When otherwise responsible adults punish children, do they sometimes exceed the bounds of their authority? Can children punish adults, and if so, can they do so justly? I hope this discussion will both deepen our understanding and loosen the grip of skepticism about the punishment of children.

Punishment and authority

What is punishment? R. A. Duff (2003) warns us against trying to prescribe what the word *must* mean:

> I do not engage in the kind of discussion of the definition of punishment that has so exercised some philosophers—a discussion that is doomed to futility if it is intended to produce a definition capturing all and only those practices that properly count as "punishment," and that must rapidly become a normative discussion of how punishment can be justified if it is to produce a useful account of what we **should** mean by "punishment." We need simply note the familiar points that punishment is, typically, something intended to be burdensome or painful, imposed on a (supposed) offender for a (supposed) offense by someone with (supposedly) the authority to do so. (pp. xiv–xv)

Duff is right to suggest that the attempt to capture "all and only those practices that properly count as 'punishment'" is a futile exercise. There are variations in understanding that a philosophical discussion must respect. On the other hand, there are limits to what punishment can mean or how the word can be sensibly used. The teacher who puts the class into detention and watches them giggling at online videos, passing round cans of beer, and begging the caretaker to let them stay when it is time to go home can hardly be said to have punished them.

Limits are important; they demarcate an area of concern. Without a broad understanding of what punishment means and what its purposes are, it is hardly possible to consider whether it should be banished or retained. In the previous passage, Duff identifies three "familiar points" about the meaning of punishment, and many philosophers substantially agree with him. Richard Peters (1966), for example, notes that

> at least the three criteria of (i) intentional infliction of pain (ii) by someone in authority (iii) on a person as a consequence of a breach of rules on his part, must be satisfied if we are to call something a case of "punishment." (p. 268)

I have suggested that (i) is correct; it demarcates a limit, and the teacher who thinks he/she has punished the exuberant class who are reluctant to go home misuses or stretches the word. (iii) is less clear; "breach of rules" is arguably too narrow (narrower than "supposed offense" or, as I prefer, "perceived wrongdoing") and begs questions by locating punishment in formally rule-governed contexts like schools and societies. The question "Can children punish?" is one we should be able to consider without supposing that *if* they can do so, they must be responding to rule breaches. It may be more a matter (as it often is with adults) of responding to vague expectations. In what follows, I shall explore this suggestion with examples.

What about (ii), "by someone in authority"? *Is* there an authority condition? Is an act that satisfies Peters's criteria (i) and (iii) but not (ii) an act of punishment in a metaphorical sense, rather than punishment proper? The first thing to consider is that the authority condition can be interpreted in at least two ways.

(1) It may mean that agents of punishment *must* be authority figures, like teachers, parents, or judges.
(2) Or it may mean that acts of punishment *are* acts of authority, even if they are not performed by authority figures. When non-authority figures impose hardship or pain on another in response to wrongdoing, they effectively *assume* authority.

(1) is the standard philosophical view. It is repeatedly endorsed by philosophers, and it aims to prescribe the correct or proper use of the word "punishment," often using words like "always" and "must." When the word "punishment" is preceded by words like "criminal," "legal," or "institutional," this makes sense. Criminal punishment *is* authorized punishment. It involves a process whereby authorized individuals deliberate on facts, gather evidence, and finally pass judgments that go on the public record. School punishment is semipublic in the sense that records are kept and schools are subject to national inspections.

This is formal punishment; the question I am exploring is whether we can talk about informal punishment without speaking metaphorically, and here interpretation (2) must be considered. Suppose your neighbor removes the fence between your houses without consultation. When questioned, she says she didn't like the fence and wants to construct another. Legally the fence is yours, and you *did* like it. You have two options. You can appeal to the court to have your fence reinstated, or you can cajole and insist that the neighbor return your fence. You decide to go the second route, but your neighbor ignores you, so you throw your rubbish into her garden, pull up her roses, throw her mail into the street.

It seems obvious to me that this is punishment. You are not authorized to punish your neighbor, but you have "donned the mantle of authority" by making a moral judgment and acting upon it. You have inflicted pain as payback for a perceived wrongdoing. When action is involved and hardship successfully imposed in the spirit of payback, it seems natural to say that punishment was inflicted.

Whether you are justified in doing what you have done is another matter. When one person punishes another, formally or informally, the question "Was it justified (or just)?" is always appropriate, given that not hurting others is a moral default position. But this does not affect the question of *whether* punishment occurred. Another example to consider is the punishment of lovers by lovers. Suppose a woman tells her partner that she has been having an affair. The partner leaves her, posts compromising photos of her online, and spreads lies about the abuse he suffered from her during their relationship. She goes into a depression, loses her job, and hears from friends that he is delighted by her downfall. She *feels* punished and indeed shamed. The person she saw for many years as her equal has become her judge and executioner. He has, in other words, assumed the mantle of authority, and she is pained not only by his lies but also by his sense of entitlement. Again, it seems natural to talk about punishment here.

A final example relates to children. It comes from George Eliot's *The Mill on the Floss* (2003), in which a thirteen-year-old boy, Tom Tulliver, hears from his younger sister, Maggie, that she neglected the rabbits he asked her to care for while he was away. They all died, and Tom is furious. He tells Maggie he doesn't love her, and she can't go fishing with him the next day. Ignoring her tears, he runs off to find his friend.

> Tom had been too much interested in his talk with Luke . . . to think of Maggie and the effect his anger had produced on her. He meant to punish her, and that business having been performed, he occupied himself with other matters, like a practical person. But when he had been called in to tea, his father said, "Why, where's the little wench?" . . .

"I don't know," said Tom . . .

"You go and fetch her down, Tom," said Mr Tulliver, rather sharply . . . "And be good to her, do you hear? Else I'll let you know better."

Tom never disobeyed his father, for Mr Tulliver was a peremptory man, and, as he said, would never let anybody get hold of his whip-hand; but he went out rather sullenly, carrying his piece of plumcake, and not intending to reprieve Maggie's punishment, which was no more than she deserved. Tom was only thirteen, and had no decided views in grammar and arithmetic, regarding them for the most part as open questions, but he was particularly clear and positive on one point,—namely, that he would punish everybody who deserved it. Why, he wouldn't have minded being punished himself if he deserved it; but, then, he never did deserve it. (p. 42)

This beautifully ironic passage depicts the hubris of a boy who is growing into his socially ordained patriarchal role. He punishes his sister, not as the head of the family but as someone who is preparing for this position by gradually assuming his father's authority. He "never disobeyed his father," but nor does he submit to him exactly. His sullenness shows him not intending to reprieve Maggie's punishment or indeed to reprieve anyone he sees as deserving of punishment.

This (I suggest) is the punishment of a child by a child, and the authority that is built into the story is not formal but assumed or "donned." If children can punish children, they can presumably punish anyone, including their parents and teachers.[2] Disruptive behavior, rudeness, or defiance may be more than mischief or fun; they can be punitively motivated, involving an assumption of authority—however desperate or strained—over the authorities children see as letting them down by not fulfilling expectations or obeying rules adults expect children to obey. Children's behavior may have a further characteristic that is typical of punishers: a fierce resolve to inflict pain or hardship and a keen eye for signs of success and failure. We shall return to this.

Why do Peters and others insist that punishment must be formally authorized if the word is to be properly used? Why do they claim that informal punishment by neighbors, lovers, or children is only metaphorical? An answer to this question has been suggested to me. "The child punished her teacher" (it was said) is rather like "Football is a religion." No one believes that football is *really* a religion; when people speak this way, they mean that football inspires quasi-religious fervor. The punishment of teachers by children, similarly, is quasi-punishment. There are other metaphorical uses of the word. People talk about having a "punishing schedule," or they might describe their job as "punishment." In neither case is it suggested that pain or hardship is inflicted in response to a perceived wrongdoing.

But "The child punished her teacher" may have precisely these implications, and philosophical concerns are not resolved by making assertions about proper and metaphorical meaning. If someone says that abortion is wrong because it's murder, little will be gained polemically by asserting that the word "murder" is used metaphorically in this context. There is no dictionary in which literal and metaphorical meanings are separately classified, for language is and must be fluid, within and beyond generally accepted limits. It must be responsive to human purposes and perspectives; the borders between literal and metaphorical meaning are determinable only to a limited extent.[3]

If, as I suggest, children can punish, can they do so justly? What could justify a negative answer, so that while asserting that they can punish, we refuse to discriminate between just and unjust instances? Maybe the concept of justice is somehow too weighty for a child, and we need to find another way of describing the instances we approve of. A further question is whether children can punish at an age when they can only process thoughts in rudimentary ways. Can very young children punish? How old must they be—how cognitively advanced—to be able to don a mantle of authority? Might one prefer to say that *some* acts of punishment involve no assumption of authority at all? Is it enough for there to be infliction of pain or hardship, intended as payback for perceived wrongdoing?

I shall not attempt to answer all these questions. My aim is to explore and conceptualize the "punitive classroom": a setting in which emotions like anger and hostility inevitably (hopefully infrequently) occur between adults and children, and acts of punishment are performed, contemplated, avoided. We need to consider the impact of emotions on our practices if we are to think well about the ethics of punishment. Might adult punishment of children become "contaminated" (rarely, sometimes) by anger? If children *are* punished in anger by adults, are they justified in punishing back? Are they justified if adult anger is (as Seneca suggests) "mad"?

Punishment and revenge

A more promising answer to my question—Why is it believed that punishment in the true sense can only be exercised by authority figures?—is suggested by Richard Peters (1966) when he says that for an act to count as punishment

> The pain must be inflicted by someone in authority, who has a right to act this way. Without authority, it would be impossible to distinguish between "punishment" and "revenge." (p. 268)

The concern, I believe, is to create a firm boundary between two kinds of scenario. In the first, punishment is a social practice, administered (hopefully justly) by authority figures. Most schools in modern times are averse to the harsh treatment of children, so if punishment occurs, it tends to be mild and civilized: after-school detentions, deprivation of minor privileges, and so on.

The second kind of scenario is less civilized and more alarming. It is driven by emotions like anger, and although anger can be rational and its expression tempered, it can also exceed all reasonable bounds. Here is Seneca (1928, Book 1):

> You have demanded of me, Novatus, that I should write how anger may be soothed, and it appears to me that you are right in feeling especial fear of this passion, which is above all others hideous and wild: for the others have some alloy of peace and quiet, but this consists wholly in action and the impulse of grief, raging with an utterly inhuman lust for arms, blood and tortures, careless of itself provided it hurts another, rushing upon the very point of the sword, and greedy for revenge even when it drags the avenger to ruin with itself. Some of the wisest of men have in consequence of this called anger a short madness: for it is equally devoid of self control, regardless of decorum, forgetful of kinship, obstinately engrossed in whatever it begins to do, deaf to reason and advice, excited by trifling causes, awkward at perceiving what is true and just, and very like a falling rock which breaks itself to pieces upon the very thing which it crushes.

Revenge is drama, as this passage flamboyantly shows, and it is rightly feared for it can inspire atrocities. It is an expression not only of anger but of intense anger that amounts to hatred and brings almost every vice in its train. It is greedy, obsessive, envious, proud. It is irrational and destructive, dragging "the avenger to ruin with itself" and "awkward at perceiving what is true and just." Revenge is the fascinating theme of many enduring literary works, from the ancient Greek dramatists to Shakespeare, Pinter, Albee, and many more. It holds us in its thrall in a way that school punishment rarely does, for it reveals an aspect of human nature that may be obscured until it emerges shockingly from the shadows. This is the aspect of humanity that dominates the politics of terror, and it appalls us, I think, not least because it reminds us of our own vengeful impulses.

In short, revenge seems like a far cry from what goes on in schools, where there is an expectation that children will be treated with fairness and respect however badly they behave. Punishment in schools, one hopes, is the expression of cool reflection by authority figures on justice and learning. Goodman says in this book, "Schools are not in the business of retribution," and she means, quite rightly, that it isn't the responsibility of teachers to ensure that children get their "just deserts." They are in the business of teaching rather than exacting penance, as vengeful people do.

But children need to learn about morality, and retributive punishment is presented by some scholars as a moral lesson, communicated practically rather than verbally for those who need this. The content of the lesson is suggested here:

> The best way to think of retributivism is as a view about free riding and equal liberty. We believe that all citizens are equal and should enjoy an equal liberty of action. The criminal offends against this basic social understanding, claiming for himself an unequal terrain of liberty. He implicitly says, I will steal, and you will continue to obey the law. I will rape, and nobody will rape me. . . . Retributive punishment brings the offender to book for that claim of unequal liberty: it says, no, you are not entitled to an unequal liberty, you will have to accept the limits that are compatible with a like liberty for others. (Nussbaum, 2004, 238)

Bringing offenders (criminal or childish) to book transmits the message: you are *not* entitled; you must, if you want to be a respected member of society, accept the limits that you expect others to obey. If a teacher has tried and failed to teach this difficult lesson, she may feel that the time has come to place the child in detention or withdraw privileges. In such a case, it may be right to describe punishment as an expression of cool reflection, not to be confused with revenge.

However, it is one thing to distinguish between punishment and revenge conceptually, and another to suppose that we can always distinguish them on the ground. It is the ground (e.g., the home or classroom) that matters practically and ethically. This is a complex place that sometimes manifests the dark side of human relations, in which expectations of respect and care are unfulfilled and anger or hatred soars. People who feel uneasy about the punishment of children are unlikely to be impressed by conceptual distinctions, for they are concerned about human psychology, especially the psychology of anger and hatred and the visible or invisible power of these emotions to disrupt reason and permeate social practices.

Tom Tulliver illustrates the impact of psychology on practice and has no inkling of his feelings (pride, anger, contempt) when he resolves to punish "everyone who deserved it," including himself (except that luckily, he never did deserve it). Here a self-serving motive masks as a fair and impartial one, and

Tom is represented as exhibiting a common human failing: the tendency to rationalize one's feelings. Teachers do not, I am sure, normally think this way, but they experience anger and their patience can be sorely tested by children. Goodman quotes the following:

> Teacher and pupil confront each other with attitudes from which the underlying hostility can never be altogether removed. (Waller, 1932)

This is a gloomy and, I think, exaggerated assessment, but it would be pointless to deny that teachers can feel hostile to, or dislike, particular children. What then? This is one of the questions I set out to discuss.

The wish to maintain a sharp distinction between punishment and revenge cannot be maintained. Like Peters, Nussbaum (2004) tries to do this. Revenge, she writes, "is typically based on personal motives and has little concern [like punishment] with general social equality" (p. 238). But a personal wish for revenge can slip through the concern for social equality *on the ground*. When this happens the conviction that a child must suffer is augmented, and there may be suspicions that the adult is being harsh because of a personal dislike. The concept of punishment is deeper and broader than the concept of formal punishment as conducted by authority figures, and I shall make some suggestions about what this means.

"Punitive logics and emotions"

Not all philosophers and legal theorists try to keep punishment and revenge apart. Joel Feinberg (1965) quotes with approval J. F. Stephen's well-known remark: "The criminal law stands to the passion of revenge in much the same relation as marriage to the sexual appetite" (p. 403). Feinberg goes on to describe punishment as a "symbolic way of getting back at the criminal, of expressing a kind of vindictive resentment" (Feinberg, 1965). Here the desire for revenge is seen as a collective response to criminal wrongdoing, symbolically underpinning the attitude of "our community" toward offenders.

I agree, but our topic is not criminal punishment. These important observations have limited relevance to school punishment, for teachers do not normally feel vindictive resentment toward their pupils. If they did, we would all join the abolitionists I hope, for children have much to learn and as Dunne (forthcoming) says:

> [childhood is] a space in which both answerability to adult codes of propriety and the full force of commitment and consequence are eased or suspended.

We would be troubled by an approach that characterized children as hardened wrongdoers *as if* they were criminals, uncritically noting our vindictive resentment toward them.

Our concern here is with personal motive rather than symbolism, and punitive or vindictive motives are relevant to this enquiry in at least two ways. First, it is often argued that these *belong* to anger; without them, we cannot intelligibly speak about anger. To be angry (it is said) *is* to have vindictive or vengeful wishes, though these may be suppressed or undeclared. This has ethical implications for our enquiry.

Second, there is a good deal of evidence that punitive or vindictive motives are on the rise. Criminologists Carvalho and Chamberlen (2016) write:

> political rhetoric, the media and arguably the public are increasingly preoccupied with an impulse to see austere punishment practiced . . . punitive emotions can be alleged as motivating authorities to feel justified in using . . . state power before an individual has even reached the courtroom (e.g., in police custody or in immigration centres) . . . we can witness punitive logics and emotions in the areas of health, welfare and housing, schooling and higher education.

The growing "impulse to see austere punishment practiced" is a serious worry. This passage suggests that there is a surge of angry feeling in the modern world, influencing personal and institutional relations in many domains. The claim is supported empirically by many psychologists, sociologists, and criminologists,[4] as well as computer scientists and journalists who attribute this "punitive turn" to social media: a space that unleashes angry feelings by protecting identity and not holding people to account.[5] Carvalho and Chamberlen suggest, in effect, that punitive feelings toward children may be more prevalent than I have allowed.

I shall refer to the thoughts, feelings, and impulses associated with the angry wish to punish simply as "punitiveness." This includes the wish for revenge and vindictive resentment as discussed by Peters and Feinberg, as well as the "punitive logics and emotions" to which Carvalho and Chamberlen refer. The latter are right to suggest that punitiveness has a logic or structure, for it includes a cognitive core, an impetus toward action, heightened emotion. Punitiveness is the motivational underbelly of *some* acts of punishment. It is not always present; a desire to punish *can* be cool and reflective, motivated by a reasonable desire to maintain order through deterrence or to teach the moral lessons of retribution as discussed earlier. The wish to keep punishment and revenge apart is understandable; most of us recoil from the idea that we are *taking revenge* every time we punish child. However, those who oppose the punishment of children are right to suggest that punishment and revenge may overlap in troubling ways.

What *are* "punitive logics and emotions"? What is the structure of what I also call "punitiveness"? This brings us to the philosophical core of the chapter, which explores the relationship between punishment, anger, and the desire for revenge in order to address what I see as understandable moral unease about the punishment of children. In the space available, I can only sketch some possible answers.

I noted that philosophers like Peters (and there are many others) *need* to keep punishment practices and punitive feelings distinct, and this is at least part of the reason why the authority condition is preserved. As Peters says (quoted earlier): "Without authority, it would be impossible to distinguish between 'punishment' and 'revenge.'" The aim (I suggested) is to drive a wedge between justifiable punishment practices in institutional settings and the kind of vengeful behaviour that can escalate into what Seneca vividly describes as "inhuman lust for blood, arms and torture." But we do not have to drive this wedge, for punishment as ordinarily and unprescriptively understood can be, but need not be, vengeful. It is likely to be vengeful when practiced by non-authority figures like children, and I gave some examples of scenarios involving such figures where "punishment" seems like the right (if not the only) word to use. It can be vengeful when practiced by authority figures too; here we stray into the territory of bullying or abuse.[6] But the good news is that punishment can also be motivated by a sincere and reasonable desire to teach children about free riding and to maintain an orderly community or society. This is good news, specifically, for those who are skeptical about punishment *because* (they think) it may be vengeful.

Two points play worryingly into the skeptic's fears. First, teachers are sometimes angry with (or dislike) certain children. Second, anger is widely assumed to be a vengeful emotion. *If* anger is always vengeful, angry teachers are not to be trusted, for it is not a teacher's job (as Goodman, quoted earlier, notes) to exact penance from children. If this is the correct understanding of anger, punishment practices had better be abolished so that punishment doesn't become an institutionalized form of bullying or abuse.

But matters are more complicated than this, and it is time to turn to Aristotle and some contemporary discussion of anger and revenge. Aristotle's *Art of Rhetoric* (1991) is a handbook of spin; it aims to initiate orators into the persuasive arts. The method is to analyze the cognitive components of emotions in order to bring them under political control. If you want to assuage anger, mold the thoughts at anger's core, suggests Aristotle (1991), and he characterizes these thoughts as

> desire, accompanied by pain, for revenge for an obvious belittlement of oneself or one of one's dependants, the belittlement being uncalled for. (1378a)

The point being made in this hard-to-translate passage is that the "belittlement of oneself or one's dependants" need not be objective or real. Anger is provoked by the perception of, or belief in, belittlement, irrespective of whether it actually occurred. This is contained in the Greek *phainomenes*, meaning "appearance." "Obvious," in the passage above, does not capture this well, and other translations (e.g., "imagined," "conspicuous") are also unsatisfactory. Aristotle's point is a good one; we are angered by what we believe, perceive or imagine[7] to be true, and we are sometimes (perhaps often) mistaken.

To count as anger, then, a feeling must include a desire for revenge on another, whether taken by oneself, witnessed by another, or believed to have taken place elsewhere. Aristotle goes on to say that this includes both pain and pleasure:

> Being revenged is . . . pleasant. For it is pleasant to achieve anything in which it is painful to fail, and those who are angry are insuperably pained by the failing of revenge, though they are delighted by the expectation of it. (1378b)

If this is right, it will be impossible for teachers and parents to feel angry with children without wanting to take revenge on them. They may suppress or redirect this desire, but it will remain present in some form as part of their anger. Moreover, they must "delight" in the expectation of revenge and be "insuperably pained" when their vengeful impulses fail. If this is too strong (we may feel that it is basically correct but exaggerated), they must at least take satisfaction in the anticipation of revenge and be disappointed when the desire for revenge fails.

I believe Aristotle is right to suggest that vengeful anger focuses intensely on success and failure (I suggested earlier that vengeful people tend to be alert to *signals* of these) but wrong to suggest that all anger is vengeful. A great deal hangs on this for the ethics of punishing children. I want to defend my unAristotelian argument by returning to Martha Nussbaum (2016), who broadly accepts Aristotle's view but adds an interesting twist.

Anger, she says, "always involves, conceptually, a thought of payback" (p. 35). (By "payback" she means a kind of revenge.) So far, so Aristotelian. She then introduces a variant on anger that she calls transition-anger, which is forward-looking rather than backward-looking and focused on welfare or well-being rather than revenge. Transition-anger occurs when we rage against an egregious example of government behavior, and instead of indulging fantasies of revenge, we think, "Something must be done! " Anger is there in the sense that we are upset by and censorious of wrongdoing, but the retaliatory impulses that are an aspect of *ordinary* anger are replaced by attention to strategies for bringing about a "better future" that (argues Nussbaum) typify transition-anger.

The latter, it is implied, is the virtue toward which we should be cultivating our own and other people's ordinary, vengeful anger. Sadly, Nussbaum adds, it is "rare and exceptional." It is odd, then, to read that

> One place it flourishes is in parents' relationships with their young children. Their behaviour is often outrageous, and yet parents rarely want payback. They just want things to get better (p. 36).

Quite so, and I would suggest that non-vengeful anger also flourishes in schools. It is not true that anger *always* involves thoughts of payback (as Nussbaum asserts, then denies) or that transition-anger (as she says) is rare. I don't believe this is typically true of adults toward children, loving friends toward friends, or indeed many other generous-spirited people toward the objects of their anger. We do not need a *variant* of anger (almost a new species of feeling with its own label, "transition-anger") to make sense of this. We need to recognize that emotions deepen and evolve as part of the developments we call moral education and growth. As Iris Murdoch (1970) says: "we have a different image of courage at forty from that which we had at twenty. A deepening process, at any rate an altering and complicating process, takes place" (p. 29). For our conception of courage to differ at forty from what it was at twenty, we must have transformed our relationship to fear. Similarly, we must transform our relationship to anger if we are to overcome the punitive impulses that are typical of the young. This is what most teachers (certainly good teachers) have been doing during their lives, and it allows us to entrust children (including the punishment of children) to them.

In classrooms one expects to find primitive childish anger (unreflective, eager for revenge); childish anger that is more developed, more reflective, less focused on revenge; and finally, the anger of adults (and possibly some emotionally mature children) who have substantially transformed their understanding of justice and wrongdoing through reflection and experience. Anger evolves, in general, through the thoughts and feelings that are characteristic of love, affection, cherishing (see Cigman, 2018). Understood as akin to the Greek *philia*, these are not feelings but virtues, involving sincere effort, truthfulness, reflection, courage, and (a Kantian rather than Aristotelian virtue) unconditional respect.

"It is impossible to cherish another from the moral . . . high ground" (Cigman, 2018, 131), and this fatally compromises the authoritarian punisher's willingness to inflict pain in vengeful, self-righteous anger. It is *right* to expect teachers to exhibit certain virtues, and concerns about punishment in schools may arise from the sense that we aren't sufficiently attentive to these or the commitments they import.[8]

A desire for revenge is not required (as Aristotle and Nussbaum claim) for an emotion to constitute anger. What *is* required is a belief in or anticipation of harm or indignity for someone (oneself or another) or something one is deeply concerned about. This is what gives anger its pain and its power, along with its tenacious and escalating tendencies. Aristotle's anticipated pleasures of revenge may be unavailable to those who are powerless or oppressed (he is showing his male aristocratic assumption of privilege here); for many, anger simply means pain or distress.

Most teachers care deeply about young people's learning and thus are primed for anger toward anyone who disrupts or devalues their work. When children persistently do this, teachers may become desperate and lose their tempers from time to time. This is part of the *ground* that I set out to explore. Most of the time, no doubt, teachers reflect wisely and practice restraint, but things are not always so straightforward.

I want to close this section by taking forward the three-part account of punishment considered earlier. According to Peters and others, punishment is

i. the intentional infliction of pain or hardship.
ii. in response to perceived wrongdoing (or rule breaches).
iii. by an authority figure.

My earlier argument was that (iii.) must be modified as follows:

iv. by an authority figure or a person who has assumed authority over another in order to punish them

And I considered Feinberg's theory that (formal) punishment is

v. a symbolic communication of censure or vindictive resentment.

I then argued that acts of punishment are worrying when they enact (albeit unobtrusively) personal punitive motives. Modifying Aristotle, we may describe the "logic and emotions" of punitiveness by saying that it involves

(1) satisfaction or pleasure in the anticipated pain or hardship of another OR a wish and longing for these.

(2) pain when this anticipation or wish is not fulfilled OR pain because it could never have been fulfilled.
(3) keen alertness to signals of success and failure, that is, the fulfillment or unfulfillment of the anticipation or wish.

This allows that Aristotle's pleasure or delight in anticipated pain or hardship (or suffering) may be impossible because of a discrepancy of status or power. In such a case, revenge is a hollow dream.

Can children punish justly?

It follows from this discussion that if a child is to punish justly, she must be able to assume authority over others justly. Children aren't normally authority figures. Authority is not conferred on them except for particular purposes, like looking after younger children or playing a role on the school council. In such cases, it is recognized that they are *on their way* to being adults and that adulthood brings responsibilities, including the responsibility to exercise authority justly. As children grow older, authority may be conferred on them from time to time as preparation for adulthood and with it the right to punish in limited ways. This is proxy authority, and when children occupy this role, the question may arise whether or not they punish justly.

Sometimes children take upon themselves the status of an authority figure. This authority may not be approved by teachers or parents; we saw this in the excerpt from *Mill on the Floss*. Children who boss or bully other children exhibit a sense of unmerited entitlement; their acts of punishment are typically motivated by punitive thoughts, feelings, and impulses and indifferent to considerations of justice. Children who act as proxy authorities, on the other hand, may punish with precisely this aim, but more is required if they are to be described as punishing justly. I do not have space to explore in detail what "punishing justly" means, but the following might be seen as suggestions for consideration and review. The person who punishes justly is

- able to reflect and in general make sound moral judgments.
- able to appreciate that rules, promises, and expectations may be poorly regulated or unfulfilled, not from hostile intent but out of weakness or error.
- aware that regret and remorse can be forms of self-punishment, rendering other forms of punishment redundant.

- aware that punishment is a form of practical communication, to be used in general when other forms of communication fail.
- able to use other forms of communication (primarily conversation) as a constructive alternative to punishment.
- able to resist one's own punitive impulses in the interests of justice.
- aware that punishment should be sparing, mild, and used as a last resort.

This list is normative; it is about what, in my view, punishment *ought* to be, how the word *ought* to be used, and I agree with Duff (quoted earlier) that this is the fundamental question. The list applies to adults as well as children, and the point is that an agent of just punishment needs to be a responsible moral agent, capable of the reflective, behavioral, and emotional dispositions that are involved in wise action. Aristotle's virtue theory, developed by philosophers like Anscombe, Foot, MacIntyre, Dunne, and Sherman, explores these concepts and provides the basis for a robust conception of children's moral agency.

Not everyone will agree that punishment should only be used sparingly, mildly, and as a last resort. I believe this is justified by considerations that *rightly* preoccupy the skeptics and abolitionists: that the punishment of children, if practiced at all, must always be attentive to their well-being and learning. Harsh punishment can be lastingly detrimental—skeptics are right about this—whereas occasional mild punishment, non-vengefully motivated as a last resort, may act as a useful reality check and aid to learning.

Understandability

What about children who are confronted with clear and persistent infractions of rules or principles by authority figures? This catastrophic experience is not as rare as we would wish. Most of the online material about child abuse refers to the abuse of children by children, but there is evidence that the abuse of children by teachers is on the rise, especially in public schools and religious institutions. This puts young people in a horrific position, and if they act disruptively in order to punish their abusers, we can hardly blame them. Might "just punishment" be an appropriate description for what happens here?

I think not. The abused, disruptive child does not typically aim to further the cause of justice, except in a crude retributive sense. This is revenge, and although I would also call it punishment if (as argued) hardship or pain is intentionally and successfully inflicted, I don't think it is properly described as just. What the abused child does may be *understandable*. Given the seriousness of the provocation, we understand why she did what she did; we do not condemn it as we might in other circumstances. One might say her behavior was wrong in a sense and right in a sense; it breached rules, but so what? We may applaud the child's fortitude in standing up to her abuser and say that she was right to assume authority *over her body* when this authority was maliciously denied. It is important to have an ample vocabulary here, so we can articulate our combined sense of rightness and wrongness with sensitivity to the circumstances and individuality of the child. The behavior was excusable, for example, given the discrepancy of power, not to mention appropriate, acceptable, even dignified. Some might want to use the word "forgivable," particularly if there are very bad consequences for other children.

Understandability is not necessarily about actions; I may find (or fail to find) a child's thoughts, wishes, or emotions understandable. The specific form of understandability under consideration here is transgressional, arising when a child breaches rules or behaves disruptively or offensively, prompting adults to consider punishment as a response. I am suggesting that transgressional understandability needs a conceptual footing in ethical classrooms, which are likely to include "punitive logics and emotions," formal but last resort acts of punishment, and inevitably in the modern age, questions and justifications. Transgressional understandability embraces other (particularly emotional) kinds of understandability, and this concept enables us to refine our uncertainties about punishment by considering when and why it may be inappropriate to punish. It is an occasion for reflection, leniency, and compassion.

Acknowledgments

My thanks to Joseph Dunne and the editors of this book for many helpful comments on earlier drafts of this chapter.

Notes

1 See, e.g., https://intouchparenting.com/punishment-5-negative-consequences/.
2 It would be odd to suggest that children can be agents of punishment, but that their targets cannot be above a certain age or have certain roles. I believe this becomes clearer as the meaning of punishment is probed (as I attempt to do here) beyond formal practices.

3 On this point, see Crary (2007) and Murdoch (1970).
4 See, e.g., Brown et al. (2005); Munn (2020) passim.
5 See, e.g., https://www.theguardian.com/lifeandstyle/2019/may/11/all-fired-up-are-we-really-living-angrier-times.
6 I would argue that we must explore this territory if we are to fulfill our conceptual duties of care toward the young.
7 "Imagined" (used by Nussbaum, op cit.) does not work, because it misleadingly suggests that the belittlement must be imaginary rather than real.
8 Murdoch (1970) addresses these issues illuminatingly.

References

Aristotle (1991) *The Art of Rhetoric*, trans. H. C. Lawson-Tancred. London: Penguin.

Carvalho, Henrique and Chamberlen, Anastasia (2016) "Punishment, Justice and Emotions." In M. Tonry (ed.), *Oxford Handbook Online in Criminology and Criminal Justice*. Oxford: Oxford University Press. Online.

Cigman, Ruth (2018) *Cherishing and the Good Life of Learning: Ethics, Education, Upbringing*. London: Bloomsbury.

Crary, Alice (2007) *Beyond Moral Judgement*. Cambridge, MA: Harvard University Press.

Duff, AKA Antony (2003) *Punishment, Communication, and Community*. Oxford: Oxford University Press.

Eliot, George (2003) *The Mill on the Floss*. London: Penguin Classics.

Feinberg, Joel (1965) "The Expressive Function of Punishment." *The Monist* 49: 3.

Goodman, Joan (2022) (this volume), "Should School Children Be Punished?"

Munn, Luke (2020) passim "Angry by Design: Toxic Communication and Technical Architectures." *Humanities and Social Sciences Communications* 7.

Murdoch, Iris (1970) *The Sovereignty of Good*. London: Routledge and Kegan Paul.

Nussbaum, Martha (2004) *Hiding from Humanity: Disgust, Shame, and the Law*. Princeton, NJ: Princeton University Press.

Nussbaum, Martha (2016) *Anger and Forgiveness: Resentment, Generosity, Justice*. Oxford: Oxford University Press.

Peters, Richard (1966) *Ethics and Education*. London: Allen and Unwin.

Pratt, John., Brown, David., Brown, Mark., Hallsworth, Simon. and Marrison, Wayne. (eds.) (2005) *The New Punitiveness: Trends, Theories, Perspectives*. Cullompton: William Publishing.

Seneca, Lucius Annaeus (1928) "On Anger." In *Moral Essays*, vol. 1, trans. John W. Basore. London: W. Heinemann. 106–355.

Waller, Willard (1932) *The Sociology of Teaching*. New York: John Wiley.

Part IV

Exploring Alternatives to Punishment

11

What We Talk About When We Talk About Punishments and Consequences

Avi I. Mintz

The people who advise teachers about classroom management and parents about discipline differ on many issues. They debate the efficacy and ethics of time-outs, reward charts, and routines, among other things. But there is near-universal agreement among the parenting and classroom management experts[1] on one topic: consequences are an important tool for guiding minors' behavior, whereas punishments ought to be avoided.

Even a casual perusal of resources for parents and teachers reveals how entrenched this advice has become. Looking at the titles of articles alone, teachers are told to embrace "Consequences Instead of Punishment" (Webster, 2019) and are advised to differentiate "Punishment vs. Logical Consequences" (*Responsive Classroom Blog*, 2011) so they can avoid the former. Sometimes related distinctions are offered. Perhaps classroom management involves discipline, but discipline need not involve punishment. That, at least, is the case made in "The Difference Between Discipline and Punishment" (Morin, n.d.), "Aiming for Discipline Instead of Punishment" (Desautels, 2018), and elsewhere.

Parents encounter remarkably similar advice, only with examples drawn from the home rather than school. Experts ask parents, "Do You Know the Difference Between Punishment and Consequences?" (Orlans, 2015); "What's the Difference Between Punishments and Consequences?" (Davis, n.d.); or "Punishments vs. Consequences: Which Are You Using?" (Pincus, 2019). These articles encourage the use of consequences and advise that punishments be reserved for oppressing prisoners in a soviet gulag. I exaggerate (though less than one might hope) but one cannot help but read the treatment of punishments and consequences in these articles as little more than a dichotomy between a good parenting practice and a harmful one, a consensus that clearly emerges in "The Difference Between a Consequence and a Punishment" (Cummings, 2018); "Consequences versus Punishment" (Levy,

2018); "Natural Consequences: Redefining Punishments for Kids" (Riebling, 2020); "The Difference Between Punishment and Natural Consequences" (Levy, 2016); and "The Difference Between Consequences and Punishments for Kids" (Morin, 2019). There are countless other examples I could add to this list (and below I discuss others and explore further some of the aforementioned sources).

On what basis are punishments and consequences distinguished in the classroom management and parenting discourse? In this chapter, I identify six issues that are frequently invoked in the advice literature to support endorsing consequences over punishments. I then show that all six fail to do so. Nevertheless, some of the concerns that experts identify and graft onto punishments and consequences are well-founded educational insights, and I conclude by exploring those.[2]

Punishments and consequences: A distinction without a difference?

Though the distinction between punishments and consequences is treated as settled in the advice literature, there are occasionally dissenters. Dennis Arjo recounts a conversation with a teacher who described punishments in her classroom but then quickly corrected herself and said "consequences" while rolling her eyes, conveying that she believed the difference is merely semantic (Arjo 2016, 113–14). Arjo, a scholar whose work I draw on further, agrees with that teacher. But perhaps punishments and consequences are conceptually distinct. Let us consider some of the ways people have made that case.

Punishments involve outcomes imposed by parents or teachers, consequences do not

In *Emile*, Jean-Jacques Rousseau imagines a defiant child, or maybe just a mischievous or curious one, who breaks his bedroom window. What should his caregiver do in response? Rousseau expected that his eighteenth-century readers—much like many parents today—would react with anger. They might yell at the child, spank him, isolate him in a room, or take away some object or privilege he enjoys. But Rousseau says such an approach is wrongheaded. The boy broke his window? Then "let the wind blow on him night and day without worrying about colds. . . . Never complain about the inconveniences he causes you, but make him feel those inconveniences first" (Rousseau, 1762/1979, 100).

Rousseau used this example to articulate a new way of thinking about discipline: "punishment as punishment must never be inflicted on children, but it should always happen to them as a *natural consequence* of the bad action" (Rousseau, 1762/1979, 101; emphasis added).

Many of Rousseau's readers saw the wisdom in this distinction. Immanuel Kant, whose *Lectures on Pedagogy* reflect a deep engagement with Rousseau's *Emile*, similarly says that punishment can be of two sorts. A "*natural* punishment," the "best" type of punishment, is something that a person "brings upon himself by his behavior—for example, that the child becomes sick when it eats too much." In contrast, "*artificial*" punishment occurs when the child or adolescent is chastised by the adult's disapproval or use of physical force (Kant, 1803/2007, 470; emphasis in original). Rousseau and Kant believed that when authority figures impose outcomes, they often teach the wrong lesson. Rather than facilitate autonomy and the ability to recognize what is problematic about one's behavior, punishments draw children into a battle of wills with their guardians. Was the minor's behavior problematic because it was not in the child's best interests or, rather, because it displeases the authority figure? Punishments obscure the issue. Better to eliminate authority from the equation, if possible.

Consider a frequent topic of concern for parents of younger children: picky eaters. Experts often advise serving the picky eater diverse foods rather than deferring to their preferences. Additionally, they advise limiting snacks before meals, as a greater appetite leads to a more adventurous palette. Some experts also advise praising children for trying new things or creating a rule that a child must take at least one bite from each food served to them.

What happens if the picky eater leaves the meal after refusing to sample any of the carefully prepared, diverse foods (regardless of whether there was a rule that she must)? She would suffer a natural consequence: hunger. An unnatural consequence would involve the authority imposing something unpleasant by scolding her or denying her of a desired item or experience. This picky eater case appears to support distinguishing punishments and natural consequences.

A critic might say that there are few cases where such natural consequences follow from a child's action. After all, parents and teachers are interested in shaping human beings, and in most cases, there is nothing natural about the behaviors we encourage or discourage. Is there something natural that occurs if one doesn't make one's bed in the morning? Or complete a geometry project by its deadline? Or join one's classmates in song during music class? And sometimes, even when natural consequences are possible, they would be unadvisable. As Arjo notes, "natural consequences can be unacceptably harsh—letting a child learn for herself why she should not play in traffic would amount to criminal negligence. Just as importantly, natural consequences can teach the *wrong* lesson, as in the case of a successful theft" (Arjo, 2016, 116).

However, if there were some cases—even an exceedingly small set of cases—where natural consequences were an ethical way of influencing a child or adolescent, consequences and punishments may be distinct. But are there? Even the seemingly clear case of the picky eater, I would suggest, does not avoid authority. Compare the picky eater as child to the adult picky eater. Say an adult picky eater is invited out to dinner at a friend's house. The meal comprises foods that the picky eater not only does not care for but finds repulsive. What might the adult do? Perhaps he'd push the food around on his plate to mask the fact that it was uneaten. Then, after the meal, the picky eater would go home and eat whatever he wants, if he hadn't already stopped for something on the way home.

Like the adult, a young child may decide to pass on eating the meal. Unlike the adult, a young child lacks the ability to procure food for herself. Perhaps at the next meal the child succumbs to her hunger and eats more of what her parents wanted her to eat. She has conformed to their ideal of a good eater, just as they hoped. But if she holds out longer, is she fighting against nature? Or is she, instead, fighting the constraints imposed upon her by her parents? I would suggest that since the parents in this case—just like parents and teachers in all cases where natural consequences are designed to influence behavior—are controlling the process, there is no meaningful conceptual distinction between punishments and consequences.

Parents and teachers are in a unique relationship with minors. Their authority is legitimate because exercising it serves minors' developmental interests; it helps minors cultivate capacities that will enable them to better manage their own lives. When parents and teachers contrive situations where minors experience "natural consequences," authority is unavoidably at play.[3] Since both punishment and natural consequences involve adults making decisions about what minors must suffer, the presence of authority and imposition does not distinguish consequences and punishment.[4]

This does not mean, however, that when a parent wants to help a child develop a more sophisticated palette or influence any other behavior, no strategy is better than another. The appeal to natural consequences is based on a well-founded psychological insight: the more an outcome seems to be based on an authority's whim, the more likely it teaches the wrong lesson. Rather than helping a child expand her palette, an "unnatural consequence" might teach solely that the parent is to be obeyed.

Punishments involve arbitrary relations between misbehaviors and outcomes, consequences do not

If natural consequences do not avoid authority as experts often assert, perhaps consequences and punishments can be distinguished on other grounds. Many experts argue that teachers and parents should embrace "logical" consequences (rather than "natural" ones). The difference, as one parenting expert puts it, is that "natural consequences are behavior outcomes that are not necessarily planned by anyone... [whereas] logical consequences are behavior outcomes that are specifically planned by parents and other adults" (Pincus, 2019). Advocates of logical consequences recognize that authority is inevitable (and perhaps even valuable). What makes a consequence logical is, above all else, that it is closely related to the problematic behavior, an idea that recurs in the expert advice ("Logical consequences are related to the child's behavior; punishment usually is not"; *Responsive Classroom Blog* 2011). If punishments are arbitrary while logical consequences are related to the problematic behavior, perhaps we have found grounds for the distinction.

Returning to the picky eater example, hunger is a more logical consequence than losing screen time insofar as it is more closely related to the problematic behavior. The minor who expands her palette because of the fear of lost screen time may not learn that it is worthwhile to try new foods as much as embrace the benefit of compliance. When there exists a close relationship between the targeted behavior and the consequence, the consequence will be more effective because the value of change will be more apparent to minors.

This may seem like a strong foundation for distinguishing punishments and consequences. Unfortunately, it is not. Punishments are not necessarily arbitrary. Indeed, a spectrum of punishments exists; some are related to problematic behaviors while some are not. The same is true for consequences, of course. Parents and teachers propose all sorts of "logical" consequences for problematic behaviors, and some are far more arbitrary than others. The issue is whether an imposed outcome is arbitrary; arbitrariness is neither constitutive of punishments nor consequences. (I consider some examples of arbitrary outcomes in the final section.) Thus other grounds for the distinction must be explored.

Punishments involve pain, consequences do not

Often in the advice literature, the distinction between consequences and punishments is based on the presence of pain. One expert writes, "Punishment is visiting something painful (physically or emotionally) on the child in the hopes that he will behave as we'd like in the future to avoid more punishment"

(Markham, n.d.). Another says, "The goal for giving consequences is to teach a lesson that leads to positive choices.... The definition of punishment is to cause to suffer. The goal is to inflict hurt, pain, and get even" (Orlans, 2015).

Is inflicting pain or suffering constitutive of punishment and absent in consequences? Consequences and punishments are both employed to change behaviors that parents or teachers deem undesirable. No one suggests that consequences, even natural consequences, are a positive experience for minors. In the two examples I've discussed so far, both the cold air from the broken window and the picky eater's hunger are by design negative experiences. Are they painful for the child? They must, at the very least, be unpleasant. But one could make the case that outcomes are often far more than that. Upon recognizing that they have disappointed a parent or teacher, many children feel acute embarrassment, guilt, or shame. Pain is clearly not only physical, and one should not lightly dismiss children's emotions. As I have argued elsewhere, students experience various kinds of pain in the process of learning and, when educators fail to recognize this fact, they risk causing students even more serious harm (Mintz, 2017).

The child's pain, therefore, cannot support a distinction between punishments and consequences because pain is experienced in either case. Perhaps, however, the experts might counter that they are concerned with a specific type of pain, one that arises from condemnation—and which occurs during punishment but is absent from consequences. But is condemnation absent from consequences? Parents and teachers impose outcomes because they hope to change minors' behavior. All outcomes therefore involve disapproval and condemnation. Any outcome that minors incur carries with it—whether explicitly or implicitly—the message that their behavior must change. If there is nothing to condemn, we would not be searching for appropriate outcomes.[5]

Punishments are retributive, consequences are not

Related to the idea that punishment involves inflicting pain is the claim that punishment is solely aimed at retribution. Consequences, on the other hand, are claimed to be imposed with developmental progress in mind. One expert writes, "parents and teachers don't like to admit that, often, the main reason they like to use punishment is to demonstrate their power to win over the child or to gain revenge by making the child suffer" (Nelson, n.d.). Another describes punishment as trying to "change kids' future behavior by making them 'pay for their mistakes'" while a "logical or natural consequence . . . aims to change behavior by helping kids learn from their mistakes," thus putting "kids in control of their behavior and decisions by teaching new skills, such as self-control and self-regulation" (Morin, n.d.). One expert puts it as follows: "A punishment is retribution (or vengeance) for a wrongful act. Punishment says to your child: you'd better think like me, or else. If you don't, I will make you pay (or suffer) until you make the choice I want you to make" (Pincus, 2019).

If punishment was inflicted solely as retribution for misbehavior, the experts would be right to say that teachers and parents should avoid punishing minors. There are scholars who argue that punishment in general should often be retributive (some of whom are uncomfortable empowering society's legal institutions to reshape citizens' character). However, other scholars argue that punishment ought to be rehabilitative. In the context of schools and homes, we ought to use the term "educative" rather than "rehabilitative"; among the measures of a legitimate outcome in schools or homes is that it ought to help students develop more robust self-control, cultivate their autonomy, and improve their decision-making.

Punishments can be retributive, but they are not necessarily so. Even those who use corporal punishment have sometimes claimed that they act in minors' long-term interest, empowering them to navigate their world more competently. In many societies, and in most historical eras, corporal punishment was widely embraced as integral to good parenting and teaching ("spare the rod, spoil the child"). Many of those parents and teachers were not primarily interested in retribution; they were invested in minors' development. Moreover, calling an outcome a consequence does mean that there was no retribution involved. The decision not to provide alternate foods to the picky eater may be made based on educative goals. But other parents could impose that same outcome as retribution.

Once again we see that one way of grounding the distinction between punishments and consequences fails to hold up. But we ought to note that the distinction arises amid concerns about what principles ought to guide the selection of outcomes. Better outcomes are educative and to the extent that an outcome is imposed as "payback," it is much less likely to be educative. But the caution against retribution is related to foregrounding authority in the outcome. When authority is central, the motive behind the imposition of the outcome is more likely to be retribution.

Punishments compel compliance, consequences do not

Punishment is sometimes assumed to be aimed at compelling compliance while consequences facilitate autonomy. Punishment is when "the powerful person can inflict some form of pain or suffering on the weaker person, in order to force them into submission," writes one expert (Schrieber Levy, 2016.). Another writes, "the goal of punishment is to enforce compliance with the rules by using external controls or authoritarian discipline.... The goal of logical consequences is to help children develop internal understanding, self-control, and a desire to follow the rules" (*Responsive Classroom Blog*, September 2011). Similar sentiments can be found elsewhere; "the motivation behind a punishment comes from a place of emotion and a need to maintain control" (Cummings, 2018) and "punishment is used to try to force compliance" (Desautels, 2018). Another writes, "we define a punishment as what is done to us (detentions, suspensions, checkmarks on public boards, calls home), and a consequence as what we do to ourselves (learning new behavior, helping others)" (Curwin, 2012).

If among the aims of schooling and childrearing is preparing minors to increasingly assume responsibility over their lives, mere compliance would be problematic. A childhood spent dominated by fear of displeasing authoritarian figures is miserable—just about as far from optimal conditions for flourishing than one could imagine. Moreover, how can minors develop their ability to make reasonable, autonomous choices about their lives if they lack the opportunity to practice doing so prior to adulthood?

We must first ask: Do teachers and parents punish primarily or solely for the sake of compliance? I think that it is reasonable to conclude many punishments are indeed designed to compel compliance; they are designed to have minors behave in accordance with the authority's vision of an ideal individual or community member. Even if compliance is not the primary goal of punishment, compliance tends to result.

If compliance is ethically and developmentally problematic, and compliance tends to be the outcome of punishment, perhaps we have found grounds for the distinction between punishments and consequences. Unfortunately, every word I wrote in the previous paragraph can be said of consequences as well. Parents and teachers impose consequences to encourage behavior that accords with their vision of an ideal individual or community member. Regardless of the teacher's or parent's intent, compliance is often the result of consequences. Thus, compliance is no more intrinsic to punishments than it is to consequences.

One further point is worth noting on this question of compelling compliance versus facilitating autonomy. Dennis Arjo points out (drawing on Jean Hampton) that punishment signifies participation in the moral world. Thus, "punishment is not inherently at odds with autonomy." Indeed, "it assumes it" (Arjo, 2016, 122–3).

Punishments are excessive and inequitable, consequences are not

Some experts suggest consequences are related to the misbehavior, respectful of the minor, reasonable for the minor to carry out, and, ideally, clearly revealed in advance, whereas punishments are none of those (Nelson, 2006; Anderson, 2018). Others echo this emphasis: "consequences are reasonable and realistic when they relate to the situation and are neither too harsh nor too lenient" (Charney, 2011). This expert understanding of consequences mirrors what scholars have sometimes said of legitimate punishments. As Randall Curren notes, a scholarly consensus has emerged that punishment should not be excessive, inequitable, or arbitrary (Curren, 2020, 117). If consequences avoid the three flaws and these flaws tend to be features of punishments, it would support a distinction between the two. In my discussion of logical consequences earlier, I challenged the claim that consequences are related to the problematic behavior while punishments are arbitrary. I will now consider inequitable and excessive outcomes.

Corporal punishment has long been criticized as excessive. Suppose Rousseau's window-breaker was governed by a different sort of person. Corporal punishment was deemed reasonable in the eighteenth century for far lesser offenses. Even those—historically and today—who employ corporal punishment identify some corporal punishment as excessive. Thus, striking a minor with a paddle, belt, or switch has been argued by some to be needlessly excessive whereas a spanking may be acceptable. But even non-corporal punishment can be excessive.

Suppose a child is hitting classmates and is punished with a time-out. A time-out of an appropriate duration may be reasonable (a popular rule of thumb recommends one minute per year of a child's age). But what if the time-out lasted an hour? Or two? Such a time-out would be excessive.

Are consequences ever excessive? Imagine a teacher devoted to employing consequences. How might he respond to a student who hits a classmate? He might impose a time-out. (Though, as time-outs have fallen out of fashion, the same outcome might go by a different name—perhaps another distinction without a difference.) After all, in a moment away from classmates, the student might have an opportunity to calm down, to reflect upon harms caused, and to consider how to make the situation right. But, just as with time-outs as punishments, the time-out as consequence could be excessive if the duration was too long. Since a consequence can be excessive just like a punishment, and a punishment might not be excessive, excessiveness is not an intrinsic feature of punishments.

Likewise, being inequitable is not an intrinsic feature of punishments and a failure to be equitable can occur among imposed consequences. In many countries, school disciplinary practices are inequitable. Suspensions and detentions are inequitably distributed by race, gender, and socioeconomic status. Do consequences avoid the problem? They do not. First, suspensions and detentions can be and are often deemed consequences. Second, "consequences" like time-outs are just as likely to be unevenly assigned by gender, race, and socioeconomic class as suspensions and detentions. One expert recognizes the risk and warns that inequitable consequences may morph into punishments: "consequences that are not perceived as fair or are not delivered consistently, can become punishing" (Antayá-Moore, 2008).

Once again, a familiar issue is at the heart of this discussion. An outcome that is not closely related to the misbehavior is problematic, regardless of whether it is called a punishment or consequence. Excessive outcomes are, in a sense, arbitrary; if the picky eater were denied food for an entire day after a meal, that would be excessive and also arbitrary as the "natural" time for the outcome to end would arguably be at the next typical meal or snack time.

Authority, arbitrariness, and outcomes

The "natural consequence" seems to be the holy grail of disciplinary systems. If a minor forgets to take her jacket to school or leaves it inside during recess, she will be cold. "Natural consequences" are appealing because, for one thing, the outcome—being cold—is directly related to the behavior—forgetting the jacket. The outcome is not arbitrary. The girl need not be scolded or forced to miss the next recess. Hence the outcome is educative; the value of a jacket becomes clear because the child feels the discomfort of its absence. What would the child learn if she was scolded or had to miss the next recess? Perhaps a different lesson: that it displeases her parent or teacher when she does not wear a jacket. The lesson is, therefore, that she ought to keep the authority figures in her life happy. This lesson points to the other thing that is important about a "natural consequence"—it removes authority from the equation significantly (but not entirely, as I argued earlier). When the girl feels cold, she is most likely to feel displeasure with her carelessness. If the girl lost recess time, she would just as likely become upset with the person who imposed the ban as with herself. Thus, parenting and classroom management experts are right to idealize an outcome that involves relatively little authority and is closely related to the problematic behavior.

Unfortunately, as I pointed out and as many experts concede, most outcomes are not "natural" in this way. They involve an outcome that is more arbitrary and is imposed more clearly by an authority figure. Consider a common classroom example. An elementary student runs around the class tipping over chairs and knocking workbooks off other children's desks. A "natural consequence" for this behavior is difficult to identify. What might "naturally" happen to a child who makes this sort of mess without any outcome imposed by an adult? Perhaps the other children would yell at him, contain him, or strike him. None of those are ideal. One might hope that the child would "naturally" want to clean up after himself. Is that a natural response though? Next time you walk through a parking lot, peek inside car windows. You will see that a car interior often resembles a frat house after a party—fast food wrappers, used napkins, and a vast array of items on the floors and seats. Cleaning up after oneself is far from a universal predilection, however much one might wish it to be. Is there a way that the behavior could be addressed where the outcome would be related to the misbehavior and would minimize the authority involved?

One solution might involve a well-established classroom rule that would prompt the student to address the misbehavior, something along the lines of "right wrongs"—that is, rectify situations in which you have harmed others. If there was such a well-established rule in the class, and a classroom culture where students reflected upon the rule when they recognize their actions are problematic and then act upon it, the student might be inclined to clean up the room. If this occurred, the result would be educative in just the way that the experts idealize—the student would autonomously exercise self-control in a way that might help him avoid similar situations in the future. Perhaps the teacher might need to prompt the student to reflect on the situation or class rule, but prompting a student into self-reflection would involve relatively little authority compared to a teacher who directly imposed an outcome.

If we were to plot outcomes according to the extent to which authority is involved and how arbitrary they are (in terms of the relation of the outcome to the infraction) as I do in Figure 11.1, this situation of the student reflecting on his misbehavior and then identifying and embracing an appropriate outcome [B] would lie in the same quadrant as the holy grail examples of natural consequences like when a forgotten coat means results in a cold child [A].

In the classroom mess case, a classroom rule might still minimize the authority involved but results in embracing an outcome that is more arbitrary. A classroom rule stating, "if you've done something that negatively impacts the

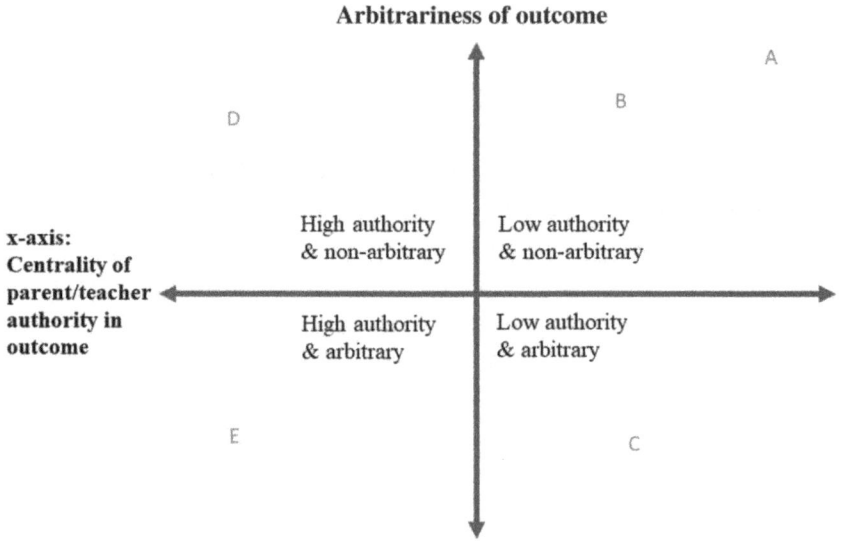

Figure 11.1 Plotting outcomes according to authority and arbitrariness. A: forgotten rain jacket, outcome is that the child is wet and cold. B: classroom mess: student cleans it, adhering to well-established rule to "right wrongs" and/or as a result of reflection upon misbehavior. C: classroom mess: student reads silently at recess, adhering to well-established rule to read silently at recess if student negatively impacts classroom community. D: classroom mess: teacher compels student to clean classroom. E: classroom mess: teacher compels student to read silently at recess.

classroom community, you must stay indoors, reading silently at recess." This case [C] would fall in the lower right quadrant. It has the virtue of minimizing authority, but the outcome is arbitrary. It is less educative in that it fails to provide an opportunity to the student to reflect on the misbehavior and to develop capacities for addressing problematic behavior. (It would also imply that reading is unpleasurable which is a considerable liability, along with denying recess to the students who likely need it most.)

Another situation [D] might address the problem of arbitrariness but rely on authority (unlike case [A]): the teacher commands the student to restore order to the classroom. In this case, the outcome is no longer arbitrary, but the authority is high. Around [D], as in any of the other cases, different variables would result in different placement. For example, authority would be slightly minimized if the teacher presented the student with a few options of how or when to clean the classroom. Or other outcomes might be proposed that are less directly related, like written apologies to classmates whose chairs or books were disturbed.

Least ideal would be a situation wherein the teacher's authority is high and the outcome is arbitrary: for example, the teacher commands the student to stay inside at recess reading silently [E]. When outcomes move toward the lower left quadrant, they are increasingly at risk of lacking legitimacy and failing to be educative.

Conclusion

I have argued that punishments versus consequences is a distinction without a difference. But I have also argued that two issues—authority and arbitrariness—lie at the heart of many of the attempts to distinguish them. The extent to which outcomes minimize the confrontation with authority and are related to the misbehavior does indeed matter; those outcomes will be more educative in that they help students develop self-control, improve their decision-making, and generally cultivate capacities that will help them manage their lives well as adults and community members. But one might concede that and still say that we should call outcomes for minors' misbehavior "punishments" if they are arbitrary and unreasonably foreground authority and call them "consequences" if not.

Have I simply offered a new way of grounding the distinction? Instead of arguing that there is no conceptual difference between punishments and consequences, perhaps I might suggest that one should label outcomes in the upper right quadrant "consequences" and deem outcomes that fall in the other three quadrants punishments.[6]

I nevertheless believe we ought to reject the distinction between punishments and consequences. First, arbitrariness and authority are never simply absent or present; they exist on a spectrum. As I argued earlier, authority is present in all imposed outcomes because minors are under the care of an adult who devises the outcome and could choose to intervene at any time. Likewise, the degree to which an outcome is related to the misbehavior is rarely perfect. Even in cases where an "eye for an eye" relationship could be identified, such an outcome would be undesirable. (If a student makes a mess in the classroom, few people would think a reasonable outcome would be for the other students to make a mess of the misbehaving students' possessions.) Instead, parents and teachers ought to search for outcomes that are most likely to be educative.

Second, any parent or teacher who embraces consequences and rejects punishments may achieve a false sense of security about the wisdom of their disciplinary practices. They are at risk of failing to recognize the complexities of any given case. As I have shown earlier, consequences can be problematic in the same way that punishments are. As the parenting and classroom management experts recognize, misbehavior can be an important occasion for learning or it can be fraught; it may bolster or threaten minors' mental health or relationships with parents and teachers. The outcome should not simply be labeled "consequence" and therefore believed to be in the minor's interests.

Third, for many teachers and parents, the appeal of consequences (and the disdain of punishments) is due to their reluctance to condemn minors' misbehavior and to impose their authority upon them. That reluctance has been central to the progressive educational tradition since Rousseau. However, as I have argued earlier, condemnation is intrinsic to outcomes. If the minor's behavior was desirable or unproblematic, there would be no need to impose outcomes. And, to reiterate, parents and teachers have authority over minors precisely because they are entrusted to shape their characters. Though the centrality of authority is problematic in outcomes, authority is the necessary condition for any disciplinary practice. Teachers and parents cannot free themselves of this precarious responsibility.

Fourth, distinguishing punishments and consequences is problematically based on parents' and teachers' perspectives of the outcome. It is all well and good for parents to feel confident about insisting that, upon receiving a call of concern from their child's school, that their child play in the cold at recess as a consequence of leaving her jacket at home. But the child may view the parent's decision not to deliver the jacket to school as an excessive or authoritarian punishment—the very sort of thing that the parent wanted to avoid imposing. Parents and teachers must be sensitive to the gap between their experiences and minors'.

For these reasons, parents and teachers ought to respond—as many already do—to a minor's misbehavior not by identifying consequences and punishments but, rather, by considering what kind of outcome is appropriate to the misbehavior while enabling the minor to assume some responsibility for addressing the misbehavior. The experts often offer sound advice about these sorts of outcomes. The extent to which outcomes foreground the authority who imposes it, and the extent to which outcomes are related to the problematic behavior, is important; reflecting upon these things can help guide teachers and parents toward more educative disciplinary decisions. These concerns are at the heart of devising educative outcomes and distinguishing punishments and consequences risks obscuring this important task.

Notes

1 I call "expert" anyone participating in the advice industry by publishing books, blogs, and magazine articles about classroom management or parenting. The experts discussed in this chapter range from individuals with PhDs to those writing based on personal experiences (and have a knack for engaging online readers). There are clearly differences in the advice offered—some are nuanced and sophisticated, some less so. However, consideration of expert advice is valuable for the purposes of this chapter because it both reflects and shapes society's understanding of punishments and consequences.

2 My focus in this chapter is on the classroom management and parenting discourse, a discourse which has virtually no contact with scholarship on the philosophy of punishment, which, generally, considers the criteria that may grant punishment legitimacy. Much of the scholarly discussion of punishment is rooted in the philosophy of law. For recent scholarly contributions on the legitimacy of punishment that focuses on schooling, see, e.g., Thompson et al. (2020) and the special issue of *Theory and Research in Education* in which it appears. See also the philosophical and historical (in an American context alone) of Scribner and Warnick (2021). See also Goodman (2006) for an argument that "punishment" should be reserved for cases that deal with moral and derivatively moral misbehavior alone. Arjo (2016, 121–3) bases a defense of punishment on its moral dimension as well (a dimension that, he argues, is obscured under the behaviorist, value-free idea of "consequence"). Yet several scholars are skeptical of the value of punishment much like in the popular expert discourse. Indeed, as I discuss further, the distinction emerged among educational philosophers, most notably in Rousseau's *Emile*. Many contemporary scholars continue to endorse the distinction. For example, Michael Hand recently wrote a paper justifying punishment for a certain set of rule violations in school—moral and scholastic rules of obligation (Hand, 2020). His embrace of, or at least acceptance of, the necessity of punishment was met with calls to distinguish punishments from "corrections, penalties, and discipline" (Goodman, 2020, 360 and 361) or from "informal or natural attempts at applying social pressure" (Martin, 2020, 356).

3 As Pieper and Pieper note in their book on parenting, "When you stand by and let bad things happen, your child experiences the twin disappointments that something went wrong and you did not seem to care enough about her to lift a finger to help prevent the mishap. The 'natural consequence' approach is really a form of punishment" (Pieper and Pieper, 1999, 208, cited in Scribner and Warnick, 2021, 20).

4 There exists a general consensus in the scholarly literature on schooling that the word "punishment" should be reserved for moral infractions alone (e.g., Goodman, 2006;

Scribner and Warnick, 2021). In the philosophy of law, the distinction of penalties (lacking moral condemnation) and punishments (involving moral condemnation) is generally accepted. Scribner and Warnick suggest that there is an analogous distinction between discipline and punishment in education (2021, 12). Though limiting punishment to moral concerns alone may be common in the scholarship, punishment in the parenting and classroom management advice literature refers to the imposition of outcomes for any undesirable behavior. Since my goal in this chapter is to address the advice literature discourse, I will continue to work with this broader definition of punishment that is not confined to moral concerns. But I might note that it is challenging to delineate the moral and nonmoral educational contexts. Even the education scholars who reserve the word "punishment" for immoral behaviors recognize how difficult it often is to distinguish violations of convention from moral infractions. For example, is a low grade simply a penalty (without any moral condemnation) or a way of conveying a moral message about effort or participation in the learning community? (Scribner and Warnick, 2021, 19).
5   As I mentioned in the previous note, I have not limited my definition of punishment in this chapter to that which involves moral condemnation, as many scholars do in the philosophy of law and the philosophy of education literature. In that literature, penalties or discipline foster social control absent of moral condemnation. But penalties and discipline, even when limited to the nonmoral, express disapproval of behavior.
6   Or one might suggest that one could draw a diagonal line from the top leftmost corner through to the bottom rightmost point (through the intersection of the x and y axes) and label those in the upper right half consequences and the left punishments.

References

Anderson, Mike (2018) "Getting Consistent with Consequences." *Classroom Management Reimagined* 76 (1): 26–33. Accessed through acsd.org.
Antaya-Moore, Dana (2008) *Supporting Positive Behaviour in Alberta Schools: A Classroom Approach*. Edmonton, Alberta: Alberta Education.
Arjo, Dennis (2016) *Paradoxes of Liberalism and Parental Authority*. Lanham, MD: Lexington Books.
Charney, Ruth Sidney (2011) "Logical Consequences Teach Important Lessons." *Responsive Classroom Strategies*.
Cummings, W. R. (2018) "The Difference between a Consequence and a Punishment." *PsychCentral.com*, September 27.
Curren, Randall (2020) "Punishment and Motivation in a Just School Community." *Theory and Research in Education* 18 (1): 117–33.

Curwin, Richard (2012) "How to Make Consequences Work." *Edutopia.org*, May 25.
Davis, Timothy (n.d.) "Discipline 101: What's the Difference Between Punishments and Consequences." *Challengingboys.com*. https://challengingboys.com/discipline-101-whats-the-difference-between-punishments-and-consequences/.
Desautels, Lori (2018) "Aiming for Discipline Instead of Punishment." *Edutopia.org*, March 1.
Goodman, Joan F. (2006) "School Discipline in Moral Disarray." *Journal of Moral Education* 35 (2): 213–30.
Goodman, Joan (2020) "Commentary: Michael Hand's 'On the Necessity of School Punishment.'" *Theory and Research in Education* 18 (3): 359–63.
Hand, Michael (2020) "On the Necessity of School Punishment." *Theory and Research in Education* 18 (1): 10–22.
Kant, Immanuel (1803/2007) "Lectures on Pedagogy." In Paul Guyer and Allen W. Wood (eds.), *Anthropology, History, and Education*, 434–85. Cambridge: Cambridge University Press.
Levy, Terry (2018) "Consequences versus Punishment." *EvergreenPsychotherapyCenter.com*, March 15.
Markham, Laura (n.d.) "Why Consequences Are Just More Ineffective Punishment." *AHAparenting.com*. https://www.ahaparenting.com/read/Consequences-Punishment.
Martin, Christopher (2020) "Punishment and the Argument from Necessity: A Reply to Hand." *Theory and Research in Education* 18 (3): 352–8.
Mintz, Avi I. (2017) "Pain and Education." In J. Corns (ed.), *The Routledge Handbook of Philosophy of Pain*, 344–53. New York: Routledge.
Morin, Amanda (n.d.) "The Difference Between Discipline and Punishment." *Understood.org*. https://www.understood.org/en/articles/the-difference-between-discipline-and-punishment.
Morin, Amy (2019) "The Difference Between Consequences and Punishments for Kids." *Verywellfamily.com*, Updated December 7.
Nelson, Jane (n.d.) "Logical Consequences." *Positivediscipline.com*. https://www.positivediscipline.com/articles/logical-consequences.
Nelson, Jane (2006) *Positive Discipline*. New York: Ballentine Books.
Orlans, Michael (2015) "Do you Know the Difference Between Punishment and Consequences?" *LinkedIn.com*, May 3.
Pieper, Martha H. and Pieper, William J. (1999) *Smart Love: The Compassionate Alternative to Discipline that Will Make You a Better Parent and Your Child a Better Person*. Boston, MA: Harvard Common Press.
Pincus, Debbie (2019) "Punishments vs. Consequences: Which Are You Using?" *EmpoweringParents.com*.
Responsive Classroom Blog (2011) "Punishment vs. Logical Consequences." *ResponsiveClassroom.org*, September 2.

Riebling, Renée Sagiv (2020) "Natural Consequences: Redefining Punishments for Kids." *Parents.com*, Updated December 21.

Rousseau, J. J. (1762/1979) *Emile, or, on Education*, trans. Alan Bloom. New York: Basic Books.

Schrieber Levy, Avital (2016) "The Difference Between Punishments and Natural Consequences." *Huffingtonpost.com*. https://www.huffpost.com/entry/punishment-natural-consequences_b_5824d86be4b021d97d31bc33.

Scribner, Campbell F. and Warnick, Bryan R. (2021) *Spare the Rod: Punishment and the Moral Community of Schools*. Chicago, IL: University of Chicago Press.

Thompson, Winston C., Beneke, Abigail J. and Mitchell, Garry S. (2020) "Legitimate Concerns: On Complications of Identity in School Punishment." *Theory and Research in Education* 18 (1): 78–97.

Webster, Jerry (2019) "Consequences Instead of Punishment." *ThoughtCo.com*, Updated July 25.

12

Praise and Positive Behavior Management

Zoë A. Johnson King

Introduction

The literature on moral responsibility is surprisingly fixated on blameworthiness. Authors in this literature chiefly propose theories about what renders someone blameworthy, about which factors mitigate blame, and about the conditions under which they do so. Indeed, it is common to see the terms "responsibility" and "blameworthiness" (or "culpability") used interchangeably. But that is absurd. Culpability is no more than half of responsibility. For, as well as blameworthiness, there is also praiseworthiness. Praiseworthiness *simpliciter* has enjoyed nothing like the sustained philosophical attention given to blameworthiness; there has been substantial discussion of the concept of virtue, and we are seeing a recent upswing of interest in the concept of moral worth, but that's about it. There isn't even a word for the positive analogue of mitigation—that is, the phenomenon whereby some consideration reduces the praiseworthiness of an aspect of someone's action, thought, or character that would otherwise be fully praiseworthy. Nor is there a word for the analogue of excuse—that is, the phenomenon whereby some consideration wholly negates the praiseworthiness of what superficially appears to be something praiseworthy. We have given so little thought to praiseworthiness and its curtailments that we don't even have ways to name the relevant phenomena.

Here philosophers might take a leaf out of the pedagogical books. Schools understand that responsibility is not all about blame; that is why they have "merit" or reward systems in addition to punishment systems. Moreover, schools and educational theorists understand that as far as the promotion of good educational outcomes is concerned, praising the praiseworthy is usually even more effective than blaming the blameworthy. Indeed, schools and educational theorists understand that praising the praiseworthy is often more effective than blaming the blameworthy even at reducing or eliminating "problem" behavior. This understanding is reflected in the gargantuan literature on "positive behavior management" (as it is known in the United Kingdom) and "positive behavioral interventions and supports" (in the United States)—a literature that is heavily emphasized in virtually all teacher training programs but has been completely overlooked in philosophical and legal work on moral responsibility. In short: schools have been seeing what happens when one tries to praise the praiseworthy as much as (if not more than) one blames the blameworthy for several decades now, and there is a wealth of research describing the results. I think that philosophers and legal theorists can learn a lot from this.[1]

In doing so, we upturn what one might think of as the typical relationship between academic theorists and teaching practitioners. Theorists of agency and responsibility who are also interested in education might assume that there is a unidirectional relationship here: the theorists take our theories, fill in their variables with propositions about what we see, imagine, or assume that school environments are like, and generate some implications about what teachers, students, administrators, or other relevant parties should do. But this unidirectional approach ignores the possibility that theorists might themselves have something to learn about agency and responsibility from schools, pedagogical research, or both.

I seek a more reciprocal relationship. I think that theorists of agency and responsibility have much to learn about praise from pedagogical research on positive behavior management, as well as from the conventional wisdom of classroom practitioners. They have found out what works and what doesn't; we would be wise to pay attention. But it is also true that while there is a gargantuan literature documenting the *efficacy* of positive behavior management techniques at improving educational outcomes and reducing instances of egregious poor behavior, there are few extended discussions of the *theoretical rationale* for a "positive" approach. The implicit argument seems to be a consequentialist one: this works better, so let's do it. Here is where theorists of agency and responsibility can help. We can provide a more robust in-principle defense of what has for decades been a regular component of on-the-ground educational practice. The point of this chapter is to begin that task.

In the next section, I will introduce the basic idea of positive behavior management and briefly summarize the extensive research on what works. This is for the benefit of philosophers and legal theorists who have little to no teacher training and are unfamiliar with the pedagogical literature. Then, in the following two sections, I will offer a theoretical rationale for placing praise at the center of our responsibility practices and praiseworthiness at the center of our theorizing, on equal footing with blame and blameworthiness rather than as a largely neglected afterthought. My view is that our reasons to blame are all matched by corresponding reasons to praise: praise and blame can be equally fitting, and both types of reactive attitude serve important communicative and expressive functions. Given this symmetry, I will suggest, we should not pay way more attention to blame and blameworthiness than we do to praise and praiseworthiness.

What is positive behavior management?

All schools have systems, of one sort or another, for *behavior management*. This phrase refers to everything that schools do to try to get students to comport themselves in a manner conducive to learning—roughly, to participate attentively in whatever classroom activities are designed for them (so as to facilitate their own learning) and to treat their peers with kindness and respect (so as to facilitate others' learning). Most schools make at least some of these systems explicit in written behavior management *policies*. And behavior management policies typically include three main components: stated expectations of student conduct, punishments for students who do not meet these expectations, and rewards for students who consistently meet expectations or who go above and beyond.

For several decades now, there has been a conspicuous trend both in pedagogical theory and in educational practice regarding the development of effective behavior management policies. This trend is known as "positive behavior management" (abbreviated PBM) or "positive behavioral interventions and supports" (abbreviated PBIS). As the latter term makes clear, there are two sides to PBM/PBIS: behavioral *interventions* and behavioral *supports*. Both are intended to contrast starkly with an approach that simply doles out punishments for failures to meet school expectations and attempts to ensure compliance through the harshness of the punishments. This is the "negative" approach with which positive behavior management is implicitly contrasted. The negative approach is now seen as somewhat Dickensian—outdated and inhumane. In contrast, PBM/PBIS systems emphasize the importance of *positive* interventions in response to failures to meet school expectations, construing "positive" interventions as those that emphasize finding out why the student acted as they did and what they or others can do to get them back on track.

PBM/PBIS systems also include positive behavioral *supports*; this encompasses anything done to facilitate students' meeting of school expectations, prior to and independent of addressing any failures to meet them. (Supports are proactive, whereas interventions are reactive.) Positive behavioral supports include clear communication of expectations for student behavior. And, crucially for this chapter, they also include explicit, planned systems of praise and reward for students who meet or exceed expectations—"supporting" good behavior by celebrating it when it occurs.

In my own teacher training,[2] the importance of praise was heavily and repeatedly emphasized. We were routinely told to "catch them being good." This phrase encourages practitioners to break cycles of defiance and admonishment by actively looking for things that students are doing well, for which one may then praise them. The underlying idea was that many of our students rarely receive any sort of encouragement whatsoever—since they come to school from unstable home environments in which not only their achievements but also some of their basic needs are frequently overlooked—and so they may struggle to develop healthy senses of self-esteem and self-efficacy if we are not actively seeking ways to point out and celebrate the small things that they are doing well.[3] Building up students' sense of themselves as someone capable of choosing to "be good," the thought goes, is crucial for preventing their development of a sense of identity built around failures to meet expectations (or hostile challenges to them, or both). And, the thought goes, since such an identity is antithetical to learning, it falls to us as teachers to prevent its development. An anecdote: I vividly recall one conversation with a senior teacher at my school who repeatedly stressed that there is no good behavior too small to be caught and praised—"It can be 'Well done for having your pen out!,'" he said. "It can be anything."

An enormous wealth of research vindicates these anecdata. Decades of studies have found PBM/PBIS programs to be effective in reducing students' rates of office disciplinary referrals (Colvin and Fernandez, 2000; Metzler et al., 2001; Nelson, Martella and Marchand-Martella, 2002; Mass-Galloway et al., 2008; Muscott, Mann and LeBrun, 2008; Bradshaw, Waasdorp and Leaf, 2012; Simonsen et al., 2012; Vincent et al., 2012; Flannery et al., 2014; Kelm et al., 2014; Bradshaw et al., 2015), in decreasing bullying (Waasdorp, Bradshaw and Leaf, 2012; Kelm et al., 2014), in improving rates of on-task behavior (Becker et al., 1967; Mayer et al., 1983, 1993; Wills et al., 2019), and in increasing prosocial behavior and emotion regulation (Broden et al., 1970; Christophersen et al., 1972; Bradshaw et al., 2012). Some studies have also found statistically significant improvements in students' academic attainment following the implementation of PBM/PBIS systems (Clark, Lachowicz and Wolf, 1968; O'Leary et al., 1969; Nelson, Martella and Marchand-Martella, 2002; McIntosh et al., 2006; Muscott, Mann and LeBrun, 2008; Horner et al., 2009; Simonsen et al., 2012; Kelm, Kent McIntosh and Cooley, 2014). These studies demonstrate the efficacy of techniques such as "good news referrals," in which teachers contact parents or carers to share good things that their children have done (i.e., the opposite of disciplinary referrals), and token reinforcement systems that use "points" or "tickets" to track students' behaviors that meet or exceed school expectations and then offer either certificates or tangible material rewards for students who accumulate a sufficient number of tokens.[4] In addition to these more elaborate techniques, though, there are also simple systems of verbal praise. One of the most widely used PBM/PBIS techniques is the aptly named "praise and ignore," in which teachers respond to low-level disruption by ignoring it entirely and instead vocally praising other students who are getting on with their work or otherwise acting well.

As mentioned, the pedagogical literature documents these strategies' *efficacy* at securing certain results. But there is little discussion of potential non-consequentialist rationales for positive behavior management. Here's where I come in. The remainder of this chapter develops just such a rationale.

Fitting praise and virtues of attention

When something is blameworthy, it is worthy of blame. Likewise, when something is praiseworthy, it is worthy of praise. So far, so tautologous. But there is an important moral upshot to these platitudes: praise and blame are either activities or attitudes[5] and are rendered *fitting* by that which makes individuals praiseworthy or blameworthy. Praising the praiseworthy is akin to blaming the blameworthy—and to fearing the fearsome, deploring the deplorable, and so on—in that they are appropriate responses to the normatively significant features of things. Now, here's another tautology: it is normatively appropriate to have the normatively appropriate responses to things. When someone deliberately acts well and/or has good motivations, praising her is normatively appropriate.[6,7]

Even this basic point gets us some way toward a case for giving praise a far more central role than it has so far enjoyed in our theorizing about moral responsibility. For, since the normatively appropriate reaction to people's moral achievements and good qualities is to praise them, ignoring such things is normatively *in*appropriate. When we focus single-mindedly on blame at the expense of praise, then we do something that is normatively inappropriate: we fail to praise the praiseworthy.

That said, we cannot have *all* of the normatively appropriate reactions to *all* of the things. This is because there are just too many features of things that render certain reactions normatively appropriate. We lack the cognitive and affective capacities to have the fitting attitudes to everything all at the same time. The combinations of attitudes that would be involved in such a state are combinations that humans cannot sustain simultaneously: we cannot simultaneously experience overwhelming grief and overwhelming joy, for instance. Moreover, the total quantity of attitudes that would be involved in a completely fitting mental state is too great for human minds: we cannot be indignant enough to respond fittingly to all of the injustices ever perpetrated, for instance. This problem is even more acute for the normatively appropriate reactions that involve action rather than mere attitude, since we have nowhere near enough time to perform all of the relevant actions. So, failing to praise the praiseworthy is not our only problem. These failures are among a litany of failures to react normatively appropriately of which each of us is guilty at all times.

Given our cognitive and affective limitations, some philosophers think that there exist *norms of attention*: norms directing us to focus on certain normatively significant features of things, and to respond to them in the ways that they deserve, at the expense of others. Norms of attention tell us which of the normatively appropriate reactions to have, since we cannot have all of them.

Indeed, norms of attention have already found their way into the literature on moral responsibility; they have been offered as putative explanations of the virtue of modesty and of what is wrong with hypocritical and meddlesome blame. Here is Nic Bommarito on modesty (2013, 115–16):

> As the thoughtless person does not attend to the needs of others, the immodest person does not attend to the goodness found in others. As the self-centered dwell on the satisfaction of their own desires and projects, the immodest dwell on their own goodness and importance. What is morally bad about immodesty is the same as what is bad about other egocentric vices—they all manifest a will that is indifferent to others in particular ways. . . . In the case of immodesty, dwelling on one's own goodness or importance manifests an egocentric will, one that cares too little about the goodness of others and the role that others play in one's own success.

According to Bommarito, the problem with immodesty is that an immodest person does not attend sufficiently to others' moral achievements and good qualities. Now, this concerns an improper balance between the extent to which one attends to *one's own goodness* and the extent to which one attends to others' goodness, rather than an improper balance between the extent to which one attends to *others' badness* and the extent to which one attends to others' goodness. But Bommarito's view does at least open the door to the idea that we ought to devote some portion of our attention to others' goodness.

Similarly, here is Matt King on meddling and hypocritical blame (2013, 1438):

> [Meddling and hypocrisy] are wrongs in which we attend to what we should ignore. For meddlesome blame, the reasons arise out of the norms that structure our personal relationships. Other things equal, we should regulate our involvement in the lives of others, restricting our concern to those with whom we share the mutual vulnerabilities of intimate relationships.... For hypocritical blame, the reasons concern our moral priorities. There is a general principle favoring attending to conducting ourselves rightly in the world over attending to the faults of others. Where hypocritical blame is objectionable, we find that the blamers have strong reason to correct their own conduct and seek self improvement. As such correction ought to be their moral priority, highlighting their own bad behavior serves to reorient their attention to the more important thing.

For King, the problem with hypocrisy is that a hypocrite does not attend sufficiently to the ways in which they are themselves capable of moral improvement. Like Bommarito's account of immodesty, this is a self-other comparison: it concerns an improper balance between one's attention to *one's own badness* and one's attention to others' badness, rather than an improper balance between one's attention to *others' goodness* and one's attention to others' badness. But King's view of hypocrisy does create room for the idea that we can pay too much attention to others' moral failings. And King's account of meddlesome blame echoes this theme, with the twist that what makes our attention inappropriate can be that our relationship to our blamee is insufficiently close for their moral failings to deserve our attention at all.

Putting these ideas together, I want to suggest that there can be improper balances between the extent to which we attend to *others' badness* and the extent to which we attend to *others' goodness*. Someone can violate norms of attention by paying too much attention to others' moral failures and bad character traits and not enough attention to others' moral achievements and good qualities. Thus, I suggest, the degrees to which one attends to others' goodnesses and to others' badnesses merit direct comparison; these degrees of attention should be compared to one another and not only to the degree to which one attends to oneself. This is a substantive, first-order proposal about the content of our norms of attention.

Developing this proposal, I want to suggest the following:

SYMMETRY THESIS: There are no reasons to attend to others' blameworthy features that are not matched by corresponding reasons to attend to others' praiseworthy features.

We can make a case for the Symmetry Thesis by surveying all the reasons one might have to attend to others' blameworthy features and observing that each of them is matched by corresponding reasons to attend to praiseworthy features. Praising the praiseworthy and blaming the blameworthy are equally fitting, as we have seen. And both can be effective in bringing about behavioral change—indeed, praise can be *more* effective than blame in this regard, as discussed in the literature on PBM/PBIS. Praise and blame can also both express or communicate our commitment to a system of moral values (on which I will say much more in the next section); we affirm these commitments just as well by recognizing those who abide by our values as by admonishing those who fall short. Similarly, just as blaming wrongdoers can be a way of standing up for ourselves or for other victims of wrongdoing, so too can praising "rightdoers"—those who treat us or others well—be a way of reaffirming the moral regard in which we and others deserve to be held (again, much more on this in the next section). I do not wish to take a stand as to which of these reasons to praise and blame are the most basic or the most explanatorily fundamental. That is because I think we can defend the Symmetry Thesis even while remaining ecumenical on this matter. On all of the most promising accounts of our reasons to praise and blame, I claim, the Symmetry Thesis holds true.

To clarify: when I speak of reasons to blame being *matched* by corresponding reasons to praise, I mean that for each sort of reason to blame that can exist, a corresponding reason to praise—one with the same underlying rationale—can also exist. Both praise and blame can be fitting, can bring about moral reform, can express or affirm our commitment to our values, can be ways of asserting ourselves, and so on. But I do not want to commit to any claim about the relative *strength* of our actual reasons to praise and to blame. This is because the strength of our actual reasons to praise and blame depends in part on how many moral failures, how many moral achievements, and how many good and bad qualities actually exist in total, as well as just how bad the badnesses are and just how good the goodnesses are. In a nightmarish world in which everyone is completely evil except for a single act of kindness one afternoon, I do not think that we would have as much total reason to praise this single act of kindness as to blame everything that is blameworthy. Surely we would have more total reason to blame the blameworthy, since there is so much more of it and it is so much more egregious. So, I cannot commit to any precise thesis about the relative strength of our actual reasons to blame and to praise, since I do not know precisely how many moral goodnesses and badnesses actually exist, nor precisely how good and bad they are. Nonetheless, the Symmetry Thesis suggests that for whichever praiseworthy and blameworthy things do actually exist, we have all of the same *types* of reasons to praise the former as to blame the latter. The same sorts of considerations that count in favor of blaming the blameworthy also count in favor of praising the praiseworthy.

To clarify further: one might think that the Symmetry Thesis is clearly false because there are certain categories of action to which only one of praise or blame is ever relevant. For example, it is often thought that supererogatory actions are praiseworthy when performed but not blameworthy when omitted. In my (ms) I explore the possibility that some actions are "morally basic" and that these actions are blameworthy when omitted but not praiseworthy when performed. And in my (forthcoming) I note that there do not seem to be any opposites of negligence and recklessness when it comes to praiseworthiness; people are not praiseworthy for doing something good without realizing that what they're doing is good, when they should have realized (as in cases of negligence), nor are people praiseworthy for being aware of the "risk" of goodness of what they're doing and doing it anyway (as in cases of recklessness). Categories of action like these could be thought to falsify the Symmetry Thesis, since the fact that someone has acted recklessly or negligently or has omitted a morally basic action might seem to be a reason to blame that corresponds to no reasons to praise, and likewise the fact that someone has acted supererogatorily might seem to be a reason to praise that corresponds to no reasons to blame. However, I don't think that this approach gets at our reasons to praise and blame at the right level of explanatory depth. When we blame a reckless act, for instance, there are deeper explanations of why we do so than the simple fact that the act was reckless, since there are further explanations of why blame is an appropriate response to reckless acts. In blaming we might be engaging in moral conversation or moral protest, for instance (on which I will discuss more in the next section). These deeper explanations identify the ultimate reasons why we blame *at all*, rather than the proximate reasons why we blame specific types of actions. I am interested in these deeper explanations—explanations of why we praise and blame *at all*. My contention is that they are symmetric.

The Symmetry Thesis, if true, suggests that those who focus on blame at the expense of praise display improper patterns of attention. For we do not, in fact, live in a nightmarish world in which the praiseworthy is far outweighed by the blameworthy. There are a lot of good people, and they do a lot of good things. Granted, the total quantity of blameworthy stuff might be somewhat greater than the total quantity of praiseworthy stuff. And perhaps some of the blameworthy stuff is a lot more evil than any of the praiseworthy stuff is good. I don't know the numbers. Nonetheless, these differences would have to be positively gargantuan for them to render fitting the monomaniacal focus on blame and blameworthiness that is currently found in the literature on moral responsibility. And I am confident that the differences are not *that* big. So, here is one non-consequentialist rationale for giving praiseworthiness a much greater role in our theorizing about moral responsibility and praise a much greater role in our behavior management practices than they have so far enjoyed: doing so would rectify an improper skewing of our collective patterns of attention.

Expressive and communicative praise

In this section, I will spend a lot more time discussing a variety of reasons to blame that one might think challenge the Symmetry Thesis. The views I will discuss all suggest, in one way or another, that blame serves a *communicative* or *expressive* function. One might think that blame is uniquely suited to serve such a function, with the result that there are reasons to blame that are not matched by corresponding reasons to praise. But I will argue that this is not the case.

Lots of philosophers think that blame serves a communicative function. Here, for example, is Jay Wallace (1996, 69):

> [the reactive emotions expressed by moral sanctions] are focused emotional responses to the violation of moral obligations that we accept. In expressing these emotions . . . we are demonstrating our commitment to certain moral standards, as regulative of social life. Once this point is grasped, blame and moral sanction can be seen to have a positive, perhaps irreplaceable contribution to make to the constitution and maintenance of moral communities: by giving voice to the reactive emotions, these responses help to articulate, and thereby to affirm and deepen, our commitment to a set of common moral obligations.

He's not the only one. Watson (1987, repr. 2010, 230) says that "the reactive attitudes are incipiently forms of communication"; Darwall (2010, 265) that "reactive attitudes . . . implicitly address their objects"; McGeer (2013, 184) that "blame . . . aims to generate a normatively valuable dialectic"; MacNamara (2015a, 2015b) that the reactive attitudes are "messages." And McKenna (2012) spends an entire book developing an account of blaming attitudes as "contribution[s] within a conversational exchange" (p. 88), in which a wrongdoer manifests ill will toward others, we interject to hold her accountable, and she is then expected to offer an excuse, justification, or apology for her behavior.

Suppose that the function of blame is indeed communicative. Start with Wallace's suggestion that its function is "to articulate, and thereby to affirm and deepen, our commitment to a set of common moral obligations." Would it really follow that the role played by blame is "irreplaceable," as Wallace suggests? Couldn't praise play the same role?

The answer is that it can. By praising those who meet or exceed our moral standards, we articulate and affirm our commitment to these standards just as well as we do by blaming those who violate them. Praise and blame express the same commitments to the same standards. Granted, these commitments are typically left implicit in instances of vocal praise; we say "That was kind of you to help her" rather than "I am committed to moral standards such that helping actions of the sort that you have performed are kind, which is a mark in their favor," for instance. But so, too, are these commitments left implicit in instances of vocal blame; we say "You can't treat people like that!" rather than "I am committed to moral standards such that actions of the sort that you have performed are cruel, which is a mark against them—one that ordinarily renders actions impermissible, as it did yours." The first-order normative theory to which we are committed is taken for granted in expressions of both praise and blame. The sense in which it is "expressed" is closer to that involved in presupposition than assertion. Nonetheless, this commitment is expressed equally well, and in the same way, by both praise and blame. And, if there is indeed a causal mechanism by means of which expressions of our moral commitments further "deepen" those commitments, as Wallace suggests, then there is no reason to expect this to occur to a greater extent for expressions of blame than for expressions of praise.

Some of the philosophers who see blame as essentially communicative think that what is communicated is not just a general commitment to a set of moral standards but rather a special sort of moral reason—a *distinctively second-personal reason* (see Darwall, 1996, and McKenna, 2012, and cf. Raz's 1979 account of authority). On this view, blame does not simply remind wrongdoers of already existing reasons to act or avoid acting provided by the standards of their moral community. Rather, blame issues wrongdoers with new reasons. When I hold you accountable for your wrongdoing, I create reasons for you to display remorse, make amends, and avoid violating moral standards in future: now you can do all of those things *because I told you to*. However, this view about blame's communicative function does not challenge the Symmetry Thesis any more than Wallace's view does, since it, too, readily extends to praise. Second-personal reasons can be issued via praise just as easily as via blame. For what is distinctive about second-personal reasons is that they enable you to take certain actions *because I told you to*. And I do not have to wait until you have failed to do something in order to tell you to do it. If you are already doing it, then I can just tell you that that's great and you should carry on. Exactly as blame can be a second-personal "Stop that!," then, so too can praise be a second-personal "Keep it up!"

Other philosophers hold a view according to which blame is expressive but not necessarily communicative. They see blame as a form of *moral protest*—an outcry in response to someone's poor behavior (see Hieronymi, 2001; Talbert, 2012; Smith, 2013; and cf. Boxill, 1979 on the relationship between protest and self-respect). On this view, it is not crucial that blame be addressed to someone receptive to its communicative message. After all, if a blamee holds sufficient ill will toward a blamer to treat her wrongly, then her complaint at his treatment may well fall on deaf ears. Rather than entering into a productive conversation about shared moral standards through one's expression of the reactive sentiments, then, one may just be shouting into the void. Nonetheless, these theorists hold, there is something morally valuable about these expressions of moral protest: they can be ways of defiantly affirming one's moral status, even if one's doing so does not change anybody's mind.

This view does not challenge the Symmetry Thesis either. That is because one can affirm one's moral status without doing so defiantly. If the point of blame is to stick up for oneself in response to a challenge to one's moral status, so too can the point of praise be to reiterate and affirm that one is being treated as one deserves. Granted, someone who is already treating a praiser as she deserves may not need a reminder of her moral status. But the blame-as-protest account is already one according to which blame serves its function independently of whether it changes anybody's mind. On this approach, then, praise can also serve its function even if no mind-changing takes place—not because the reactive sentiments fall on deaf ears but because praiser and praisee already agree about how the praiser deserves to be treated. Both praise and blame can be affirmatory regardless of who is or is not convinced by them.

One aspect of one version of the expressive view might seem particularly challenging to the Symmetry Thesis. Here is Hieronymi (2001, 546):

> I suggest that a past wrong against you, standing in your history without apology, atonement, retribution, punishment, restitution, condemnation, or anything else that might recognize it as a wrong, makes a claim. It says, in effect, that you can be treated in this way, and that such treatment is acceptable. That—that claim—is what you resent. It poses a threat. In resenting it, you challenge it. If there is nothing else that would mark out that event as wrong, there is at least your resentment.

According to Hieronymi, people's deliberate actions make claims about how those affected by the actions may be treated. If a claim is negative and goes unchallenged, then it poses a persistent threat. One might think that this makes the negative claim particularly *challenge-worthy*; a claim that we may be treated well is not similarly threatening, so there is nothing to challenge. So, blame's ability to repudiate a persistent threat might provide a reason to blame that is not matched by reasons to praise. In the sea of demands on our limited attention, a persistent threat adds some urgency to our reasons to blame.

This might be right. But it takes us only so far. For, when Hieronymi addresses the objection that we should not get worked up about the threats posed by others' actions, she articulates a more fundamental underlying rationale for her view that does extend to praise (2001, 549):

> [W]e ought to care about what other people think. To not care about what you think is to not care about you. To disregard your evaluation is to disregard you. Respect for you as a fellow human being commits me to caring about your evaluation.

We should pay attention to threatening claims about how we may be treated, according to Hieronymi, because we ought in general to care about others' evaluations of us. And we ought in general to care about others' evaluations of us as a matter of respect for those others. But if we ought in general to care about others' evaluations of us, then we ought to care about those evaluations regardless of whether they are negative (and thus threatening) or positive. And, in that case, if we have reasons to protest false claims about how we or others deserve to be treated then we also have matching reasons to celebrate true claims. Indeed, one might think that the goal of respecting you and your evaluations makes it especially important to acknowledge and credit those of your evaluations that are *correct*, rather than skipping over them until we find one that is incorrect and then blaming you for it. This might make our reasons to praise even stronger than our reasons to blame. But, at any rate, even if there is some urgency to our reasons to pay attention to others' threatening evaluations, it remains the case that we also have reasons to pay attention to others' correct, non-threatening evaluations. And these reasons to praise have the same underlying rationale as our reasons to blame—namely, the general importance of what other people think. That is exactly what the Symmetry Thesis predicts.

Conclusion

Praise is often more effective than blame at ensuring compliance with the standards of our moral community, as the literature on PBM/PBIS shows. Moreover, I have argued that there are no reasons to blame that are not matched by corresponding reasons to praise: when someone is genuinely praiseworthy, praising her is fitting, is a way of communicating our commitment to the moral standards that she upholds, and—if her praiseworthiness involves treating us or others well—is a way of affirming and reiterating the moral status that her actions afford to people. Since there is much out there that deserves to be praised, it is normatively inappropriate to focus monomaniacally on that which deserves to be blamed, directing a disproportionate amount of our attention toward blameworthiness at the expense of praiseworthiness. As well as blaming the blameworthy, we should praise the praiseworthy.[8]

Notes

1   N.B. I am concerned with *moral* praise and blameworthiness. I take it that schools' behavior management systems are primarily attempts to respond to that which is morally praiseworthy and that which is morally blameworthy in their students' conduct; for example, helping a peer with their work is praiseworthy (when well-motivated) and making a snide remark intended to damage a peer's self-esteem is blameworthy (when done without justification or excuse). This is complicated by the fact that schools' reward systems often include rewards for academic achievement as well as for good behavior. We might think that what is rewarded is in fact some mix of the *morally* praiseworthy and the *academically* praiseworthy. If that is so, then I should be understood as talking only about the moral parts of the picture. Notice, though, that schools do not typically punish poor academic performance itself—just the morally suspect behavior that might lead to it. I suspect, then, that rewards that are ostensibly for good academic performance are in fact best interpreted as rewards for the morally praiseworthy efforts that led to it.

2   I have a PGCE, the UK's main teaching degree, and used to work at an academy in South-East London.
3   The concept of self-efficacy is now widely used in pedagogical theory but has its roots in the work of psychologist Albert Bandura (1977, 1986, 1997, 2000). Roughly, someone's sense of self-efficacy is her sense of her own ability to revise her behavior and/or alter her surrounding circumstances so as to be successful in accomplishing a goal—something that is crucial to maintaining students' motivation to focus on learning and helping their peers in class, especially if they have in the past behaved poorly and/or been academically unsuccessful. Bandura argues that "social persuasion" can be an effective tool in developing individuals' senses of self-efficacy: "people who are persuaded verbally that they possess the capabilities to master given activities are likely to mobilise greater effort and sustain it than if they harbour self-doubts and dwell on personal deficiencies when problems arise" (2000, 302). In addition, Bandura suggests that "vicarious experiences" provided by observations of peers can increase self-efficacy: "[s]eeing people similar to oneself succeed by sustained effort raises observers' beliefs that they too possess the capabilities to master comparable activities to succeed" (2000, 302). Thus public verbal praise of either students or their peers—whoever is "caught" being good—can serve to increase students' sense of self-efficacy.
4   It should be noted that there may be important differences between immaterial and material rewards when it comes to securing student motivation long term; Edward Deci and Richard Ryan's "self-determination theory" (1985) emphasizes the importance of autonomous motivation, suggesting that attaching *extrinsic* rewards to behaviors can undermine the extent to which individuals are then *intrinsically* motivated to engage in the behaviors when rewards are no longer offered. Deci and Ryan's account suggests that schools would do better to focus on good news referrals, verbal praise, and certificates than on material reinforcement.
5   We can use the term "praise" to refer either to the private mental state of giving positive moral credit or to outward expressions of that mental state (e.g., saying "well done!"). The former is an attitude, the latter an activity. Likewise, blame is either an attitude (cf. Scanlon, 2008; Wolf, 2011; Wallace, 2011 for accounts of this attitude) or an activity.
6   This assumes the substantive account of what we are praiseworthy for that I have defended elsewhere (Johnson King *fc*). Subsequently, I will speak generally of praiseworthy "features" when I want to talk simultaneously about praiseworthy features of one's actions and praiseworthy motivations.
7   One fascinating set of questions concerns the extent to which young children can really *deserve* praise and blame, given their limited moral understanding and the limited control that they have over their actions. One might suspect that much of our blame of very young children is "proleptic" in Williams's (1995) sense—and the same may be true of praise. But I don't think that this remains plausible as children

get older. Perhaps elementary-school-age children are universally excused when they act poorly, and perhaps their moral motivations are insufficiently robust for them to deserve praise even when they act well, but that is dubious for most middle schoolers and surely false of high schoolers. Children's moral agency is burgeoning, but they often have more than enough of a grasp of the morally relevant aspects of what they are doing for them to be fitting targets of at least some degree of praise and blame.

8   I am grateful to the editors of this volume for helpful comments that improved the chapter's argument in several places, as well as to Chris Howard and Jamie Fritz for helpful conversations about the fittingness parts. But my highest debt of gratitude is to my wonderful research assistant, Meghana Maddali, who helped me to collect and organize all of the empirical material that appears in this chapter.

References

Bandura, Albert (1977) "Self-Efficacy: Toward a Unifying Theory of Behavioral Change." *Psychological Review* 84 (2): 191–215.

Bandura, Albert (1986) *Social Foundations of Thought and Action: A Social Cognitive Theory*. Englewood Cliffs, NJ: Prentice-Hall.

Bandura, Albert (1997) *Self-Efficacy: The Exercise of Control*. New York: W. H. Freeman.

Bandura, Albert (2000) "Health Promotion from the Perspective of Social Cognitive Theory." In Charles Abraham, Paul Norman and Mark Conner (eds.), *Understanding and Changing Health Behavior: From Health Beliefs to Self-Regulation*, 299–339. Reading: Harwood.

Becker, Wesley C., Madsen, Charles H., Arnold, Carole Revelle and Thomas, Don R. (1967) "The Contingent Use of Teacher Attention and Praise in Reducing Classroom Behavior Problems." *The Journal of Special Education* 1 (3): 287–307.

Bommarito, Nicolas (2013) "Modesty as a Virtue of Attention." *Philosophical Review* 122 (1): 93–117.

Boxill, Bernard R. (1979) "Self-Respect and Protest." *Philosophy and Public Affairs* 6 (1): 58–69.

Bradshaw, Catherine P., Waasdorp, Tracy E. and Leaf, Philip J. (2012) "Effects of School-Wide Positive Behavioral Interventions and Supports on Child Behavior Problems." *Pediatrics* 130 (5): e1136–45.

Bradshaw, Catherine P., Waasdorp, Tracy E., Tracy, Philip J. Leaf and Graham, Steve (2015) "Examining Variation in the Impact of School-Wide Positive Behavioral Interventions and Supports: Findings from a Randomized Controlled Effectiveness Trial." *Journal of Educational Psychology* 107 (2): 546–57.

Broden, Marcia, Bruce, Carl, Mitchell, Mary Ann, Carter, Virginia and Hall, R. Vance (1970) "Effects of Teacher Attention on Attending Behavior of Two Boys at Adjacent Desks." *Journal of Applied Behavior Analysis* 3 (3): 199–203.

Christophersen, Edward R., Arnold, Caroline M., Hill, Diane W. and Quilitch, Robert H. (1972) "The Home Point System: Token Reinforcement Procedures for Application by Parents of Children with Behavior Problems." *Journal of Applied Behavior Analysis* 5 (4) 485–97.

Clark, Marilyn, Lachowicz, Joe and Wolf, Montrose (1968) "A Pilot Basic Education Program for School Dropouts Incorporating a Token Reinforcement System." *Behavioral Research and Therapy* 6 (2): 183–8.

Colvin, Geoff and Fernandez, Elizabeth (2000) "Sustaining Effective Behavior Support Systems in an Elementary School." *Journal of Positive Behavior Interventions* 2 (4): 251–3.

Darwall, Stephen (1996) *The Second-Person Standpoint: Morality, Respect, and Accountability*. Cambridge, MA: Harvard University Press.

Darwall, Stephen (2010) "Authority and Reasons: Exclusionary and Second-Personal." *Ethics* 120 (2): 257–78.

Flannery, K. Bridgid, Fenning, Pamela, McGrath Kato, Mimi, and McIntosh, Kent (2014) "Effects of School-Wide Positive Behavioral Interventions and Supports and Fidelity of Implementation on Problem Behavior in High Schools." *School Psychology Quarterly* 29 (2): 111–24.

Hieronymi, Pamela (2001) "Articulating an Uncompromising Forgiveness." *Philosophy and Phenomenological Research* 63 (3): 529–55.

Horner, Robert H., Sugai, George, Smolkowski, Keith, Eber, Lucille, Nakasato, Jean, Todd, Anne W. and Esperanza, Jody (2009) "A Randomized, Wait-List Controlled Effectiveness Trial Assessing School-Wide Positive Behavior Support in Elementary Schools." *Journal of Positive Behavior Interventions* 11 (3): 133–44.

Johnson King, Zoë (ms). "The Slow Clap Phenomenon." Unpublished manuscript.

Johnson King, Zoë (forthcoming). "What Are We Praiseworthy For?" In Ruth Chang and Amia Srinivasan (eds.), *New Conversations in Philosophy, Law, and Politics*. Oxford University Press.

Kelm, Joanna L., Kent McIntosh, Kent and Cooley, Sharon (2014) "Effects of Implementing School-Wide Positive Behavioural Interventions and Supports on Problem Behaviour and Academic Achievement in a Canadian Elementary School." *Canadian Journal of School Psychology* 29 (3): 195–212.

King, Matt (2020) "Attending to Blame." *Philosophical Studies* 177 (5): 1423–39.

Macnamara, Colleen (2015a). "Reactive Attitudes as Communicative Entities." *Philosophy and Phenomenological Research* 90 (3): 546–69.

Macnamara, Colleen (2015b). "Blame, Communication, and Morally Responsible Agency." In Randolph Clarke, Michael McKenna and Angela Smith (eds.), *The Nature of Moral Responsibility: New Essays*, 211–36. New York: Oxford University Press.

Mass-Galloway, Robin L., Panyan, Marion V., Smith, Carl R. and Wessendorf, Suana (2008) "Systems Change with School-Wide Positive Behavior Supports: Iowa's Work in Progress." *Journal of Positive Behavior Interventions* 10 (2): 129–35.

Mayer, G. Roy, Butterworth, Tom, Nafpaktitis, Mary and Sulzer-Azaroff, Beth (1983) "Preventing School Vandalism and Improving Discipline: A Three-Year Study." *Journal of Applied Behavior Analysis* 16 (4): 355–69.

Mayer, G. Roy, Mitchell, Lynda K., Clementi, Tamara, Clement-Robertson, Erica, Myatt, Rosalind and Bullara, Daniel Thomas (1993) "A Dropout Prevention Program for At-Risk High School Students: Emphasizing Consulting to Promote Positive Classroom Climates." *Education & Treatment of Children* 16 (2): 135–46.

McGeer, Victoria (2013) "Civilizing Blame." In D. Justin Coates and Neal A. Tognazzini (eds.), *Blame: Its Nature and Norms*, 162–88. Oxford: Oxford University Press.

McIntosh, Kent, Chard, David J., Boland, Joseph B. and Horner, Robert H. (2006) "Demonstration of Combined Efforts in School-Wide Academic and Behavioral Systems and Incidence of Reading and Behavior Challenges in Early Elementary Grades." *Journal of Positive Behavior Interventions* 8 (3): 146–54.

McKenna, Michael (2012) *Conversation and Responsibility*. New York: Oxford University Press.

Metzler, Carol W., Biglan, Anthony, Rusby, Julie C. and Sprague, Jeffrey R. (2001) "Evaluation of a Comprehensive Behavior Management Program to Improve School-Wide Positive Behavior Support." *Education & Treatment of Children* 24 (4): 448–79.

Muscott, Howard S., Mann, Eric L. and LeBrun, Marcel R. (2008) "Positive Behavioral Interventions and Supports in New Hampshire: Effects of Large-Scale Implementation of Schoolwide Positive Behavior Support on Student Discipline and Academic Achievement." *Journal of Positive Behavior Interventions* 10 (3): 190–205.

Nelson, J., Martella, Ronald M. and Marchand-Martella, Nancy (2002) "Maximizing Student Learning: The Effects of a Comprehensive School-Based Program for Preventing Problem Behaviors." *Journal of Emotional and Behavioral Disorders* 10 (3): 136–48.

O'Leary, K. D., Becker, W. C., Evans, M. B. and Saudargas, R. A. (1969) "A Token Reinforcement Program in a Public School: A Replication and Systematic Analysis." *Journal of Applied Behavior Analysis* 2 (1): 3–13.

Raz, Joseph (1979) "Legitimate Authority." In his *The Authority of Law: Essays on Law and Morality*, 3–27. New York: Oxford University Press.

Scanlon, Thomas (2008) *Moral Dimensions: Permissibility, Meaning, Blame*. Cambridge, MA: Belknap Press.

Simonsen, Brandi, Eber, Lucille, Black, Anne C., Sugai, George, Lewandowski, Holly, Sims, Barbra and Myers, Diane (2012) "Illinois Statewide Positive Behavioral Interventions and Supports: Evolution and Impact on Student Outcomes Across Years." *Journal of Positive Behavior Interventions* 14 (1): 5–16.

Smith, Angela (2013) "Moral Blame and Moral Protest." In D. Justin Coates and Neal A. Tognazzini (eds.), *Blame: Its Nature and Norms*, 27–49. Oxford: Oxford University Press.

Talbert, Matthew (2012) "Moral Competence, Moral Blame, and Protest." *The Journal of Ethics* 16 (1): 89–109.

Vincent, Claudia G., Tobin, Tary Jeanne, Hawken, Leanne S. and Frank, Jennifer L. (2012) "Discipline Referrals and Access to Secondary Level Support in Elementary and Middle Schools: Patterns Across African-American, Hispanic-American, and White Students." *Education & Treatment of Children* 35 (3): 431–58.

Waasdorp, Tracy E., Bradshaw, Catherine P. and Leaf, Philip J. (2012) "The Impact of Schoolwide Positive Behavioral Interventions and Supports on Bullying and Peer Rejection: A Randomized Controlled Effectiveness Trial." *Archives of Pediatrics & Adolescent Medicine* 166 (2): 149–56.

Wallace, R. Jay (1996) *Responsibility and the Moral Sentiments*. Cambridge, MA: Harvard University Press.

Wallace, R. Jay (2011) "Dispassionate Opprobrium." In R. Jay Wallace, Rahul Kumar and Samuel Freeman (eds.), *Reasons and Recognition: Essays on the Philosophy of T. M. Scanlon*, 348–72. Oxford: Oxford University Press.

Watson, Gary (2010) "Responsibility and the Limits of Evil: Variations on a Strawsonian Theme." In his *Agency and Answerability: Selected Essays*, 219–58. Oxford: Oxford University Press.

Williams, Bernard (1995) "Internal Reasons and the Obscurity of Blame." In his *Making Sense of Humanity*, 39–45. Cambridge: Cambridge University Press.

Wills, Howard P., Caldarella, Paul, Mason, Benjamin A., Lappin, Amanda and Anderson, Darlene H. (2019) "Improving Student Behavior in Middle Schools: Results of a Classroom Management Intervention." *Journal of Positive Behavior Interventions* 21 (4): 213–27.

Wolf, Susan (2011) "Blame, Italian Style." In R. Jay Wallace, Rahul Kumar and Samuel Freeman (eds.), *Reasons and Recognition: Essays on the Philosophy of T. M. Scanlon*, 332–47. Oxford: Oxford University Press.

Nudging School Discipline

Viktor Ivanković

Introduction

Nudges have recently made their way into schools. Long lists of tested techniques (Lavecchia, Liu and Oreopoulous, 2014; Levitt et al., 2016; Damgaard and Nielsen, 2018) are now giving us a sense of how certain educational goals may be more effectively pursued by predictably steering students' decision-making. But as nudges break new policy ground, the standard moral concerns remain on their tail: Are they manipulative (Wilkinson, 2013)? Do they treat targeted individuals as rational agents (Rozeboom, 2020)? Since they are employed covertly, do they in fact threaten individual autonomy as much or even more than coercive means (Hausman and Welch, 2010)?

In the context of the classroom, there is a different flavor to these questions. For one, since very young children and adolescents do not have fully developed personal autonomies, they might be considered appropriate targets of paternalistic intervention. Furthermore, we standardly permit and perhaps even expect educators to put psychological insights and techniques to use in the educational process (hence why prospective teachers must often take courses in educational and developmental psychology). One seemingly appropriate aim of nudging for the educator is maintaining an orderly atmosphere in the classroom that facilitates learning and limits the infractions of rules to a minimum. If nudges prove effective in this regard, they can reduce the need for some disciplinary measures that both educators and students may want to avoid and some of which may raise their own moral concerns.

This chapter offers moral considerations for using nudges to facilitate school discipline. I argue that the normative approach to school-discipline nudges ought to be attuned to the broad age-related differences of children at different stages of their development. Since children at an earlier school age cannot fully appreciate the importance of school discipline in education, there is little controversy in exposing them to nudges, which may be helpful in forming good habits. Middle and late adolescents, I argue, require a more sensitive approach. Because of the duty to support adolescents' developing autonomy (Tucker, 2016), their possible resentment to being nudged, and considerations of classroom trust, educators should nudge carefully and conservatively, and refrain from it altogether when they can.

Classroom nudges

The typology of classroom nudging

There are two important empirical observations behind the incorporation of nudges: one is the fact that humans make numerous predictable errors that defeat their perceived ends (e.g., despite caring more about long-term goals, they focus on short-term consequences); the other is that the changes in environmental surroundings influence individuals in logically irrelevant ways (by changing the order of items, their color, their shape, etc.) (Blumenthal-Barby, 2013, 178). "Nudging" is an attempt at harnessing these predictable behavioral traits and the environmental influences that trigger them. A default registration into pension saving or organ donation harnesses the status quo bias. Placing healthy food at eye level in cafeterias harnesses the salience effect.[1]

Permissible nudging, in the original account of its main advocates, Richard Thaler and Cass Sunstein (2008), is constrained along three moral lines. The first is that nudges should be incorporated transparently and defended publicly (Thaler and Sunstein, 2008, 242–3).[2] The second is that individuals should be influenced so they are made better off by their own lights (Thaler and Sunstein, 2008, 80).[3] Finally, nudges must be "easy and cheap to avoid" (Thaler and Sunstein, 2008, 6), in the sense that they should not effectively close off alternatives. Let's take these requirements to be generally helpful in assessing whether using a particular nudge respects the autonomies of those targeted.[4] We consider it valuable that individuals are autonomous in governing their own lives, that is, that they, in Rawlsian terms, have the capacity to form, revise, and pursue their conceptions of the good life. As we shall see later, one of the main goals of education is to gradually build up this capacity in young children and adolescents.

However, given the range of very diverse examples of nudges offered by Thaler and Sunstein, their three constraints seem more relevant for the moral assessment of some nudges compared to others. A number of influences listed as nudges, such as GPS navigation or the "look right/left/both ways" signs in the UK, seem to be transparent by design. Pelle Hansen and Andreas Jespersen suggest that these belong to a distinct category of nudges (so-called Type 2 nudges) that do not bypass their targets' reflective capacities (2013, 20), while Robert Baldwin claims that such nudges "respect the decision-making autonomy of the individual and enhance reflective decision-making" (2014, 835). The three aforementioned constraints do not seem obviously applicable to Type 2 nudges, which seem compatible with autonomy. Not only do they automatically pass the transparency test, but even if it is difficult for their targets to easily resist them or the ends they promote (upon reflection), the manner in which they promote them is not apparently morally objectionable. This is because they highlight information that grounds reasons for action, which targeted individuals may find convincing. On the other hand, "Type 1" nudges seem more threatening to autonomy since they tap into psychological mechanisms (i.e., "trigger heuristics" [Barton and Grüne-Yanoff, 2015]) without highlighting reasons for action. For example, reducing plate size in a school cafeteria so that students eat less does not highlight any reasons for eating less.[5]

The predictable tendencies to commit errors mentioned by Blumenthal-Barby are just as present if not more pronounced in the reasoning and decision-making of minors. Lavechia, Liu, and Oreopoulous (2014) note that students manifest systematic biases in discounting long-term consequences (e.g., the difficulty of picking certain classes or taking them seriously given distant rewards), in sticking to established routines (e.g., problems with transitioning from involuntary to voluntary attendance), and in giving into peer pressure (e.g., not deviating significantly from the predominant behavior in their social circle). The classroom environment exacerbates some of these aspects further. For instance, putting in a lot of effort in class may often come at the cost of socializing opportunities (short-term rewards) or being ridiculed and/or rejected by less ambitious peers (peer pressure). If students are allowed to act on these biases throughout education, they may often come to regret such decisions after the fact and wish they were given more guidance at the time (Bridgeland, DiIulio and Morison, 2006).

The distinction between Type 1 and Type 2 nudges also translates quite neatly onto the different kinds of techniques tested in the classroom. This typology has already been used for classroom nudges by Weijers, de Koning, and Paas (2021). Consider first a few examples of effective Type 2 techniques. Students can be instructed to anticipate the temptations that distract them from studying (such as receiving text messages on their phones) and removing the source of temptation from the study area (Duckworth, Gendler and Gross, 2014). Or they could do an exercise in which they are asked to think about and write down long-term goals and ways of achieving them (Morisano et al., 2010). They could also be taught about the differences in earnings among adults that result from different levels of education (Jensen, 2010).[6] Type 1 nudges act more subtly. Weijers et al. mention the possibility of automatically enrolling students for exams (and requiring them to opt out if they wish to do so) (2021, 894). Quite a few other Type 1 nudges, which I describe shortly, regulate student behavior that might otherwise be sanctioned in standard educational circumstances.[7]

Weijers et al. recommend Type 2 nudges for occasions where educational goals are oriented toward long-term behavioral change. Type 1 nudges, on the other hand, are to be utilized only when students are expected to be cognitively overloaded in the face of demanding learning tasks (2021, 890–1). The expectation of Weijers et al. that Type 1 nudges will likely result in transient, rather than stable behavioral changes is somewhat understandable, given that such nudges do not highlight reasons for action that the targeted individuals could endorse. But this supposition would require further empirical evidence. It is possible, first, that if Type 1 nudges remain in place for a while, they would support the forming of desirable habits and norms that students would incorporate into their established routines. After all, going back as far as Plato, the development of virtues with a distinctly moral character cannot be obtained merely through contemplation, but also requires practice and habituation (Jonas, 2017). For instance, an opt-out nudge into exam enrollment could well establish a norm over time that students should resist procrastination and aim to take as many exams early. Second, it is also possible that while Type 1 nudges do not engage targeted individuals with reasons, individuals may still reflectively endorse the resulting shifts in behavior and in a way that could ground stable behavioral change and good habits. Students may sometimes be unable to say why their behaviors have changed, or they might confabulate; yet, if they endorse the behavior, it would be difficult to say why the forming of habits in such a way would be less plausible than through Type 2 nudges.

It remains the fact that Type 1 nudges are more morally threatening. It is Type 1 nudges that critics standardly have in mind when raising objections pertaining to autonomy, manipulation, and respect. In the case of children, there is the additional risk that Type 1 nudges could negatively affect the abilities of individuals to reach reflected decisions (Binder and Lades, 2015, 18), a skill that should be fostered and not undermined within the classroom. The permissibility of Type 1 nudges in the classroom (or perhaps on school grounds more generally) should be assessed in view of how they affect the autonomy and flourishing of students on balance and how they may help to realize educational values.

School discipline

One possible aim of (Type 1) nudging could be to achieve and maintain school discipline. By "discipline," here I mean the adherence of students to rules and regulations set by the school authority, the purpose of which is to protect students from harm and create an environment conducive to the promotion of students' educational interests. If these rules and regulations are violated, they are often met with sanction. Now, there might be different conceptions of which rules should be enacted and which sanctions practiced, so that educational goals could be achieved. Some believe that if students are to be self-determined, sanctions should be "educative whenever possible" and avoid to "delay or derail the emergence of decisional competence" (Curren, 2020, 126). The kinds of educational goals that they should be compatible with are, for instance, the aim of developing in students a wherewithal to lead independent lives as adults, which includes arriving at one's own conception of a good life and one's own sense of justice and morality (Clayton, 2015). Most agree that severe disciplinary measures (particularly exclusionary ones [Costenbader and Markson, 1998]) should be avoided, as they not only seem to correlate with bad academic performance and later criminal activity (Balfanz, Byrnes and Fox, 2014; APAZTTF, 2008; Nance, 2020) but, due to the stress they introduce, may "inhibit students' attainment of the intrinsic goods of childhood" (Schouten, 2019, 352).

Imagine now that the government delivers the best school disciplinary system, one in which each sanction is "diagnostic, educative, community building, and restorative" (Curren, 2020, 120). One might think it would still be preferable if the need for sanctions was altogether minimized, and if the students were able to learn their lessons in another way.[8] What if nudges could be a means of controlling student behavior, so as to bring us closer to such goals? This can be attempted either *indirectly* by getting students to focus on long-term goals and deterring them from opportunities for rule infractions (see nudges earlier) or by promoting rule-abidance *directly*. Consider a few examples of the latter kind. Arranging seats in a classroom is certain to affect student behavior (Wannarka and Ruhl, 2008) and may be successfully used to prevent victimization and promote more positive social relations between students (Van den Berg, Segers and Cillessen, 2012). In a study by Chalmers et al., playing classical piano music in a lunchroom reduced the need for the staff's disciplinary intervention by 65 percent (1999, 44).⁹ Engelen et al. have also argued recently that the stories about morally exemplary individuals that educators can use in class have some aspects of nudges—they frame moral choices, personalize information, and make options more salient (2018, 351); doing so facilitates children's moral education, the aims of which are avoiding and preventing harm, truth-telling, benevolence, and discipline (knowing what our society demands of us) (2018, 347–8).

Now, even if these school-discipline nudges turn out to be effective and morally justified, this would not relieve philosophers of education from the normative task of finding an appropriate model of student sanctioning in schools. Similar to how it is often objected that nudges cannot replace structural reform (Schmidt and Engelen, 2020, 8), it could be stated here that even the most effective school-discipline nudge would still need to be backed by a justifiable system of school sanctions. As in general debates about nudging, this objection is convincing but does little to disqualify the use of nudges. Nudges can be used alongside justified sanctions and can initiate behavioral shifts that may prompt institutional change (Schmidt and Engelen, 2020, 8). There is thus no obvious tension between using school-discipline nudges and a justifiable system of school sanctions. It might even be suggested that school-discipline nudges might be part of the coercive system, as they are in two senses more difficult to avoid than standardly conceived nudges. First, children cannot opt out of school, so they cannot avoid nudges applied in the classroom. Second, classroom nudges are hardly easily resistible for children, since they may have a harder time noticing the nudge than adults or appreciating the workings of their cognitive heuristics and since resisting the behavior the nudge promotes often implies sanction.

Yet, one possible suggestion might be that at least at some stages of schooling, students should be required to follow rules in compliance with reasons to do so and not as a result of triggering heuristics. Covert nudges, insofar as they are manipulative, are less "honest" or respectful of their targets' rational agencies than coercive rules (Coons and Weber, 2014, 15), so autonomy that reaches a certain level of development might fit better with "honest coercion." I discuss adolescent schoolgoers as potential candidates for this kind of treatment in the following section.

The autonomies of very young and adolescent schoolchildren

The constraints on permissible nudging, pertaining to transparency, easy resistibility, and sensitivity to agent preferences, might not apply to children as it does to adults. This is because children seem to lack the autonomy to govern their own lives and depend for this on adults. For instance, on a Kantian account offered by Tamar Schapiro (1999), children lack a unified self, capable of harnessing, in a principled way, the various motivational forces that steer their behavior. In an important sense, we take schooling to be one of the primary means of developing autonomy, through cultivating the competences one requires to become a self-governing agent (Brighouse, 2000, 2006) and through making children familiar with the "range of meaningful life options from which to choose" (Reich, 2002, 92).

Even more importantly for considerations of school discipline, children are often thought to be incapable of autonomous *moral* conduct. Matthew Clayton and Andrés Moles have argued that children's lack of capacity to recognize moral reasons and act on them is their crucial distinctive trait compared to adults, "which suggests a wider scope for permissible interference in children's lives to improve their moral conduct" (2018, 250). Children can very well understand what rules apply to them and what the consequences are for breaking them, but they have a harder time understanding the moral reasons that explain why breaking these rules is wrong. This corresponds to what developmental psychologist Lawrence Kohlberg calls the "preconventional stage" of moral development (1984).

But this capacity for understanding develops over time. In fact, most authors agree that there are significant differences in autonomous agency between young children and adolescents. As Sarah Hannan notes,

> children's autonomy develops gradually. It begins in very limited domains to limited extents in early childhood, and slowly becomes very close to adult autonomy later in childhood. [. . .] For instance, children's ability to assess risks of failure, or to formulate and execute plans, increases as they age. (2019, 118)

It could be argued that adolescents are not only comparatively more autonomous than very young children but that there are domains of decision-making in which adolescents are autonomous, whereas young children are not. In fact, young children can seemingly be autonomous in some domains, such as choosing who to play with. But adolescents become autonomous in many other areas as they mature. Many of these entail the possibility of taking responsibility for their actions, making the requirement to practice autonomy more powerful in their case than in the case of younger children.[10] On Kohlberg's understanding (1984), adolescents enter into the "conventional stage" of moral development, in which they attain a better grasp of moral standards and responsibilities within relationships; some adolescents may even enter the stage of "postconventional morality," in which they develop personal moralities and notice the shortcomings of social rules and norms.

Thus, if autonomy is the primary criterion upon which we test the permissibility of classroom nudges, it hardly seems appropriate to reach the same moral conclusions for exposing young children and adolescents. Adolescents are not only more competent to make self-governing decisions and to weigh options and tailor plans about the kinds of persons they want to become. Being allowed to act in these ways without interference is at least sometimes important as a formative exercise and for how their relationships with adults develop over time. An important social condition of autonomy, says Hannan, is that children have "opportunities to practice or express their developing self-governance skills" (1984). Hence, I argue in what follows that in the case of adolescence, educators should nudge them into discipline carefully and conservatively, and refrain from it altogether when they can.[11]

To understand the kind of special treatment required in the case of adolescents, a particularly instructive account of how autonomy develops as minors mature is offered by Faye Tucker (2016). According to Tucker, autonomies of adolescents flourish when they are enabled to take part in important decisions that were previously made for them and when they can take responsibility for their actions. This inclusion makes it possible for them to cultivate their self-governance (Tucker, 2016, 759), giving educators (and adults more broadly) a duty to ensure conditions for such cultivation (Tucker, 2016, 761). The importance of this process for autonomy is that it develops in adolescents "a set of skills and attitudes," including "the ability to reason, to appreciate different points of view, and to debate with others," but also that it establishes "a sense of self-worth and self-respect" (Tucker, 2016, 762). The process also fosters their capacity for choosing well by helping adolescents to develop "a deliberative perspective," which consists in "learning about choices" and "understanding [. . .] what matters to [them]" (Tucker, 2016, 763).

Tucker's account shows not only why the emergent autonomy of adolescents requires they be included in decisions they may not be entirely ready to make, but it also hints at why the utilization of Type 1 nudges in the case of adolescent students raises sensitive issues. When possible, it will be preferable to approach adolescents openly about the kinds of influences that could be applied to their educational context and to give them a say in what kinds of influences will regulate their behavior.[12] If students collectively insist on not being influenced in some way that optimally promotes discipline, then by that act they can take responsibility for their possible rule infractions in the future.

Autonomy in development and exposure to nudges

Let's consider several moral concerns about the use of Type 1 nudges on adolescents.

First, the covert use of a Type 1 nudge may fully divert students from engaging with reasons, thereby failing to cultivate their autonomy-specific skills and attitudes. The transition that we seem to expect from adolescents as they mature is that they gradually become more compliant, rather than merely conforming with moral reasons (Raz, 1999, 178–9).[13] For instance, a student who merely conforms with a moral reason not to bully her classmate is deterred by threat of detention, whereas a student who is compliant with the moral reason acts *from* that reason (e.g., that bullying classmates seriously harms them and is thereby wrong). While trying to establish discipline through seating arrangements does not necessarily damage compliance with reasons, it does not promote it either and is thereby a missed opportunity. Moral exemplars could highlight such reasons but might inspire nothing more than conformity, if students are not told why they are being taught about the exemplar.

Second, favoring the inclusion of adolescents in the decisions about whether and how they should be nudged also considers the vehement "demands for autonomy" (Benporath, 2003, 132) so commonly associated with adolescents. Matthew Clayton's independence view of autonomy (2012), which emphasizes not only the agents' capacities for decision-making but also a requirement for self-authorship, seems particularly fitting in the case of adolescents. Cultivating a budding autonomy at least sometimes entails leaving the choice entirely to the developing agent, even if the supervising agent is significantly more knowledgeable or the consequences of misconduct somewhat unpleasant. In the case of nudging school discipline, it makes sense, as part of putting the independence principle into practice, to sometimes refrain from steering adolescent students and allowing them to arrive at reasons to uphold rules by themselves, even if they do so suboptimally. Not doing so may come at a cost to the kind of self-worth and self-respect that Tucker points to (2016, 762), especially if educators are discovered in their covert activities.

This leads me to the third and related point, which is that nudges might undermine classroom trust and damage the relationships between adolescents and adults. On relational accounts of autonomy, an agent's capacity for autonomy depends crucially on the kinds of social relationships and modes of socialization; these may impede the capacity for autonomy, say, by undermining the agent's sense of self-respect, self-worth, and self-trust (Mackenzie and Stoljar, 2000,

22). Any such impediments on autonomy arising from social relationships are considered "oppressive" (Mackenzie and Stoljar, 2000, 22). Can triggering heuristics be oppressive toward adolescents? And if so, in what way? Consider that an adolescent's is a nascent sense of self-worth and is for that reason still fragile. The educator's decision to bypass the adolescent's reasoning capacities, where these capacities could have been engaged, communicates to adolescents that they cannot expect to be treated as reasons-giving stakeholders or trust the educators to be honest about their intentions. This outcome is potentially damaging not only in a general sense, creating an image for the adolescent of a world in which adults are not to be trusted, but particularly in the intimate context of the classroom, where educators and adolescents spend many hours together and cooperate with each other in a multitude of ways.[14] Admittedly, nudge transparency does not always require advance disclosure of this kind in order for Type 1 nudges to be permissible (Ivanković and Engelen, 2019), but this is more easily established in the "adult world," where targeted individuals can appreciate how they make predictable errors in view of the goals that they autonomously endorse. The same levels of self-awareness about psychological leanings should not be expected from adolescents, who are more interested in the newly forming capacities that earn them a "place at the adults' table." Thus, covert heuristics triggering is more damaging to the autonomy of adolescents compared to that of adults, as well as to the relationships they form with one another.

The fourth and final concern about covertly exposing adolescents to school-discipline nudges is that they steer adolescents toward abiding by rules that they would more likely challenge if they were overtly given reasons to abide by them. As Engelen et al. point out, one aim of moral education is to enable individuals to criticize and surpass the moral norms that concern them (2018, 357). If adolescents are truly to engage with moral reasons behind norms that have become formal disciplinary rules and that regulate their behavior under threat of sanction, then these rules and norms are bound to be occasionally challenged as well. And not for naught—student perspectives are crucial in morally assessing the fairness and proportionality of many different school rules. If schools are to come up with diagnostic, educative, community building, and restorative sanctions (Curren, 2020, 120), they will surely require the input of students. While some nudges, like the moral exemplars proposed by Engelen et al., arguably preserve and cultivate the capacities of adolescents to challenge rules and norms, other heuristic-triggering nudges will unlikely have the same effect. In this case, it is not only the cultivation of adolescent autonomy that suffers but also the process of arriving at just and proportionate disciplinary rules and sanctions.

Concerns about exposing adolescents are alleviated at least to an extent if the transparency condition is satisfied in ways other than via the teacher's direct disclosure in the classroom and if the nudge itself is easily resistible or made easily resistible by virtue of such transparency. For instance, students can find out about the nudges in use on a website, during school open day events, or within school-discipline rulebooks. But these alternative ways of satisfying transparency are inferior to direct disclosure for several reasons. First, they do not leave room for renegotiating the nudge with the students, in effect preventing them from assuming responsibility in their interactions with teachers. Second, the teachers must have a justified expectation that students will consult these alternative sources. Finally, the alternative sources might not help if nudges are stacked and students cannot keep track of their many occurrences.

Thus, exposing adolescents to school-discipline nudges should be avoided, or they should at least have a say in whether they accept exposure. But are covert school-discipline nudges otherwise impermissible? While students could flourish from taking part in how their surroundings are modified in order to facilitate rule-abidance, school-discipline nudges are not always inappropriate all things considered. Sometimes the student behavior that these nudges are supposed to correct is so far off from satisfactory rule-abidance that it effectively cancels the duty of educators to refrain from covert influences. And after all, sometimes it might be more important to ensure that adolescents discharge their enforceable duties toward others than attempting that they engage reflectively with such duties, so as to protect students from harm and safeguard an environment that facilitates learning.

Adolescence as transition

Once more, we can take note from Tucker's instructive account of adolescent autonomy. Tucker seeks to articulate a transitional kind of paternalism that allows adults to interfere when adolescents are struggling with their newly gained independence and when they are putting their interests at risk. Transitional paternalism, in her view, is an "intermediate step, between a time when an individual has no normative power and a time when they have unshared normative power, [which] prepares young people to be able to take on increased normative powers in adulthood" (2016, 761). As Tucker notes, adolescents are only "*becoming* self-governing, and adults have a duty to help them work their way out of childhood" (2016, 762). Tucker's example of permissible interference is in the clinical context, where it is desirable for the development of adolescent autonomy that they are able to consent to a number of clinical actions, but where their refusal can be overruled if it risks significant harm or death (2016, 760). Similarly in the context of the classroom, adolescents should be able to take part in shaping the environment that steers their behavior in relation to rule-abidance and should be allowed to reject the behavioral arrangements that do so optimally. But they should not be allowed to insist on environments that are potentially harmful to some or those that cannot possibly facilitate learning and thus promote the interests realized through education.

Tucker further illustrates transitional paternalism through the analogy of dual controls in a driving instructor's car. The learner is given some space to make and gradually improve her driving decisions, but the additional set of controls enables the instructor to take over when the learner's decisions risk very bad outcomes. The learner gets to exercise her newly acquired skills (which she will put to use once she is recognized as a fully self-sufficient driver) but without the danger of making the worst kinds of mistakes (2016, 755). Back in the classroom, the adolescent may undoubtedly resent educators in some situation for prematurely "taking control" over the environment to ensure rule-abidance and promote better learning outcomes. But while some interferences will undoubtedly be premature, the relationship in which such boundaries are openly established is more respectful and takes better consideration of the adolescent's burgeoning autonomy.[15]

Finally, consider the objection that some of the influences that we have considered as part of the Type 1 nudge category are inevitably chosen by educators. An educator reading this chapter may think she is hardly wronging adolescent students when picking this or that seating arrangement, since *some* seating arrangement, with *some* predictable effect, will have to get picked. Surely, we may think, her only obligation is to pick an arrangement that contributes to school discipline and facilitates learning, or at the very least, rule out those available arrangements that plainly undermine these goals. But on the conception of adolescent autonomy that I have adopted, this would not be sufficient. Students could still plausibly be told about the available arrangements (pertaining to seating or other matters on school premises) and their predictable effects, as well as be made participants in the decisions that concern them—namely, to be exposed to one arrangement or the other. When resisting the choice of an optimal arrangement for keeping an orderly classroom, I argued, adolescents can take responsibility for resulting deviations from school discipline and thereby develop their budding autonomy. This is preferable to merely steering adolescents via Type 1 nudges in the way that very young children would be steered in these kinds of circumstances. Still, the educator might insist that there are many such decisions to be made; surely, adolescents cannot be consulted in every single case. My response is that if there are indeed many such decisions in an average classroom, then surely educators would not be neglecting the development of adolescent autonomy or the forming of trusting relationships between adolescents and adults by failing to include adolescents in all such decisions. It would suffice, for the aforementioned purposes, to have adolescents participate in the most important decisions of this kind.

Conclusion

My analysis of classroom nudges in this chapter remains well short of being exhaustive. There is still a lot more to be said, for instance, about how nudges fare morally compared to coercive sanction or how classroom nudges fare compared to other nudges given their mandatory setting. We should also explore in greater detail whether educators and other school workers should seriously be expected to "keep up with the science" and reliably produce nudges with predictable effects. But I have at least managed to point to an important possible moral pitfall in the case of adolescents.

This is not to suggest that classroom nudges do not have a lot going for them. They may be able to prevent the use of sanction that all parties would want to avoid, protect students from the possibly harmful infractions of others, and, ultimately, contribute to and maintain a classroom that facilitates learning. But if I am right that classroom nudges might also frustrate the development of adolescent autonomy, cause resentment, and erode classroom trust, then too much is at stake for our approach to be carefree. Concerns of this kind might seem minor to some, but if they are indeed minor, then they are a fitting occasion to acknowledge the developing adolescents as partners in the educational process.

Acknowledgments

Many thanks to Lovro Savić, John Tillson, and Winston Thompson for their valuable comments and suggestions.

Notes

1 Following Schmidt (2019), I use the notion of "harnessing" rather than "exploiting" cognitive heuristics, since it seems a less normatively question-begging term.
2 Nudges can be transparent by design, be it before or after they take effect. In addition, they can be made transparent through disclosure; we can be told about them explicitly, or we can learn about them through an easily accessible source, like a website or pamphlet. See Ivanković and Engelen (2019) for a detailed account.
3 However, many nudges mentioned in the literature do not obviously promote the interests of the person they target, or promoting the interests of the targeted individual is hardly the primary purpose behind the nudge (as opposed to, say, preventing harm to others or reducing costs). For instance, the oft-cited organ donation nudge seems primarily about helping people in need of organs rather than getting organ donors to do what they really want to do. For a similar point, and examples of how nudges could be used in other-regarding ways, see Kelly (2013), Nagatsu (2015), and Moles (2015). Along these lines, an unruly student could be nudged to act in line with her background aim to behave, but it seems just as, if not more significant, to thereby benefit other students adversely affected by the student's unruliness.
4 However, for a sophisticated account of how these requirements are to be further modified for nudges to be "interpersonally justified" to their targets, see Kiener (2021). I will assume, in line with Kiener, that these requirements may at the very least still serve as useful rules of thumb for safeguarding important moral principles.
5 "Type 1" and "Type 2" are references to dual-process and dual-systems theories in behavioral science. The notions of "Type 1" and "System 1" refer to quick and effortless cognitive processes for the most part not consciously controlled, while "Type 2" and "System 2" refer to slow and labored processes of conscious reflection. These theories are contested in behavioral science and often conflict with one another, but I do not need to take a stand on the correctness of any of them for the purposes of this chapter. For more detailed accounts of these theories, see Evans and Over (1996) and Kahneman (2011).
6 Note, however, that some Type 2 techniques may contain predictable Type 1 effects, and secondary aims can be formulated accordingly. For instance, in the goal-setting exercise of Morisano et al., educators may come to expect that students will, to some extent, share how they have handled the exercise with their friends. This may, for instance, reveal to students that others have ambitions similar to theirs and make them more socially comfortable about their goals.
7 One important difference between my account and that of Weijers et al. is that on their conception, which follows Hansen and Jespersen's (2013), Type 2 nudges can be non-transparent (2021, 894). Although the examples of Type 2 nudges they mention do engage with targeted individuals reflectively, it is not obvious that

they thereby highlight information relevant for deciding whether to engage in the given activity (e.g., priming students' relationships with family members in order to relax them into discussing sensitive issues [PIS, 2019]). The purpose of engaging reflection here is to trigger a heuristic. I remain skeptical on the tenability of this category but do not explore the issue further here.
8   However, I revisit this possibility in the second part of the chapter.
9   Behavior may also be influenced by neurochemical and environmental factors that may not be classified as nudges but would similarly bypass the engagement with moral reasons if used. Granström (1996) mentions the effects of temperature and lighting, while Clayton and Moles (2018, 248) hypothesize about influencing behavior through controlling student diets.
10 But for a more nuanced view about child autonomy and the differences (or lack thereof) in autonomous will between children and adults, see Grill (2019). Grill argues that because children normally do not create coherent life plans, interferences do not violate self-creation, as they would in the case of adults.
11 The primary scope of normative analysis in this chapter is nudging school discipline, but much of what I claim here could apply to other domains, such as adolescents' academic performance.
12 Students could also disagree with each other. But arguably, facing disagreement and arriving at compromises in the classroom may also be relevant for developing adolescent autonomy. I thank Lovro Savić for highlighting this important point to me.
13 This is not to suggest that compliance with reasons always has an upward trend in adolescence. At certain stages, adolescents may resist engaging with moral reasons despite their content, for instance, when adults impose harsh sanctions for their violation or when they see the rule as an expression of someone's control over them. Be that as it may, rebelliousness is usually only a temporary deterrent from engaging with moral reasons.
14 The classroom is also a far more intimate environment than the usual sites of nudging discussed in the nudge literature.
15 Note that Tucker believes that the interference in transitional paternalism does not violate but is compatible with adolescent autonomy because it helps develop the normative powers of adolescents down the line (2016, 766). I remain agnostic on this issue here.

References

American Psychological Association Zero Tolerance Task Force (2008) "Are Zero Tolerance Policies Effective in the Schools? An Evidentiary Review and Recommendations." *American Psychologist* 63 (9): 852–62.

Baldwin, Robert (2014) "From Regulation to Behaviour Change: Giving Nudge the Third Degree." *The Modern Law Review* 77 (6): 831–57.

Balfanz, Robert, Byrnes, Vaughan and Fox, Joanna (2014) "Sent Home and Put Off-Track: The Antecedents, Disproportionalities, and Consequences of Being Suspended in the Ninth Grade." *Journal of Applied Research on Children* 5 (2). https://files.eric.ed.gov/fulltext/EJ1188519.pdf.

Barton, Adrien and Grüne-Yanoff, Till (2015) "From Libertarian Paternalism to Nudging—and Beyond." *Review of Philosophy and Psychology* 6 (3): 341–59.

Benporath, Sigal R. (2003) "Autonomy and Vulnerability: On Just Relations Between Adults and Children." *Journal of Philosophy of Education* 37 (1): 127–45.

Binder, Martin and Lades, Leonhard K. (2015) "Autonomy-Enhancing Paternalism." *Kyklos* 68 (1): 3–27.

Blumenthal-Barby, Jennifer S. (2013) "Choice Architecture: A Mechanism for Improving Decisions While Preserving Liberty?" In Christian Coons and Michael Weber (eds.), *Paternalism: Theory and Practice*, 178–96. New York: Cambridge University Press.

Bridgeland, John M., DiIulio, John J. Jr. and Morison, Karen B. (2006) *The Silent Epidemic: Perspectives of High School Dropouts.* Civic Enterprises. https://docs.gatesfoundation.org/documents/thesilentepidemic3-06final.pdf.

Brighouse, Harry (2000) *School Choice and Social Justice.* Oxford: Oxford University Press.

Brighouse, Harry (2006) *On Education.* New York: Routledge.

Chalmers, Lynne, Olson, Myrna R. and Zurkowski, Joyce K. (1999) "Music as a Classroom Tool." *Intervention in School and Clinic* 35 (1): 43–52.

Clayton, Matthew (2012) "Debate: The Case against the Comprehensive Enrolment of Children." *The Journal of Political Philosophy* 20 (3): 353–64.

Clayton, Matthew (2015) "Anti-perfectionist Childrearing." In Alexander Bagattini and Colin Macleod (eds.), *The Nature of Children's Well-Being*, 123–40. Dordrecht: Springer.

Clayton, Matthew and Moles, Andrés (2018) "Neurointerventions, Morality, and Children." In David Birks and Thomas Douglas (eds.), *Treatment for Crime: Philosophical Essays on Neurointerventions in Criminal Justice*, 235–51. Oxford: Oxford University Press.

Coons, Christian and Weber, Michael (2014) "Introduction: Investigating the Core Concept and Its Moral Status." In Christian Coons and Michael Weber (eds.), *Manipulation: Theory and Practice*, 1–16, New York: Oxford University Press.

Costenbader, Virginia and Markson, Samia (1998) "School Suspension: A Study with Secondary School Students." *Journal of School Psychology* 36 (1): 59–82.

Curren, Randall (2020) "Punishment and Motivation in a Just School Community." *Theory and Research in Education* 18 (1): 117–33.

Damgaard, Mette T. and Nielsen, Helena S. (2018) "Nudging in Education." *Economics of Education Review* 64: 313–42.

Duckworth, Angela L., Gendler, Tamar S. and Gross, James J. (2014) "Self-Control in School-Age Children." *Educational Psychologist* 49 (3): 199–217.

Engelen, Bart, Thomas, Alan, Archer, Alfred and van de Ven, Niels (2018) "Exemplars and Nudges: Combining Two Strategies for Moral Education." *Journal of Moral Education* 47 (3): 346–65.

Evans, Jonathan S. B. T. and Over, David E. (1996) *Rationality and Reasoning.* Hove: Psychology Press.

Granström, Kjell (1996) "Private Communication Between Students in the Classroom in Relation to Different Classroom Features." *Educational Psychology* 16 (4): 349–64.

Grill, Kalle (2019) "Paternalism Towards Children." In Anca Gheaus, Gideon Calder and Jurgen De Wispelaere (eds.), *The Routledge Handbook of the Philosophy of Childhood and Children*, 123–33. London and New York: Routledge.

Hannan, Sarah (2019) "Childhood and Autonomy." In Anca Gheaus, Gideon Calder and Jurgen De Wispelaere (eds.), *The Routledge Handbook of the Philosophy of Childhood and Children*, 112–22. London and New York: Routledge.

Hansen, Pelle G. and Jespersen, Andreas M. (2013) "Nudge and the Manipulation of Choice: A Framework for the Responsible Use of the Nudge Approach to Behaviour Change in Public Policy." *European Journal of Risk Regulation* 4 (1): 3–28.

Hausman, Daniel M. and Welch, Brynn (2010) "Debate: To Nudge or Not to Nudge." *Journal of Political Philosophy* 18 (1): 123–36.

Ivanković, Viktor and Engelen, Bart (2019) "Nudging, Transparency, and Watchfulness." *Social Theory and Practice* 45 (1): 43–73.

Jensen, Robert (2010) "The (Perceived) Returns to Education and the Demand for Schooling." *Quarterly Journal of Economics* 125 (2): 515–48.

Jonas, Mark E. (2017) "Plato on the Necessity of Imitation and Habituation for the Cultivation of the Virtues." In David Carr, James Arthur and Kristján Kristjánsson (eds.), *Varieties of Virtue Ethics*, 233–48. London: Palgrave Macmillan.

Kahneman, Daniel (2011) *Thinking, Fast and Slow.* London: Penguin.

Kelly, Jamie T. (2013) "Libertarian Paternalism, Utilitarianism, and Justice." In Christian Coons and Michael Weber (eds.), *Paternalism: Theory and Practice*, 216–30. New York: Cambridge University Press.

Kiener, Maximilian (2021) "When Do Nudges Undermine Voluntary Consent?." *Philosophical Studies* 178 (12): 4201–26.

Kohlberg, Lawrence (1984) *The Psychology of Moral Development: The Nature and Validity of Moral Stages, Essays on Moral Development Volume 2.* San Francisco: Harper & Row.

Lavecchia, Adam M., Liu, Heidi and Oreopoulous, Philip (2014) "Behavioral Economics of Education: Progress and Possibilities." *National Bureau of Economic Research: Working Paper 20609.* http://www.nber.org/papers/w20609.

Levitt, Steven D., List, John A., Neckermann, Susanne and Sadoff, Sally (2016) "The Behavioralist Goes to School: Leveraging Behavioral Economics to Improve

Educational Performance." *American Economic Journal: Economic Policy* 8 (4): 183–219.

Mackenzie, Catriona and Stoljar, Natalie (2000) "Introduction: Autonomy Refigured." In Catriona Mackenzie and Natalie Stoljar (eds.), *Relational Autonomy: Feminist Perspectives on Autonomy, Agency, and the Social Self*, 3–31. New York and Oxford: Oxford University Press.

Moles, Andrés (2015) "Nudging for Liberals." *Social Theory and Practice* 41 (4): 644–67.

Morisano, Dominique, Hirsch, Jacob B., Peterson, Jordan B., Pihl, Robert O. and Shore, Bruce M. (2010) "Setting, Elaborating, and Reflecting on Personal Goals Improves Academic Performance." *Journal of Applied Psychology* 95 (2): 255–64.

Nagatsu, Michiru (2015) "Social Nudges: Their Mechanisms and Justification." *Review of Philosophy and Psychology* 6 (3): 481–94.

Nance, Jason P. (2020) "The Intersection between Schools and the Criminal Justice System." In James G. Dwyer (ed.), *The Oxford Handbook of Children and the Law*, 665–700. Oxford: Oxford University Press.

Platform Integration and Society (2019) *Primen in de Praktijk? [Priming in Practice?]*, Utrecht: Kennisplatform Integratie & Samenleving.

Raz, Joseph (1999) *Practical Reasons and Norms*, 2nd ed. Oxford: Oxford University Press.

Reich, Rob (2002) *Bridging Liberalism and Multiculturalism in American Education*. Chicago, IL: University of Chicago Press.

Rozeboom, Grant J. (2020) "Nudging for Rationality and Self-Governance." *Ethics* 131 (1): 107–21.

Schapiro, Tamar (1999) "What Is a Child?" *Ethics* 109 (4): 715–38.

Schmidt, Andreas T. (2019) "Getting Real on Rationality—Behavioral Science, Nudging, and Public Policy." *Ethics* 129 (4): 511–43.

Schmidt, Andreas T. and Engelen, Bart (2020) "The Ethics of Nudging: An Overview." *Philosophy Compass* 15 (4). https://compass.onlinelibrary.wiley.com/doi/full/10.1111/phc3.12658.

Schouten, Gina (2019) "Schooling." In Anca Gheaus, Gideon Calder and Jurgen De Wispelaere (eds.), *The Routledge Handbook of the Philosophy of Childhood and Children*, 351–61. London and New York: Routledge.

Thaler, Richard H. and Sunstein, Cass R. (2008) *Nudge: Improving Decisions about Health, Wealth, and Happiness*. New Haven, CT: Yale University Press.

Tucker, Faye (2016) "Developing Autonomy and Transitional Paternalism." *Bioethics* 30 (9): 759–66.

Van den Berg, Yvonne H., Segers, Eliane and Cillessen, Antonius H. (2012) "Changing Peer Perceptions and Victimization through Classroom Arrangements: A Field Experiment." *Journal of Abnormal Child Psychology* 40 (3): 403–12.

Wannarka, Rachel and Ruhl, Kathy (2008) "Seating Arrangements that Promote Positive Academic and Behavioural Outcomes: A Review of Empirical Research." *Support for Learning* 23 (2): 89–93.

Weijers, Robert J., de Koning, Björn B. and Paas, Fred (2021) "Nudging in Education: From Theory Towards Guidelines for Successful Implementation." *European Journal of Psychology of Education* 36 (1): 883–902.

Wilkinson, T. Martin (2013) "Nudging and Manipulation." *Political Studies* 61 (2): 341–55.

14

Making Sense of Student (Mis)behavior
A Critical Pragmatist Alternative to Pedagogies of Punishment

Barbara S. Stengel, Elizabeth A. Self, and Rebecca A. Peterson

Herbie Hancock tells a story about Miles Davis, the great jazz trumpeter, who was quoted as saying, "When you hit a wrong note, it's the next note you play that determines whether it's good or bad." Hancock describes his own error in the middle of a Davis solo and records Davis's response: "Miles paused for a second . . . and then he played some notes that made my chord right . . . Miles was able to turn something that was wrong into something that was right."[1] This was in contrast to Hancock's distraction, paralyzed by his own ideas about "right" and "wrong" notes. Miles Davis's approach—a focus on the "next note you play"—is an object lesson for educators. Davis isn't fazed by errant notes but concentrates on responding constructively to what is given, making sense of and transforming might-be missteps into moments on the way toward a high-quality performance. It is this type of pragmatist and improvisational approach to student (mis)behaviors that we argue for in this chapter. It is an approach that views apparent student errors and transgressions as opportunities for growth rather than as triggers for punishment. It is, quite simply, a commitment to the education of students rather than to control them.

Careful inspection reveals that well-intentioned educators practice punishment far more frequently than we would care to admit, following an instrumental logic that is more juridical than educative. This is so because (a) regimes of discipline and pedagogies of punishments are built into societal and educational status quos, (b) we (i.e., well-intentioned educators, including the authors) too often separate feelings, thoughts, and behaviors in pedagogical deliberation and action, and (c) educative purposes are not foregrounded. That is, we are not attuned to the feelings that move students, nor do we appreciate the institutional pushes and pulls that make their actions make sense to themselves and their peers. Most damning, and despite our good intentions, we forget why we are there in the first place.

While understandable, this is not an educative stance. An educative stance, one that is developmental and growth-oriented, requires a different logic, a logic of interpretation and response that accounts for these affective and institutional considerations, a logic that strives to make sense of what students do rather than focus on what they *should* do. Such a critical, pragmatist, and improvisational logic enriches possibilities for interpretation of students' and teachers' actions, enabling the educator to respond in a fitting way to whatever students offer. It enables the educator to participate in sense-making with students on the path to growth.

In this chapter, we (all three with experience in both K-12 and university-level teaching, and with responsibility for university-level teacher candidates' learning to teach) admit to our own unwitting habits of punishment, describe institutional constraints framing habits of punitive interpretation and reaction, unveil the affects embedded in seemingly reasonable practices, and explore how we can and why we should reconstruct habits of reaction in the direction of a critical pragmatist ethic.

Unwitting habits of punishment

To ground our argument, we invite the reader to recall typical instances of student "misbehavior": disrupting learning, disrespecting others, harassment/bullying, threatening physical danger, not knowing, and knowing too much. These are types of missteps that appear across educational levels (primary, K-6; secondary 7-12; tertiary, 13+) and that too often elicit punishing reactions.

As we sketch some examples throughout this chapter, it will become both more and less clear what counts as punishment here. Our pragmatist view is quite simple though perhaps counterintuitive to some. Any response to student behavior that is not educative—even if pleasant—is punishing, that is, depriving a student of what they expect, deserve, and need. It is only possible to determine whether a student's behavior is misbehavior after the fact, based on the outcome of the student's act and the teacher's response. Similarly, it is only possible to determine whether a teacher's action is punishing rather than educative after the fact. Students' growth (or lack thereof) marks the meaning of the teacher's action. (To clarify, this does not suggest that obviously hurtful actions in response may be rendered acceptable if they result in seemingly desirable behaviors—or learning achievements—in the short run. The goal is the *education* of the student, that is, an increase in the students' capacity for growth. It is likely impossible to avoid *all* instances of hurtful action as teachers respond to very different students, but it is never acceptable to impose pain, separation, or helplessness on students for instrumental purposes except perhaps when the purpose is preservation of immediate safety.)

We, the authors, readily admit that this foregrounds the judgment of the teacher and complicates that teacher's decision-making. Even the helpful and hard-to-dispute principle that teachers should be "firm, fair, and consistent" is devilishly difficult to implement and always revisable in specific circumstances. To address this reality, we focus here on student *behaviors*, never assuming that a specific (type of) behavior is *mis*behavior. We also try not to assume that what a teacher or administrator expects is always the best guide for assessing what students are doing. We leave open the possibility that what we, though well-intentioned, fail to expect (or even initially appreciate) might be just the right move to advance student growth *if* we can respond in a fitting, and ultimately transformative, way.

This approach challenges the assumption that (a certain kind of) order precedes learning and development as well as other assumptions of and about practice. It is simply not the case that obedient children who do as they are told will live the fullest lives. It is not the case that formal testing results in more effective learning. It is not the case that getting the right answer is the best indicator of either intelligence or achievement. Challenging adult thinking is a rite of passage toward maturity. Testing takes up time that might be spent investigating. Error is an opportunity to think anew and differently. These are educative outcomes that become more difficult to attain when we view student behavior through a lens that assumes misbehavior.

More often than we would like to admit, educators enact habits that are rooted in a juridical logic of blame and punishment ("do the crime; do the time") rather than an educational framing of growth and development. Here we counter a logic of blame and punishment with a more expansive view: what does not educate punishes. Sometimes a student action *is* a transgression, literally a student's attempt to test the lines/limits by crossing them. And when the system of behaviors understood to be appropriate is well thought out and educationally conceived, and the stipulated consequences seem to fit the break in communal possibilities for growth, such events serve the purposes of student growth and do no harm. They are simply a stop on the pathway toward self-regulation.

However, what if a student's transgression is, in fact, educationally useful? What if a student who transgresses is actually the canary in the coal mine alerting us to some inequity, inequality, or unsafe condition? These are the questions that become ripe for consideration when we begin to think through a critical pragmatist frame toward an educative response.

Below we take up questions of affect and institutional assumptions accounting for documentable inequities and obvious failings. We maintain that we can't tell whether an educator's action constitutes punishment or constructive redirection without contextualizing it in the light of educational purposes. Too many responses are punishing, and most punishments are forms of disinvestment in our students, reflecting our failure to actually educate in the name of an artificial sense of order. Punishment *may* control students' behavior but at the price of defeating the educational impulse toward growth, especially when it causes students to question whether they deserve to be taught.

Institutional assumptions shaping the practice of control

A variety of myths, values, habits, and expectations control what it is possible for teachers and students to think/do. Primary among those is the belief that control in the classroom precedes learning, an assumption enacted almost universally by teachers who spend the first days of a school year or a semester stipulating rules and procedures, co-constructing norms, reviewing syllabi to highlight dates and expectations, and "building community." These constitute the ground-laying work that justifies punishing consequences for those who don't abide by the rules, stick to the schedule, learn at a predictable pace, and maintain disciplined behavior.

Today, a fifth grader who can effortlessly recite the five "stages" of discipline (scolding, call home, write up, in-school suspension, out-of-school suspension) came home to report that her class was "not behaving." As a result, the teacher scrapped a plan for a Socratic seminar and assigned the entire class a three-paragraph response to a question (typed in twenty minutes) that would be graded. Clearly, the teacher felt that the students were no longer under control. Her reaction was to punish them in multiple ways: by replacing an engaging activity with a rote, boring exercise, *and* by linking their misbehavior to grades (and, in an unfortunate twist, privileging those who already knew how to type and could answer quickly rather than thoughtfully), all in the service of order rather than growth.

It is admittedly the teacher's responsibility to design the conditions for organization in the learning environment. Organization matters so that interaction and continuity are possible as students and teachers pursue growth together. Finding the effective source of authority requires thorough interpretation, anticipation of options and the likely consequences associated with each, and fitting response. The fitting response is the one most likely to generate enough organization to move toward growth, but not so much as to unnecessarily constrain the possibilities that individual freedom brings. In the instance cited here, the teacher meets the students' disruption with her own abandonment of rich pedagogical possibilities.

Obscured by the obvious, and dominant, focus on external control in schools are a host of related institutional assumptions that give rise to the apparent need for control and that shape how we both read and respond to students' actions. These include societal (and institutional) conservativism, physical and emotional security, and a presumption that the game of achieving in school is fair and equitable.

Schooling functions analogous to a game with rules. Many of the rules of the game of schooling—including what counts as appropriate behavior—have been designed to serve the interests of the status quo. Maintaining schooling in its current form—designed to privilege White, socioeconomically, and educationally well-off students—legitimates the system's winners (academically and economically). So, it is unsurprising that elites at the local, state, and federal levels think that schools are just fine pursuing the practices and policies that enabled *them* to rise to the top of the heap.

What counts as fairness is also built into the rules of the game. If the rules favor those who can type quickly, for example, there is no recourse for the student who types slowly other than failure or disruption. If the rules favor the student who has a parent at home providing and checking their clothing for dress-code compliance, then other students may struggle under the perception that they are "problem children." If the rules favor the student who comes to school or college ready to learn, then those who come without the benefit of readiness will be categorized (and penalized) as not knowing. They are seen as unworthy through no fault of their own.

Further, there is an undercurrent of concern for school security in this era of mass shootings. Lynda Stone (2011) suggests that this has so infected our school imaginary that instead of a teaching-learning dyad, we think in terms of a teaching-learning-security triad. Even those teachers who recognize that a little organized disorder can be quite educative are compelled to prioritize safety and security, a stance that engenders and supports suspicion of the other, even when the other is a member of the school community. Students who are minoritized (even sometimes when they constitute the majority of the school population) and students who are marked as different (particularly students who identify as LGBT or those with disabilities) are burdened with proving that they are not a threat or a problem. Perhaps predictably, the importance of safe space, especially from bullies and harassers, for those students who are "othered" has become a topic of much conversation. Advocates argue that educators must create safe space where students are protected and unburdened (or alternatively, brave space where they are able to advocate for themselves). However, as Stengel (2010) explains, there is no space that is safe for all persons at the same time. Only a both/and response, an educative encounter, can move teacher and students through this kind of impasse. Punishing one or the other (or both) likely results in neither safety nor growth.

Schools are ultimately conservative institutions, reproducing the power relations already in place in society. This means that as students learn to go along, to be compliant, they also learn their own place in a socioeconomic system that values persons based on what they can contribute to economic development. The narrowly conceived achievement that is the mark of school success is a proxy for (and just as distorted as) the valuing that imagines Jeff Bezos and Bill Gates as our wisest citizens because they are our richest citizens. If that is knowing then, as educators, we have to at least consider the possibility that "not knowing" is something we should be encouraging rather than punishing.

Punishment's affects

Students and teachers are moved to new understandings and new possibilities by affects associated with cultural and communal ideas and rituals. The affects associated with typical interactions, with specific (categories of) persons or with objects exchanged, constitute the *infrastructure* of the social entity that is school (Berlant, 2016), and we take those up here. It is important to stipulate that "affect" in our telling always involves embodied response and is autonomic rather than willed. Nonetheless, it is best understood as a relational habit, a nexus of thinking, feeling, and doing, fused in prior social relations. The question that links this section to the previous one, borrowed from Berlant, is "when do norms become forms?" That is, when do the ways that we act based on our typified modes of interaction become fixed, legitimated, and institutionalized?

We begin by asking, who are the students who know too much? Or at least are characterized in that way? It is still the case that White male students are socially positioned as knowers, epistemically competent, and worthy of a full hearing, while others, especially male, female, and nonbinary people of color, may be the objects of epistemic injustice. Are those who apparently know too much experiencing the bumptiousness of (over) confidence or the false bravado of uncertainty, or both? We cannot know unless we ask. Asking doesn't always mean a direct question; it may mean indirect questioning or attention to a student's background or past experiences in school. In either case, whether the student is truly confident or compensating for insecurity, the most educative response is one that extends the affect and its meaning in a constructive direction.

Confidence is a good thing but bludgeoning your peers with your confidence is not. Every student should learn this lesson in communication at one time or another. Momentary insecurity is a passing phenomenon that is unavoidable—and potentially productive—in learning; if we are teaching students to learn, we don't want to shame their insecurity. We want to normalize it and encourage persistence until the insecurity passes into increasing competence. Persistent insecurity is a more intransigent problem, of course. Again, however, it's an opportunity to learn to check one's feelings against one's thinking and one's performance. When insecurity is matched by a lack of competence (e.g., in the notorious case of young girls and mathematics), that calls for a carefully designed pedagogical intervention to address the lack of competence. In that case, the insecurity, masked by false bravado, is not the problem. Punishing the annoying student won't make any difference in whether or not they grow in the ways they need to.

Further, how is it ever possible for a student to know too much, at least if what they know is accurate? Surely the teacher wants to know all that their students think about in order to plan next instructional steps and/or differentiate instruction to meet their needs. One can only assume that the teacher is experiencing either a lack of confidence in one's own understanding and authority or a desire for authoritarian control. Neither have educative value. Instead of normalizing error and correction, instead of learning to fail productively, the fear of the instructor can be seen in reactions that move their fear to their students. To identify what a student is feeling in a given situation moves a teacher in an educative direction and away from punitive judgments or consequences precisely because it allows us to recognize that shame may leave no room for joy in learning, that frustration and anger are, educationally at least, unsatisfying.

We might take a similar cut at the students who don't know (when we, as their teachers, think they should). Again, teachers experience frustration or anger, prompted perhaps by a sense that they simply don't have enough time to respond to a student's real need or perhaps by a failure of their own confidence in their previous teaching. While teaching and learning proceed together and a teacher is never solely responsible for a student's failure to grow, it is also true that blaming a student doesn't move either closer to the shared goal. Taking a moment to check one's own state of mind and heart can prevent a turn to punishment. Interrogating the possibility that students are bored or frustrated themselves might point toward a generative educational tack. Even understanding that a student seems apathetic opens up a set of options (e.g., referral to a counselor or social worker) that do not involve punishment.

In general, it has to be remembered that any student actions that seem disruptive or disrespectful or even harassing are only so in the context of preset patterns of acceptable behavior that themselves may or may not be educative in the moment. It is easy to characterize a fistfight or a food fight as disruptive, but why is it disruptive for young students to walk around the classroom? Such students are typically responding to some not-so-obvious imperative. Perhaps she just thought of something she needed to tell her classmates, or he hasn't yet been vision tested and wants to see the blackboard or screen, or she simply has a hard time sitting still and needs a break from trying to concentrate on being still so that she *can* think. Rarely is there defiance or a desire to disrupt or disrespect. Instead, the behavior makes sense to the student in the context of what needs to happen in the moment.

Similarly, why is it disruptive for a college student to consult a cell phone? One might use the phone to check an allusion about which one is uncertain or "phone a friend" who can clarify an assignment. Who is disrupted when the cell phone appears? It's possible of course that the affect experienced is not urgency or interest but boredom. But that is its own pedagogical problem.

What motivates the teacher who does not allow walking around, calling out, consulting the cell phone, or in general, interaction between and among students. Just what is the teacher worried about? It probably doesn't matter exactly, but the fact that the teacher frets about the possibility that a single instance of disruption and disrespect can turn into a maelstrom of disorder—and, therefore, has to be nipped in the bud—is indicative that the teacher trusts neither their own pedagogical capacity nor the students' curiosity about the world and interest in worthwhile tasks. The teacher's distrust is enacted as fear, as a negative feeling in the face of uncertainty. It is this fear that turns the student-teacher interaction into an agonistic relation. Rather than working from an assumption and construction of shared goals, the teacher views the students as working against the stated standards, and ironically, working against their own best interest. Captured in zero-tolerance prohibitions of specific behaviors no matter what the meaning or intent, such constraints are counterproductive, defeating the teacher and punishing the student.

Educators who are not able to identify and connect with their own affective experience in such situations will almost always react punitively rather than respond constructively. They will project fear and distrust onto their students without figuring out which students, if any, are actually distrustful or untrustworthy and without considering how to develop the needed trust. One of our informants, a normally "well-behaved" seventh grader, reported on a cafeteria experience in which an adult approached a table of noisy boys, saying, "You should know I'm with the administration." No matter what the boys were doing, that kind of provocation will generate either puzzlement or defiance.

Consider also the affects associated with learning in process and learning achieved: curiosity, joy, vulnerability, satisfaction, pride, and a growing sense of self. Contrast those with shame, embarrassment, boredom, apathy, guilt, frustration, and a wavering sense of self that accompanies the personally diminishing experience of punishment. Educators worthy of the name never terrorize their students. To terrorize is to attack, and this results in rejection of what the teacher offers. The result is counterproductive: learning failure.

Nothing stated earlier suggests that students do not want and need academic, moral, emotional, and behavioral direction. But direction is not judgment. Direction, even correction, can prompt dynamic movement toward the better. Judgment fixes a student's actions as a function of a character found wanting. Moreover, judgment is often imposed on those students who seem different in some way: too Black, too brown, too active, too noisy, too poor, too physically unable, too linguistically or culturally "other." When we assign that judgment and then take away labs and replace them with worksheets, or shame individuals, or practice passive-aggressive responses, we deny rich educational opportunities, punishing students educationally because of those differences.

Above all, perhaps, we project onto students a capacity for free will that we as educators don't expect of ourselves. As educators, we are only too aware of the contexts—structural and infrastructural, institutional and affective—that move us and that constrain the movements available to us. At the same time, we assume that students *could* act otherwise, that their actions are a function not of constrained circumstances but of flawed character. It is, of course, a question not of circumstances *or* character but of circumstances *and* character. This is yet another aspect of classroom discipline that a pragmatist perspective keeps in focus.

Critical pragmatism for situated response-ability

The circumstances and cases described earlier suggest two dispositions that are part of a teacher's critical pragmatist mindset:

(1) shift away from a break-the-rule-and-suffer-the-consequences logic focused on misbehaviors and toward a constant, conscious awareness of the quality of relation and interaction that is growth-encouraging, and
(2) employ a logic of interpretation and response that is emblematic of intelligence co-constructed by and in the service of communities of learners who desire growth.

We begin by acknowledging that any teacher at any level is always juggling general educational goals, specific curricular and pedagogical purposes, multiple students who bring different kinds and present different needs, time, space, and place constraints, limited resources, and all the things that both teacher and students are bringing with them on *this* day. Sometimes, it is necessary to shut one opportunity down in order to make another possible. Because the task of the teacher is so complex at any given moment, educators have, by necessity, developed dispositions appropriate to various kinds of events. They have habits of reaction. And if a habit has been carefully formed, it will generally serve the moment.

When a third grader tells a peer, "you're so gay," it demands a reaction. But whether that reaction is an acknowledgment that this is a teachable-stop-everything-and-address-it moment, or an oh-wait-a-minute, look-at-what-just-happened,-we-have-to-address-this-eventually moment, has to be determined by the teacher given who is involved, what past experience in the classroom has been, and what's happening in the background institutionally and socially. There *are* habits for moving on that keep open possibilities for growth. If the student speaking is one with whom you have worked this through before, then it's possible that a quick "we don't talk that way" is what is needed. But in general, when inappropriate and/or unnerving slurs occur, it is important to note the speech act, enjoin it firmly for now, but also note that this will be a topic for our class meeting on Friday morning since, of course, we, as a community of learners, want to avoid insulting each other or using hurtful language. In the process of resolving a problematic situation, a teacher is demonstrating to students how to turn problems into responses that make things better.

The adolescent (usually male) who uses homophobic slurs in casual conversation or in targeted harassment is up to something quite different. The first challenge, of course, is to nip this language in the bud. That may involve a remarkably simple "Stop it please" accompanied by what has been called the "hairy eyeball," but only if there are already established relationships of respect as well as norms that proscribe homophobic behavior and speech. In a school environment where homophobia is an open wound, this kind of speech demands a careful campaign to carve out and legitimate classroom norms so that safe space is a kind of regulative ideal even if not attainable for all at once. The immediate reaction has to enjoin homophobic speech here and now, but make it clear that we *are* going to work this out (and maybe we should have worked it out a long time ago). Perhaps the most difficult context in which to address this speech act is the community in which heterosexual privilege is in full flower, but homophobic resentments are silenced in public. Affects (and ideas infused with those feelings) gone underground are generally more destructive than affects openly expressed. Determining the quality of community precedes any capacity to react positively or respond thoughtfully.

Situations like this are impacted, of course, by *why* an individual student employs a form of aggressive and offensive language—and how the offending student feels when he says it. It may be a habit carried from home or neighborhood, spoken with little thought or feeling. It may be an effort to demonstrate his own masculinity, a masculinity that is somehow in question or in development, spoken out of insecurity. It may be a misguided effort to impress the "cool kids." How we react will only be effective if we read this right. How we respond will only be fitting if we take the time to understand what is actually going on for the "offending" student.

Teachers' reactions and responses are also impacted by how *we* hear any microaggressive speech in use. A teacher who is themselves LGBT may hear the term as a personal threat. The teacher who has an LGBT son or daughter may experience anger at the ignorance and cavalier treatment of another human being. A teacher with their own adolescent children may recognize the predictable flailing of an adolescent and react with compassionate concern—but clear limits.

We cannot know the meaning of an individual behavior or of an interaction until and unless we have developed realistic, but nonjudgmental habits of reaction in advance and unless we are prepared to take the time and space to reinterpret affective and institutional realities that are not foregrounded in our set routines.

The college student who knows not to use insulting terms openly may nonetheless internalize discriminatory attitudes. The exclusion of a classmate from one's group suggests a dangerously judgmental attitude on the part of the student and, more damning, may also suggest an important educational failure, that is, the failure to recognize that the *other* is the source of my growth. The instructor may experience less immediacy of react and/or respond since students of that age are often able to stick up for themselves the threat of disruption is lessened. But it may also be *more* important to determine and design a fitting response because the incident points so clearly to the heart of our educational purpose.

The point in rehearsing immediate reactions and more thoughtful responses to this set of events is not to say that our interpretation and response is the only correct one. Rather, it is to point out that there will always be immediate reactions and, when needed, thoughtful responses. The immediate reactions will be more or less effective *and* more or less punishing depending on whether careful consideration of the affects of interaction (infrastructure) and the demands of institution practices (structure) have been factored into the dispositions we practice with regularity. The thoughtful responses—that is, the deliberate effort to think things through when our immediate reactions or habits fail—will be more beneficial depending on how well we engage (with students) in transparent interpretation, creative generation of alternative interactions, imaginative rehearsal of what each alternative might yield, and action that, if successful, informs a renewed set of habitual reactions. And all of this proceeds in the context of concrete communities of learning and the shared (though too often unstated) purposes for that learning.

This kind of critical pragmatist approach enables us to acknowledge rules as structurally important *and* consequences as factors for consideration without suggesting that one or the other controls our reactions. It privileges individual concerns *and* communal values. It allows for social dislocation *and* restoration. It integrates what is academic *and* what is ethical in our educational intentions. It recognizes institutional constraints and affective motivations. In short, it calls out pedagogical responsibility and highlights it as response-ability, that is, the capacity to respond richly. It does not call for retrospective punishment but the prospective enactment of what is growth-generating. This is the model that Herbie Hancock offers teachers: when a sour note arises, play the note that turns this occurrence into growth.

Note

1 Adapted from Jones (2018).

References

Berlant, Lauren (2016) "The Commons: Infrastructures for Troubling Times." *Environment and Planning D: Society and Space* 34 (3): 393–419. doi:10.1177/0263775816645989.

Jones, Josh (2018), "Herbie Hancock Explains the Big Lesson He Learned From Miles Davis: Every Mistake in Music, as in Life, Is an Opportunity." *Open Culture*. Retrieved January 14, 2022 at https://www.openculture.com/2018/04/herbie-hancock-explains-the-big-lesson-he-learned-from-miles-davis.html.

Stengel, Barbara (2010) "The Complex Case of Fear and Safe Space." *Studies in Philosophy and Education* 29 (6): 253–540. doi:10.1007/s11217-010-9198-3.

Stone, Lynda (2011) "Outliers, Cheese and Rhizomes: Variations on a Theme of Limitation." *Educational Theory* 61 (6): 647–58.

Contributors

Abigail J. Beneke is a PhD candidate in the Department of Educational Policy Studies at the University of Wisconsin-Madison, United States, where she studies school discipline and its reform. Through her research, she seeks to understand: (1) how students, school-based educators, and community members challenge, reproduce, or exacerbate social injustice through school discipline and its reform and (2) how these processes are shaped by the broader sociocultural and political-economic contexts in which schools are situated. She uses critical, sociocultural theories and qualitative methods to examine these questions.

Ruth Cigman is Honorary Senior Research Fellow at IOE, UCL's Faculty of Education and Society, University College London, UK. She was a doctoral student in philosophy at Cambridge University, UK, with Bernard Williams and spent several years in the United States, first as a Fulbright scholar, then as a university lecturer. She has published widely in ethics and educational philosophy, writing on moral epistemology, animal rights, special educational needs, medical ethics, philosophies of well-being, and other topics. In 2016, she cofounded a charity for asylum seekers and refugees called the Cotton Tree Trust, and she is currently developing an ethical perspective on UK immigration policy that is informed by both academic research and her experiences at the trust. Ruth is the author of *Cherishing and the Good Life of Learning: Ethics, Education, Upbringing* (2018).

Todd A. DeMitchell is Emeritus Professor at the University of New Hampshire, United States. Prior to this role, DeMitchell served as an elementary school teacher, principal, director of personnel and labor relations, and superintendent in California. At the University of New Hampshire, he has held two endowed professorships, one in education and one in justice studies, in addition to being named University Distinguished Professor. DeMitchell has authored/coauthored eleven books and over 220 law review articles, education articles, case commentaries, and book chapters. DeMitchell's work has been cited in a *writ of certiorari* submitted to the US Supreme Court, plus motions before state and federal courts, as well as quoted by federal and state supreme courts and state attorneys general, in addition to major law reviews. DeMitchell holds master's degrees in American intellectual history and philosophy of education, a doctorate specializing in education law and policy, and postdoctoral study in education law and labor.

Joy Dangora Erickson is Assistant Professor of Education in the School of Education at Endicott College, United States. She received the Student Outstanding Research Award from the Literacy Research Association in 2018 for her work examining young children's motivation. In addition to exploring children's motivation to read within intervention programs, Erickson is interested in issues of early education for citizenship. Her work has been featured in numerous journals including *The Reading Teacher*; *Literacy Research: Theory, Method, and Practice*; *Reading & Writing Quarterly: Overcoming Learning Difficulties*; *Journal of Early Childhood Literacy*; *Democracy & Education*; and the *Journal of Curriculum Studies*.

Joan F. Goodman is Professor of Education at the University of Pennsylvania, United States. Over a forty-plus-year career, Goodman's work has spanned clinical psychological services for children, research and teaching on developmental disabilities, and some of the controversies around moral issues confronted by teachers and students in K-12 grades. She has authored numerous articles on the psychology of mental retardation in children and on moral issues that schools must address. Her books include *When Slow Is Fast Enough* (1992) and, coauthored with Howard Lesnick, *The Moral Stake in Education* (2001).

Viktor Ivanković is a postdoctoral researcher at the Institute of Philosophy in Zagreb, Croatia. He holds a PhD in political theory from Central European University. Following up on his doctoral research, he focuses on several prominent topics in the ethics of nudging and behavioral influence. His other interests are in distributive justice and bioethics.

Zoë A. Johnson King is Assistant Professor of Philosophy at the University of Southern California, United States, and a former secondary school teacher. She holds a PGCE (the UK's main teaching degree) as well as a BA, M.Phil, and PhD in philosophy, and she completed the Teach First program in 2012, working full-time for two years at the Quest Academy in Croydon before returning to academia for her PhD. During the PhD she also cofounded an outreach program that partners with a local community organization to run grad-student-led

Ethics classes in high schools across Michigan. Her academic research focuses primarily on motivation and praiseworthiness.

Avi I. Mintz is a member of the Philosophy Faculty at Newlane University, United States. Mintz has broad interests in the history of educational philosophy and has published work on ancient Greek educational thought, Jean-Jacques Rousseau, and progressive educational thought. He is the author of *Plato: Images, Aims, and Practices of Education* (2018) and the editor of *A History of Western Philosophy of Education in Antiquity* (2021). He has also drawn on the history of educational philosophy to address contemporary topics such as teaching metaphors, parenting, and the role of struggle in education.

Rebecca A. Peterson has a dual appointment as a Lecturer in the Department of Teaching and Learning at Vanderbilt's Peabody College and in the Department of French and Italian. With over two decades working in a variety of education-oriented settings, she currently spends her time in the secondary education licensure program working with pre-service and in-service educators.

Jenna Scaramanga is Honorary Research Associate in the Department of Curriculum, Pedagogy and Assessment at IOE, UCL's Faculty of Education and Society, University College London, UK. Scaramanga completed her PhD on the experiences of students in fundamentalist Christian schools. She has written articles critiquing Accelerated Christian Education in the *Oxford Review of Education* and the *Journal of Curriculum Studies*. She came out as trans in 2021 and is trying to escape academia, not altogether successfully.

Elizabeth A. Self is a teacher educator in the elementary and secondary education licensure programs and a teacher education researcher in the Department of Teaching and Learning at Vanderbilt University's Peabody College. Dr. Self regularly teaches social and philosophical aspects of education, classroom ecology, and other social foundations courses, along with elective courses that focus on identity, positionality, and systems of oppression. Her current research and publications focus on designing and using simulated encounters, modeled after standardized patient encounters in medical education, to prepare pre-service teachers for anti-oppressive teaching.

Clio Stearns is Assistant Professor of Education at the Massachusetts College of Liberal Arts, United States. In this position, Stearns works with pre-service and in-service elementary and early childhood teachers. Her teaching focuses on the emotional and ethical dimensions of learning, particularly in childhood. Her recent book, *Consent in the Childhood Classroom* (2022), focuses on what young children choose to engage in when they enter school. She is currently working on a project about how children make sense of narratives of "learning loss" associated with the educational fallout of the Covid pandemic. Stearns is consistently interested in methodologies that foreground children's voices and other ways of expressing their will.

Peter Stearns is University Professor of History at George Mason, United States. He has written widely on the history of emotions and the history of childhood, with particular interest in providing historical perspective on contemporary patterns. He is coauthor of *Education in World History* (2022).

Barbara S. Stengel is Professor Emerita of Philosophy of Education and Teacher Education at Vanderbilt University, United States. She is the author of several books, most recently (with Elizabeth Self), *Toward Anti-Oppressive Pedagogy* (2020), and (with Gert Biesta) is the coauthor of "Thinking Philosophically about Teaching" in the American Educational Research Association's *Handbook of Research on Teaching* (2016). Currently at work on a book project that focuses on responsibility as the orienting concept for understanding education as moral practice, she is also collaborating on "Chasing Bailey," a podcast representing the transformation of a school in Nashville, Tennessee.

Larisa Svirsky lectures at Brandeis University, United States. She received her PhD in philosophy from UNC–Chapel Hill, United States, in 2019. Following this, she completed a postdoctoral fellowship at the Ohio State University, United States, focused on the treatment and regulation of addiction. Her work is primarily in ethics, bioethics, moral psychology, and philosophy of psychiatry. Her long-term research has centered on social practices of holding others responsible and how those practices involve vulnerable populations, such as children and people, with mental illness. She is also interested in the impact of trauma on responsibility and forgiveness.

Winston C. Thompson is Associate Professor in the Department of Educational Studies and in the Department of Philosophy (by courtesy) at the Ohio State University, United States. He received his PhD (*with distinction*) in philosophy and education from Teachers College, Columbia University. Thompson's scholarship explores ethical/political dimensions of educational policy and practice. His work on justice and the role of education in a pluralistic, democratic society has appeared in *Educational Theory*, *Philosophy of Education*, *Teachers College Record*, *The Journal of Philosophy of Education*, *Educational Philosophy and Theory*, and *Studies in Philosophy and Education*. He is the editor of *Philosophical Foundations of Education* (2023). Alongside his collaborator John Tillson, he is a PI on the Pedagogies of Punishment project.

John Tillson is Senior Lecturer in Philosophy of Education at Liverpool Hope University, UK. He is the author of *Children, Religion and the Ethics of Influence* (2019). His work on educational aims, curriculum theory, school exclusion, and the ethics of influence has appeared in *Educational Theory*, *Philosophy of Education*, *The Journal of Philosophy of Education*, *Educational Philosophy and Theory*, and *Studies in Philosophy and Education*. He has an entry on "Wrongful Influence in Educational Contexts" in the *Oxford Research Encyclopedia of Education*. He discusses his research in "Children, Religion and Influence in Philosophy of Education," an interview with Richard Marshall for his 3:16 *End Times* series (2020). Alongside his collaborator Winston C. Thompson, he is a PI on the Pedagogies of Punishment project.

Kartik Upadhyaya is Visiting Lecturer at the Dickson Pool School of Law, King's College London, UK. He completed his doctoral thesis, entitled "What's Wrong with Hypocrisy?," at the University of Warwick. His areas of specialization are applied moral and political philosophy, the morality of hypocrisy, and the ethics of blame.

Index

Abington Township, Pennsylvania v. Schemp (1963) 144
academic cheating 24
accountability, value of 162–4
acknowledgment 168, 171
acts of punishment 180, 183, 187, 191–2, 194
adolescence 42, 44
   nudging, autonomy and 246–8
   social transition 77
   as transition 246–8
adulthood
   vs. childhoods 93–4
   imagination 94
   play 94
adultification 92
   Black children subject to 92–3
   punishment, consequences for 92–3
affects, punishment's 260–4; *see also* emotions
agency 94, 98–101
anger 188–91, 262
Annamma, Subini A. 92
anti-perfectionism 58 n.16
arbitrariness 208–11
Aristotle 188–91
Arjo, Dennis 200, 206
Art of Rhetoric (Aristotle) 188
authority 50, 208–11
   and logical consequences 203
   with minors 202
   and punishment 179–83
autonomy 9, 20, 42–4, 54
   of adolescents 241–8
   capacities for 110
   and consequences 205–6
   global 44
   vs. heteronomy 44
   and nudging 241–8

Baldwin, Robert 238
behavior management 218–21

Beneke, Abigail J. 6
Black children/people 91–4, 99–100, 107
Black girls 92–3
Blake, Jamilia J. 92
blame/blaming children 51, 161–4, 175 n.5, 176 n.22, 217, 257
   accountability, value of 162–4
   affective *vs.* detached 174 n.1
   communicative blaming 175 n.5
   expressive 228
   hypocritical 161–7, 171, 223
   mutual deliberation 169–71
   non-hypocritical 161–2, 167–74
   and school rules 165–7
blameworthiness 217–18, 221, 223–6
Bommarito, Nic 222–3
Bonhoeffer, Dietrich 144
Brighouse, Harry 100
Brophy, Jere 29
Brown v. Board of Education case 144
bullying 77, 79–81
Burden, Paul 21

"Calm Down Corner" 134–5
Carvalho, Henrique 187
Chalmers, Lynne 240–1
Chamberlen, Anastasia 187
charter schools, United States 96
chattel slavery 91
Chicago Tribune 107–8
childhoods
   vs. adulthood 93–4
   developmental view of 93
   education 108–9
   educational goods 93–4
   expulsion 114–15
   features of 92
   goods 93–4
   nondevelopmental view of 93–4
   racialized 91–4
   suspensions in 116–17

children
    adolescents, *vs.*   42, 44, 52, 54, 77, 236–7, 242–8
    anger   188–91
    as autonomous   9, 42–5
    blame/blaming   51, 161–74
    communication to   70
    as heteronomous   9, 44–5
    holding responsible   65–7
    infants   51
    locking in isolation rooms   107–8
    moral rights   108–21
    older   54, 92
    punishing, prospect of   69–70
    punish justly   192–3
    punitive feelings   178–9
    responsibility   62–70
    self-direction   111
    young   9, 48, 51, 64, 66, 69, 98, 100, 106–20
Cigman, Ruth   7
classroom management   199, 209–11, 213 n.2
Clayton, Matthew   242, 244
codes of conduct, school   24
coercion   30, 42
Columbus Public School System   145–6
commonwealth/community   144
confidence   261
consequences   199–212
    logical   203, 206
    natural   201–2, 208
    vs. punishments   200–8
        compliance, compel   205–6
        excessive   207
        inequitable   208
        misbehaviors and outcomes, arbitrary relations between   203
        pain, presence of   203–4
        parents/teachers, outcomes imposed by   200–2
        retribution   204–5
context control   52
control   42–3, 51–2
    practice of   258–60
critical childhood studies   91–2
critical pragmatist approach   264–6
culpability   26, 217
Curren, Randall   207

Darwall, Stephen   226–7
Davis, Miles   255
de Koning, Björn B.   238–9
DeMitchell, Todd A.   7
Dewey, John   25, 30, 132
discipline, educative   13–14, 95
    behavioral control   95
    deprivation and   20
    and due process   144–5
    as fields of study   15
    interventions   15
    vs. punishment   15–18
    as submission to rules   14–15
    in theory   14–16
disincentivizing behavior   6, 66–70
Dobbie, Will   96
Dreikurs, Rudolf   21
Driver, Justin   155
due process   143–56
    Clause   146–7
    conscience   153
    and discipline   144–5
    and education   144–5
    and ethics   144–5, 156
    fair treatment   150–1
    Goss v. Lopez, student rights   145–9
    legal rights   156
    overbroad rule   153
    procedural   151–2
    in public schools   149–56
    responsibilities   156
    and student activities   155–6
    and student rules   153–5
    substantive   152
    and US Constitution   144–5
    vague rules   152
Duff, R. A.   179
Dumas, Michael J.   92

early childhood education   6, 108, 113–20
East Asia   132, 136–7
educational goods   93–4
    claims   95–101
Eliot, George   181
Emile (Rousseau)   200
emotions; *see also* affects, punishment's
    of anger   179
    and punitive logics   186–92
enablement   49

Engelen, Bart   241, 245
Epstein, Rebecca   92
equality   26, 31, 186
exclusionary practices in schools
    113–19
  expulsions   114–15
  suspensions   116–17
  time-out   117–19
expressive praise   226–30

fair laws   150–1
Faye, Shon   75
Feinberg, Joel   25, 186
Feinberg, Mike   95
Foucault, Michael   95
Franklin-Hall, Andrew   44–5
Fryer, Roland G.   96

Gender
  cisgenderism   79–81
  cisgender people   76
  cisnormativity   80
  gender binary   81–2
  gender deviance   82
  Gender Euphoria (Dale)   78
  gender identity   76–8, 82–5
  gender ideologies   79–80
  gender-punitive schools   84–5
  nonbinary children/people   76, 83–4
  trans youth   75–9
    and anti-trans sports
      legislation   75–6
    bullying with   77, 79–81
    conversion therapy for   82–3
    depression, rates of   78
    joy, power of   78
    justice for   75–9
    media coverage of   75
    nonpunitive education   84
    peer violence with   81
    pronouns for   75–6
    punishments of   78–9
    recommendations for schools
      on   85
    in schools   77–8
    sexual assault in schools   77
    suicidality, rates of   78
    support to   77–8
    and teachers   77–8

    trans girls   75–6
    uniform/dress codes for   81–2
  Gheaus, Anca   93
  global autonomy   44
  Golann, Joanne   90, 95–100
  González, Thalia   92
  Good, Thomas   29
  Goodman, Joan F.   2, 5–6, 46
  "good news referrals"   221
  Goss, Norval   146
  Goss v. Lopez case   145–9
  GSAs (Gender & Sexuality or Gay-Straight
    Alliances)   80
  guidance   21

Hampton, Jean   18, 30, 50
Hancock, Herbie   255
Hand, Michael   49
Hannan, Sarah   93, 242–3
Hansen, Pelle   238
harms   58 n.17
Hart, Herbert   38, 51
heteronomy *vs.* autonomy   44
heuristics   238–45
Hieronymi, Pamela   228–9
Hispanic children   107
history   130–3
Hobson, Peter   49
Holder, Eric H.   154
hypocrisy   161–7, 171, 223
hypocritical blaming   161–7, 171, 223

identity   1, 6, 76–8, 82–5, 93, 187, 220
imagination   94
immodesty   222–3
insecurity   261
insult   25
integration   135–7
intentional shaming *vs.* shaming in
  schools   126
interpretation-response logic   266
Islamic schools   130
Ivanković, Viktor   8, 56 n.2

Jespersen, Andreas   238
Johnson King, Zoë A.   8
justice   31–2, 183
  distributive   52–4

just punishment 192–3
  for trans youth 75–9
justification for school punishment 27–31, 38, 45–9, 65, 67
  backward-looking 46–7
  deterrence (decreasing behavior) 21
  forward-looking 47–8
  hybrid 48–9
  "just deserts" 46–7
  moral education 18–19
  retribution 16–18, 46, 185
  Tadros's duty view of 46–8

K-12 harassment 77
Kant, Immanuel 201
King, Matt 223
Knowledge is Power Program (KIPP) 95
Kohlberg, Lawrence 242

Lavecchia, Adam M. 238
Lectures on Pedagogy (Kant) 200
legal requirements 57 n.7
legitimacy 9
Levin, Dave 95
Levin, James 20–1
LGBTQ+
  "Don't Say Gay" law (Florida) 76–7
  homosexuality 77
  nonbinary children/people 76, 83–4
  people 77–8, 80
  Section 28, British laws 77
  societies 80
  Trans youth (*see* Gender)
liberty 147
life-stage 44
literacy skills 97
Liu, Heidi 238
Locke, John 131

Macleod, Colin M. 93–4, 97
Macnamara, Colleen 227
Magna Carta Libertatum (Great Charter of Freedoms) 150
maturation 106, 110
McGeer, Victoria 227
McKenna, Michael 227
Meiners, Erica R. 92
Messner, Michael 80
Mill on the Floss, The (Eliot) 181–2

Mintz, Avi I. 8
misbehavior 205, 256–7
Moles, Andrés 242
moral education 18, 44, 62–3, 190, 241
  theory of punishment 18–19
moral/morality 24–6
  communication 2
  complying with 3, 24–6
  conforming with 2–3
  issues 164
  principles 39–40
moral protest 228–9
moral responsibility 108, 217–22, 226
moral rights of young children 108–21
  exclusionary practices violate 113–19
  morally significant status 109–11
  and NAEYC 109
  Reggio Approach 108–9
  and UNCRC 111–13
Morrissey v. Brewer (1972) 151
Moskowitz, Eva 127
motivation 231 n.4
mutual deliberation 169–71

National Association for the Education of Young Children (NAEYC) 109
natural consequences 201–2, 208
Nelkin, Dana Kay 51–2
Nelson, Joseph D. 92
No Excuses school model 90, 95–101
  adequacy 97
  behavioral control at 95
  call-and-response chants in 98
  discipline 96–7
  educational goods 96–101
  guidelines 95
  play/agency, capacities for 96–8, 100–1
  students access to agency 98–9
  systemic racial oppression 99–100
  test scores 96
  vs. traditional public school 100
Nolan, James 21
non-exclusion time-outs 119
non-hypocritical blaming 161–2
  mutual deliberation 169–71
  pedagogic advantage of 167–71
  pedagogic duty of 172–4
nonpunitive education 84

normative expectations 63, 71 n.3
norms, relationships as sources of 63–4, 71 n.4
norms of attention 222
nudges/nudging 236–48, 249 n.2
　autonomies of 241–8
　　adolescence 246–8
　　in development/exposure 244–6
　category of 238
　classroom 237–40
　permissible 237
　school discipline 240–1
　Type 1 238–40, 249 n.5
　Type 2 238–40, 249 n.5
Nussbaum, Martha 186, 189

Ohio Rev. Code Ann. § 3313.66 (1972) 146
Oreopoulous, Philip 238
Oxley, Laura 52–4

Paas, Fred 238–9
pain 18, 23–4, 48
　consequences vs. punishments 203–4
　criteria for punishment 23–4
parent-child relationship 63–4
parenting discourse 199–200, 213 n.2
paternalism 42–5
　paternalistic punishment 49–51, 57 n.10
PBM/PBIS systems 219–21
peer hazing 83
peer pressure 83
peer violence 81
penalties 29
perceptionism 41
perfectionism 41, 57 n.9, 58 n.16
Peters, R. S. 14–15, 180, 183
Peterson, Rebecca A. 8
play 94, 97–8, 100–1
positive behavior management 218–21
praise/praiseworthiness 217, 231 n.5
　communicative 226–30
　expressive 226–30
　fitting 221–6
　importance of 220
ProPublica 107–8
Prynne, Hester 133
public education 144–5

punishment, school 1–5, 31–3
　as actions thought to communicate 49
　acts of 180, 183, 187, 191–2, 194
　adultification consequences for 92–3
　advantages 2–4
　affect 260–4
　artificial 201
　as an aspect of discipline 16
　and authority 179–83
　communicative aim 65
　compliance, and 49
　complying with morality, for 3, 24–6
　conforming with morality, for 2–3
　conformity, and 49
　consequences, vs. 199–208
　corporal punishment 207
　criteria for 23–7
　definitions of 38–9, 179, 206
　distinctiveness of 65–7
　vs. educative discipline 15–18
　emotional experience of 125 (see also shaming in schools)
　ethical concerns 178
　Goodman's views on 46
　justification of 27–31, 38, 45–9, 65, 67
　liability for 37, 43, 48–9, 51–4
　　focus on intention 26–7
　mixed theory of 18–19
　objections to 30
　paternalistic 49–51, 57 n.10
　penalties, vs. 214 n.4
　prospect of 69–70
　for reform 30
　and retribution 16–18, 46, 185
　and revenge 183–6
　and school practice 19–23
　seclusion 107–8
　Tadros's duty view of 46–8
　of trans children 78–9
　unwitting habits of 256–8
punitive classroom 183
punitive feelings 178, 187–8; see also affects, punishment's; emotions
punitive logics 186–92
pupils 13, 55
queer 77

racial oppression   99–100
Reggio Approach   108–9
reintegration, role of   135–7
relationship-based norms   63–4, 71 n.6
resentment   13, 17, 29, 161, 179, 186–7
response costs   29
responsibility   110, 217–18
   blame/blaming children, and   164–5
   blameworthiness   217–19, 221, 224–6, 230 n.1
   capacities for   51–2
   children   62–70
   community   67–8
   culpability   26, 46, 48, 99, 217
   degrees of   62
   moral   108, 217–22, 226
   praiseworthiness   217–19, 221–2, 224–6, 230 n.1
   for wrongdoing   51
retribution   16–18
   consequences *vs.* punishments   204–5
   school punishment as   16–18, 46, 185
revenge   183–6
   and anger   188–91
   and punishment   183–6
rights
   human   110–11
   legal   156
   moral   108–21
   UNCRC   111–13
risk   67–9
Rochin v. California (1972)   153
Rousseau, Jean-Jacques   200–1
rule-breaking   38; *see also* school rules

Sandel, Michael   144
Scaramanga, Jenna   6
Schapiro, Tamar   68, 242
school discipline; *see* discipline, educative
School punishments
   expulsions   114–15
   school seclusion   107–8
   Shaming (see 'shaming in schools')
   suspensions   116–17, 146
   time-out   117–19
      non-exclusion   119
school rules   14–15, 19–20, 24, 31–2, 39–40, 165–7

behavior, requirements   39–42
   ethical   40
   moral   39–40
   prudential   40
   codes of conduct   24
   dress codes/uniform   81–2
   impositions   38
   swearing   25
   zero-tolerance rules   154–5
Self, Elizabeth A.   8
self-control   52, 62
self-direction   110–11
self-efficacy   220, 231 n.3
self-esteem   220
self-other comparison   223
SEL (social and emotional learning) programs   134
Seneca, Lucius Annaeus   184, 188
shame   130–3
shaming in schools   29–30, 125–38
   case studies   127–30, 135–7
   corner, going to   133–5
   definition   125
   ethical nature of   129
   future directions   137–8
   history of   130–3
   vs. intentional shaming   126
   and Islamic schools   130
   as punitive practice *vs.* pedagogical intent   128–9
   role of   127
   and Success Academy   127–30
   teacher engaged in   127–30
Shapiro, Tamar   93
Spiegel, Alix   83
sports   29, 75–7, 80, 84, 133
Stearns, Clio   7
Stearns, Peter   7
Stengel, Barbara S.   8, 260
Stephen, J. F.   186
Stone, Lynda   259–60
Success Academy   127–30
Sunstein, Cass   237
Svirsky, Larisa   6
Symmetry Thesis   224–6

Tadros, Victor   9, 46–8
teachers   13
   blaming   161–74

critical pragmatist mindset 264–6
obligations 13
professionalism of 178
shaming in schools, engaged in 127–30
training 220
and trans students 77–8
Thaler, Richard 237
Thompson, Winston C. 4, 6
Tillson, John 4, 6–7, 52–4
token reinforcement systems 221
Tomlin, Patrick 93–4
Torres, A. Chris 96
trans youth (*see* gender)
trust 166
Tucker, Faye 243–4, 247
Tulliver, Tom 185–6

uncertainty 67–9
United Nations Convention on the Rights of the Child (UNCRC) 111–13
   Article 12 112, 118
   Article 19 112, 118
   Article 28 112, 118
   Article 37 112–13, 118
Upadhyaya, Kartik 7
US Constitution 144–5, 150–1
   Fourteenth Amendment right, US Constitution 143, 146, 148, 150–1

Wallace, Jay 226
Wallace, John M., Jr. 92–3
Waller, Richard 13
Watson, Gary 226
Weijers, Robert J. 238–9
welfare 42
West, Benjamin 131
White, Byron 146
White children 92

Young v. Price (1983) 155

Zucker, Ken 83